BUS PEOPLE

30 Days on the Road
with America's Nomads

MIKE PENTECOST

Abby!
Enjoy the
bus ride!

Best
Mike Pentecost

Published and Printed in the United States of America

ISBN 978-0-9851415-0-9

Blevins House Publishing

Brentwood, TN

To my loving wife Erica Stone Pentecost.
Thank you for always believing in me and
convincing me to follow my dreams, even on a bus.

CONTENTS

PROLOGUE

"We're in college now . . . I don't know . . . I just feel like we need to see other people. I really want to experience college."

This was the conclusion of her well-crafted salvo that ended it all. There were more words exchanged, something about wanting us to still be friends, but I don't remember much after she said those words. I held the sweaty, cream-colored dorm room phone against my cheek and rested my head against the door jam, wishing it hadn't come to this. We had been through so much. Ellen was my first true love. We were going to get married. She had promised me that we'd be together forever, the antithesis of my parents, who had just announced their impending divorce after twenty-eight years of marriage.

We would be a throwback love story for the ages. But it had all ended before Thanksgiving of my freshman year.

Admittedly, ours had only been a ten-month relationship. But, at eighteen, those months were like dog years. Ellen and I were as good as married in my mind. We had gone to prom together. We spent a weekend camping in the Michigan dunes. She and I had gone to baseball games and county fairs. We studied together. We were best friends. There was no doubt in my mind that this was a

rare, lasting kind of love. I knew that high school sweethearts sel-
dom end up together, especially when headed to different colleges,
but we were destined to be different. We would beat the odds.

That August my father had helped me carry my clothes, stereo, records, a few books, and my refrigerette up to room 408 in the
"A" wing of Haggin Hall, where most of the freshman boys attend-
ing the University of Kentucky were housed. This eight-by-twelve
space was what I would call home for the next nine months. It was
a depressing excuse for a dorm room—white cinder blocks and a
bunk bed better suited for a medium-security correctional facility.
I kept a picture of Ellen on my desk. I looked at it often. We spoke
on the phone almost every day and we made great plans for seeing each other on weekends here and there. My father knew that I
was crazy about this girl, so, he generously gave me enough airline
miles that I could fly from Lexington to North Carolina at the end
of September. But waiting to see her was agony. About three weeks
into school, I decided I couldn't stand it any longer. I didn't have a
car, and I only had enough money in my account to get me through
the semester, if I rationed everything very carefully. So one night,
while splitting a six-pack of Milwaukee's Best with my high-school
friends Crisanne and Kelli, a plan was hatched.

"How much do you think a bus ticket to North Carolina
costs?" I asked them.

None of us had ever ridden a bus, other than a school bus, but
the idea of a surprise road trip sounded very romantic to the girls.

"That would be so sweet! You could go down there this weekend and surprise Ellen. She would love that!" gushed Kelli.

I thought that if these two girls loved the idea, then Ellen
would surely be blown away by the gesture. *This will show her just
how much I love her,* I thought. *But how to pay for the ticket?* Then came
my next brilliant plan. Girls in general are romantic creatures,
right? Maybe, if they heard my story of love and separation, they
would be so taken with my plea that they would gladly help me out.

I got excited. I grabbed my plastic shower bucket and wrote a sign that said, "Bus Trip to See My Girlfriend." I taped the sign to the side of the bucket and Crisanne and I headed out, with a slight beer buzz, on a mission to raise the money that night. We started knocking on doors at Donovan Hall, the girls' dorm. At each door I launched into a long spiel about my intentions to take a Greyhound bus to North Carolina to see my beloved. Some girls were rude and shut the door in our faces, but most were open and receptive as I asked them for the spare change off their dressers. Crisanne, my patient and loyal sidekick, held the bucket.

We made it through all four floors of Donavan Hall, and then headed back to Kelli and Crisanne's dorm room. We dumped our booty on the bed like a couple of excited trick-or-treaters. At the end of the tallying process, we counted just over $80. Not too bad for a Tuesday night's work.

I called Greyhound and found out that a round trip ticket from Lexington, Kentucky, to Winston Salem, North Carolina, where Wake Forest University is located, was $140. I figured I could cover the difference out of my semester's savings account. This was a worthy cause, after all. The bus would leave at 5:00 pm on Thursday afternoon and would get there around noon on Friday. I wondered why this trip, which I estimated was only a seven- or eight-hour car ride, would be a nineteen-hour bus ride, but I didn't really care. It would be worth it.

On Wednesday and Thursday I couldn't pay attention in class. All that was on my mind was getting to see Ellen. She would give me a big hug and we would cuddle together all weekend. I couldn't wait. All that mattered was getting on that bus. Thursday afternoon I packed my suitcase and walked from my dorm to downtown Lexington to pick up a city bus that would take me to the Greyhound station. I had a smile on my face that wouldn't go away. I felt so grown up. I hadn't asked anyone's permission to do this. It was a crazy idea, and I felt wild and free.

I arrived at the Greyhound station off of Russell Cave Road in Lexington and saw a group of people gathered on the side of the building under an overhang. They were standing next to their suitcases, most of them smoking. I went inside, plopped down the $140, and got my bus ticket. I noticed a teenager, who looked to be a little younger than me, standing by himself. He was an African American kid wearing a black Raiders ball cap.

"Where you headed?" I asked him.

"San Jose, California," he replied.

"My name's Mike." I reached out my hand.

"Chris," he introduced himself.

"Why are you going out to San Jose?"

"My aunt's out there. I'm going to live with her."

Chris and I stuck close to each other for the next five hours on our way to Knoxville, Tennessee, where Chris would pick up a different bus for his roundabout journey out to California. Like me, he seemed a little nervous. We didn't know anyone on the bus, and we were young. But we had each other to talk to. We talked about sports and school. I learned that Chris was sixteen and had a pretty crappy home life in Lexington. His mom was in trouble with the law and his dad was out of the picture. He was apprehensive about going to a new city where he knew no one other than family, but he was excited about the possibility of starting over. It seemed pretty sad to me that he felt he needed to "start over" at sixteen years old.

Our bus was heading down I-75 toward Tennessee when I noticed that the driver started pulling over frequently. It seemed like we were getting off the interstate every ten miles. Chris and I were wondering why we kept stopping, but at every stop–Richmond, Mt. Vernon, Berea–somebody was always getting off the bus and somebody else was getting on. At most stops people would file off the bus to go smoke in some parking lot. We stopped for about thirty minutes in Corbin as the driver went into Burger King and bought a cup of coffee and a burger. Chris and I stayed on the bus, complaining about how long this was taking, when an older gentleman walked up to us.

"Do you boys want some whiskey?" he asked. He was wearing dirty clothes and had gray stubble protruding from the lower half of his weathered face.

"No, thanks," we told him.

"Well, how about some beer?"

"No, really, that's ok."

"Well, do you have some money so that I can get some whiskey?" he asked.

Again, Chris and I politely declined. Everyone loaded back on the bus and before long we were in Tennessee. I remember the driver talking to us like he was a pilot. "Ladies and gentlemen, we're beginning our descent into Knoxville. We should be there in about a half hour." By "descent" he meant that our bus would be climbing through the mountains and then going downhill on a windy, scary trajectory. The older man who had tried to talk us into drinking with him had evidently found a buddy because he was now soused. Chris and I saw him stumble back to the bathroom and for the remainder of the trip we heard him throwing up. The toe-curling vomiting sound was so loud that the entire bus could hear. The driver did nothing. When we got to Knoxville the man just stumbled toward the front of the bus and exited, wandering around the bus station without purpose or direction.

Chris and I said goodbye in Knoxville. He was finally headed west, and I had to wait three more hours for the connecting bus to take me to Charlotte, North Carolina. In Charlotte, where I waited four more hours for the bus to take me back up north to Winston-Salem, a man approached me and asked if I wanted to buy some crack. This scared me. I was way out of my comfort level, but the prize—Ellen, my love—was waiting just a few hours away. It would be worth it.

When I arrived in Winston-Salem, Ellen was waiting for me

in the bus station. I expected her to come running toward me and throw her arms around me, welcoming me like a soldier who had just returned home after a long stint overseas. Instead, she slowly approached me with an odd look on her face.

"You look dreadful," she said.

We spent the weekend on campus at Wake Forest. It was a beautiful campus, and Ellen seemed to be having the time of her life there. It felt so comfortable being there with her and her friends. We went out for Mexican food and told stories all night. Ellen seemed proud to have me with her, which pleased me to no end. But Sunday morning rolled around sooner than either of us wanted. I got a ride to the bus station and said a tearful goodbye to Ellen.

The bus ride back to Lexington was only going to be twelve hours long this time—it was an "express" bus. For the entire ride I sat next to a man named Carl. He was hard-looking and seemed about seventy years old, though he was probably fifty. Carl talked my ear off.

"I've got two grown sons. One's in prison. He's made some big mistakes, but he'll get out someday. My other boy is doing great. He works with the carnival. He's living the good life. They travel around from town to town. He's in charge of one of the rides. He's been doing that for years . . ." Carl continued on for four hundred miles.

By the time I got home I was exhausted. I hadn't done any homework and I had a mountain of it waiting for me. All I could think about was my weekend in North Carolina. I called Ellen as soon as I got to my dorm. We recapped the weekend and talked about how we couldn't wait to see each other again.

It was only a short month later that the infamous we-can-still-be-friends phone call from Ellen came. I was devastated. The sting of that breakup lasted well into the winter, as our phone calls got shorter and letters less frequent. Eventually Ellen and I stopped speaking altogether.

But while the experience of being dumped by my high-school sweetheart faded in my rearview mirror a long time ago, that bus trip to North Carolina has stayed with me. I wonder where Chris is now. By now he'd be in his late thirties. Did he ever make it to California? I wonder about his story. What about Carl? Did his son ever get out of prison? Is the drunk guy from the bathroom still alive?

If there were an era of my life that I would choose to go back and do over again, even with all the angst, it would be my college years. I can remember, at the time, feeling that the weight of the world was on my shoulders, but as I soon learned, an eight-page paper is nothing compared to a nine-to-five job with a boss and mortgage payments. In college, there was always something going on—a stereo blaring from someone's dorm room and a cold beer at the ready. I miss those days, that in-between time of still being a kid yet feeling very much like an adult. There was nobody checking where I was going and what I was doing. I could stay up as late as I wanted. I could eat Doritos and drink Pepsi for breakfast. But I also found myself wanting to lean on my parents from time to time.

Their divorce the summer before my freshman year made that difficult. Home was no longer home. After their split my mom moved to Florida and my father joined a lonely hearts' singles club and later remarried. My JC Penney stereo was put in storage as my folks sold the old house and my dad moved in with his new wife. Home became Haggin Hall. That was a depressing reality. I didn't look forward to going "home" for the holidays, as I found them to be increasingly awkward, always feeling like a guest in someone else's home.

Luckily I found the church to be a safe haven for me during my college years. No matter how rough Saturday night might have been, I found my way to the sanctuary on Sunday morning, buoyed by the faith that had been nurtured in me during my high school years. Maxwell Street Presbyterian became a home away from home for me for the better part of the next decade.

Maxwell Street was very active in local and foreign mission work, which really appealed to me. Some of my most formative experiences were mission trips with my youth group in high school. During each of those trips, I was inevitably haunted by the question: "Why was I so lucky?" I can remember going on a mission trip in the summer of 1988 to a Native American reservation in Northern Wisconsin. We were there to help build houses and paint a church. I saw children living in dilapidated homes, spreading ketchup on Wonder bread for a meal, while tick-infested litters of puppies played at their feet. I remember thinking, *That could have been me. Why was I so lucky to be born into a family that could provide pretty much anything I needed and most of what I wanted?* It didn't seem fair then, and it still doesn't seem fair now.

These annual mission trips were an opportunity for me to escape my own sheltered environment, and there was something that attracted me to being a guest in someone else's world. Though the point of the mission projects was to feed, build, clothe, teach, and encourage, I always felt a sense of exhilaration about being away from my home, my world as I knew it—a suburban upbringing full of homogenous homes and schools where everyone pretty much looked the same. We had sports, activities, safe places to play—pretty much all of the niceties of middle-class suburbia. But I always longed to see what was outside my little world. I never felt more alive and such a deep sense of purpose and humility as when I was a stranger in someone else's community.

Maxwell Street was also where I met my wife, Erica. While she hadn't grown up in the church, she responded to an ad in the school newspaper and soon found herself babysitting at the church almost every night. She was beautiful and nurturing with the children. I mustered the courage to ask her out, and we hit it off from the get-go. After dating only six months, I proposed, and we married as soon as I finished my degree. Our first son was born two years later; the next followed a few years later. And we were off—into the land of adulthood.

Today I wouldn't change any of that for the world, but I have always envied those students who were in no hurry to get going with their lives, studying abroad or backpacking and hitchhiking and staying in foreign hostels after graduation. There was nothing like kids, a job, and a mortgage to make me realize that ship sailed for me long ago. But the wanderlust remained.

So when I found myself, at age 38, in the midst of a job transition that afforded me a month's worth of downtime, I was reminded of my long-ago ride on the bus, and I knew this was the time to do something spontaneous. Here was my chance.

Throughout my adult life, I have sought ways to tiptoe into other communities and try and belong, if only for a short while, taking pleasure in being exposed to a different part of the country or the world. Once I visited the Grand Canyon, and sitting on edge of the abyss, I was reminded that I am very small in the great, vast scheme of things. Oddly enough, that's also the way I felt riding the bus so long ago. Being an outsider on that bus gave me some perspective and reminded me that the world does not and should not revolve around all of my needs and wants. And I felt I could use a good dose of perspective. Surely riding a Greyhound bus for thirty days, with no other purpose in mind other than to be an observant passenger, would give me some perspective, right?

I wanted to take a break from my world for a little while. I wanted to ride the bus again, to reengage with a very odd, but very interesting community who had welcomed me so very long ago—a nearly invisible pocket of nomadic Americans who live in transition and on the fringe. They are on the bus every day. Most of them we don't even see; most of them we choose not to see. And that is a shame. Because, as I learned, everyone on the bus has a story to tell.

DAY ONE

Nashville, Tennessee

Riding the Greyhound bus is about as American as it gets. Since the invention of the car, America has had a love affair with the road. We have a pioneering spirit. We want to know what's out there. Greyhound has afforded countless people the opportunity to seek answers to that question. It has become a symbol for adventure, freedom, and nostalgia. It's even been documented in song: "I was born on the backseat of a Greyhound bus, rollin' down highway forty-one" (The Allman Brothers) and "She fell in love on the backseat of a Greyhound bus" (Sara Evans).

The Greyhound bus has been romanticized through lyrics like these, described as a place of escape, the open road, and new beginnings. But for all who have actually traveled at length on the Greyhound bus, they know it's not romantic at all. It's a grind. The bus is set up as a low-cost mode of transportation to get people from point A to point B, and not in the most efficient manner. Unlike the airplane, the bus forces passengers to spend long hours, sometimes days, together, traveling and stopping. The bus is far less predictable than other forms of travel–road construction, accidents, breakdowns, and unforeseen incidents with passengers make the bus the ultimate wild card of interstate travel.

"Are you really serious about this? The bus is disgusting. What if you only make it five days and want to come home? Are you having a mid-life crisis?" These were the fair questions thrown my way by my wife and children.

None of my immediate family, and very few of my extended family, has ever ridden the Greyhound bus. So their initial concern and confusion over this proposed road trip were understandable. But, I thought, *that's exactly the point.* My family is like a large majority of our country: disengaged from and widely uninterested in that steel tube with the dog logo on its side barreling down the highway. *Does America have any idea about the bus and her passengers?* I wondered. I knew the only way to find out was to climb back on the "pooch," as the bus is affectionately called. My wife was pretty sure I'd lost my mind, but was reluctantly supportive. I told her it was an itch that needed to be scratched, and if I didn't do this now, while I had the time, I knew I would regret it forever.

My only experience with the Greyhound bus twenty years ago was what had stuck in my mind–this time I anticipated finding a whole cast of hardscrabble characters with interesting stories. But when I started looking into the origins of Greyhound, I discovered that the bus hasn't always been what it is today. In fact, it turns out that the origins of the Greyhound bus are utilitarian and entrepreneurial. In 1914 an unemployed Swedish immigrant named Carl Wickman was living in Hibbing, Minnesota, and looking for a way to make a buck. He began transporting iron mine workers from Hibbing to nearby Alice. It was a short ride, but he charged the tired miners fifteen cents a pop to ferry them back and forth between the mines in Hibbing and the hotels in Alice. He clearly was on to something and started making good money almost immediately. I can imagine these exhausted miners debating among themselves: "Hey, Larry, do you want to hoof it back to Alice?" "No way, Stan, my ass is draggin'. Let's fork over the 30 cents and ride back to the hotel."

A year later Wickman joined forces with a guy named Ralph Bogan, who owned a transit service that ran between Hibbing and Duluth, Minnesota. They called their new venture the Mesaba Transportation Company and recorded first-year profits of $8,000, which was a princely sum in those days. Their fledgling company started buying up buses and driving people all over Minnesota, and three years later they had eighteen buses and were earning $40,000 in profits per year. Like a successful player in Monopoly, Wickman started merging with and gobbling up other companies, and by 1930 Greyhound, complete with dog logo, was born.[1]

I don't know that Carl Wickman or any of his business partners back in the day could have envisioned what Greyhound would become today. At present the active Greyhound fleet consists of about 1,800 buses, serving more than 3,800 destinations in North America, and the company employs more than 7,800 people. In 2010 Greyhound operated nearly 5.5 billion passenger miles and transported almost 18 million riders to their destinations. Greyhound prides itself on their safe travel record, claiming to be the safest mode of transportation over cars, trucks, trains, and planes. They are also quick to point out that each bus takes an average of 19 cars off the road and gets about 170 passenger miles per gallon of fuel.[2]

Bus travel, however, is considerably less popular than air travel. While 18 million people take the bus each year in this country, U.S. airports transported over 717 million passengers in 2010.[3] That makes bus travel about 2.5 percent as utilized as air travel. And while almost everyone seems to have a story about getting pulled over in their car by a police officer, or about a bumpy flight or getting delayed in the airport or seeing someone famous on an airplane, few people have stories about bus travel. You just don't hear someone say, "Boy, I was on the Greyhound the other day, heading to Chicago on business . . ." But there was an era, not long after Wickman and company started the bus line, when bus travel was very popular. This luxurious form of travel was viewed as an adventure, an experience to be savored. At various Greyhound stations there are photos from yesteryear, usually black-and-white, showing nattily dressed passengers posing outside buses. The men wore suits and ties and the women had pillbox hats. It looked like they were all going to church. Riding the bus was a special occasion since automobile travel was still reserved for the relatively wealthy. The old pictures exude an air of prestige and class. My, how times have changed. Well-dressed passengers have now morphed into scruffy men in long gym shorts and tank tops and women wearing low-rider jeans that show off an array of tattoos. During my trip I saw no one–not one person–who dressed up to ride the bus. I doubt the founders of Greyhound could have seen this coming.

Greyhound has had to change over the years to meet their market. While air travel exploded in popularity and accessibility, bus travel went in the other direction. In the early 60s Greyhound found that they needed to target certain groups and markets to keep their business afloat. They had a campaign that appealed to the "Freedom Riders" who protested segregation, and Greyhound actually wound up on the cutting edge of the Civil Rights movement at that time. The popularity of bus travel in the South and in urban centers soared during those years. Since then, Greyhound has had to transition from a mainstream form of transportation to a niche carrier that gets people from one place to another in an affordable manner.

What Greyhound conveniently fails to mention on their website or in their literature is that riding the bus is also exponentially more inconvenient than traveling by car, truck, train, or plane. While a flight from Nashville to Seattle takes five hours (including security pat-downs and rental car procurement), a Greyhound makes the same trip in two days and nine hours. (That calculation is based on an actual trip I took, which was probably faster than most since it was uncharacteristically void of any missed buses or mechanical problems that often add further delay.) Greyhounds have no special "get out of my way" lanes or magical powers to circumvent the same construction and accident traffic that plagues any other driver. I remember once, as a college student, sitting for the better part of eight hours on the Tri-State Toll way, the victim of road construction and heavy holiday traffic on my way back home to Chicago for Thanksgiving. In comparison, riding in an airplane makes me feel like George Jetson, swiftly getting to my destination from high above, glad that I'm not one of those poor bastards stuck in traffic down below. There is both risk and reward for those willing to accept Greyhound's enticing offer to "Go Greyhound and leave the driving to us."

There is also a myth that bus travel is rock-bottom cheap. While that may hold true for short jaunts (the average price of a Greyhound ticket is reported to be only $45), for cross-country travel the rates are really no better than air travel. An average plane ticket, with two weeks' advance purchase, roundtrip from Nashville to San Diego is about $280 plus fees. A round-trip Greyhound ticket between those two cities for the same dates and with the same advance purchase time is $377. Most Greyhound passengers aren't buying round-trip tickets, though. Bus travel seems to be more impulsive than air travel. Whereas I have thoroughly researched and mapped out most of the vacations or business travel I've done in my adult life, it's different for bus travelers. I've never had an occasion, outside of one family emergency, where I've woken up and said, "I think I'm going to fly three states away tomorrow morning." Conversely, most of the bus passengers I met along the way had no idea forty-eight hours before I met them that they would be on the bus that day. They had gotten evicted, had a fight with a girlfriend, or just flat-out decided to blow out of town. Based on my experience, this is Greyhound's target market: folks needing to leave town quickly. For example, with only a day's notice you could take the 19-hour-and-35-minute trip from Nashville to Omaha for only $138.60. For last-minute travel, Greyhound is indeed the cheapest game in town.

So there I was, out to ride alongside the passengers of the bus, the last-minute travelers who were all heading somewhere, for some reason, all with a story to tell. In my mind, I imagined plopping down in the backseat of the bus and interacting with a revolving-door series of nomadic travelers, eager to hear their stories. But I quickly learned that the very backseat of the bus is not always the place to be. The fact that the backseat of the Greyhound bus is documented in two well-known songs is interesting because the backseat is next to the toilet. It usually smells back there. As far as a destination to fall in love or as a place to be born, I could think of a million other better places besides the backseat of a Greyhound bus.

It was a hot August day when my wife, Erica, and my neighbor Pat Madden took me to the Nashville Greyhound station to begin my trip. I was excited. I had spent the past two days packing. I purchased a cheap duffel bag from a local sporting goods store and started loading it with T-shirts and jeans. I tried to pack light, taking only the necessities. I figured I could find a Laundromat to use here or there, and I knew that it didn't much matter what I wore. I wasn't trying to impress anyone; I just wanted to get to know people.

Before I left home my wife and kids and I gathered on our front steps for a family photo. My oldest boy Russ hugged me hard. I was expecting him to start shedding some tears that his dad was going to be gone for the next month, but instead he started laughing. "Have fun on the bus, Dad," he said. I leaned over and got a somewhat limp hug from my youngest boy, Mitch, who, at nine years old, couldn't really figure out what this bus trip was all about. We shared a family group hug before saying goodbye. I have no idea what my boys really thought about their dad getting on a bus for thirty days, but they seemed excited for my adventure.

I had passed the Greyhound station in Nashville many times in the years that I've lived here, but a few days before my trip, when I had mentioned to a friend what I was getting ready to do, he said, "You know they moved the bus station, right?" I hadn't known that. I got on the Internet and found that the new location, on Charlotte Avenue, was about a mile from the old one. I also learned, when looking up the location of the new station, the move was not without controversy. Residents of the neighborhood surrounding the new terminal were royally pissed the station was coming to their area. There were letters to the editor, town meetings, petitions, and all sorts of other futile opposition proposed. My lack of awareness that the bus station had even moved was a sign to me that this was a necessary trip. The location of the Greyhound station was not even a blip on my radar. I try to stay up to speed with respect to community events and local news, but somehow I had missed this year-old fracas over the location of a bus depot. The debate had come and gone fairly quickly and was not well publicized. The fact that the new location of the bus station was met with the same level of excitement neighbors might have in welcoming a new landfill or a prison gave me an even stronger desire to find out why. What was it about buses, bus stations, and bus people that cause folks to cringe? Was the distaste based on stereotypes or was there validity in the citizens' outrage? Well, I was about to find out.

When we arrived at the Greyhound station, Pat, Erica, and I immediately noticed dozens of people standing outside smoking near a row of port-a-lets that had been placed in the parking lot during the construction of the new terminal some six months earlier. I later would learn that this was just a typical scene for a Greyhound station. We walked into the terminal and saw eight people waiting in line to buy tickets for the bus. We had gotten there in plenty of time, so the line wasn't a problem, but the wait gave us all a chance to assess the situation. Pat and Erica just shook their heads. They were supportive, but clearly feared for my safety and sanity as I embarked on this journey. Erica was on her lunch break, so she couldn't linger. She gave me a hug and a kiss and told me to be careful and that she loved me. Pat snapped a picture of us and they headed back out to their car, leaving me to begin this trip on my own.

I was excited, nervous, and a bit uneasy. Would I stick out like a sore thumb? Would I be safe? Would I be able to get people to open up to me and share their stories with me the way they had twenty years earlier?

Finally it was my turn at the ticket counter.

"May I help you?" asked a pleasant, young African American woman. Her name was Christa.

"I'd like to buy a 30-day discovery pass. Have you ever sold one of those before?" I asked her.

"No, I don't think I ever have. I've sold a 7-day and a 14-day, but never a 30-day. What are you going to do? Are you going on vacation?" she asked me.

"No, actually, I'm just going to ride the bus around the country for a month and write a book about my experiences and the people I meet," I cheerily replied.

There was silence. She just started smiling. "You are crazy. But I want to read the book. Have you ever been on the bus before?"

"A long, long time ago. Once I took a bus to go see my college girlfriend."

"Oh, so you're like a virgin. This is so exciting!" she gushed.

While the virgin imagery is something I could have done without, I was pleased that she was excited about the idea. This told me that maybe I was on to something. "That's $439," she told me. I gladly handed over the money, considering it a relative bargain to have an entire month to see as much of the country as I could.

Turns out that Christa had been working for Greyhound for several years. She was a student at Volunteer State Community College, studying to be a nurse. This job was just something to help pay the bills and to squirrel away a little cash to put toward her education.

"I bet you've seen it all," I told her.

This wound up being a handy statement to use during the bus trip—everyone likes to consider themselves as the one who's "seen it all."

"I sure have," she told me. "The bus is crazy. There's crazy people on there. I could write a book about all the stuff *I've* seen . . . This is so exciting! You've got to come back in here when you're done with the trip and tell me how it went . . . Now, you've got to be careful. Watch your stuff. There's people who steal out there." The line behind me had grown to over a dozen but Christa didn't want to say goodbye. Clearly I was a break in the monotony of her day. She wanted to hear more about what I was doing, but finally shook my hand, and with a beautiful smile, wished me good luck.

I rolled my duffel bag with me into the men's room. Recalling my parents' advice to always use the restroom before we hit the road, I made my way to the urinal. In the restroom was one stall with an "out of order" sign taped to the door, a yellow cone warning us of a wet floor, and two weary travelers brushing their teeth in the sink and applying deodorant. It did remind me a bit of the common john on the fourth floor of Haggin Hall, except the travelers were significantly older than college freshmen. It smelled like a bowel movement and I didn't really want to touch any door handles or knobs in the sink. I just held my breath, did my business, and headed back out to the terminal.

Surveying the scene, I saw that there were a few empty seats on the black iron benches lining the walls. I sat down next to a large African American man that I had spotted earlier when I was in line. "Where you headed?" I asked him.

"Memphis. You?" he responded.

"Oh, I'm headed the other direction. Actually, I'm going to be riding around the country for thirty days and writing a book about the trip." He raised his eyebrows, and then a huge smile and a deep chuckle followed.

"You're crazy, man. I ain't never heard nothin' like that before."

"I'm Mike. What's your name?" I asked.

"Marcus," he said, extending his right hand for a firm shake.

Marcus was wearing large, baggy blue jeans and a white T-shirt. He carried only a small duffel bag that was sitting at his feet. He was on his way back to Memphis after having worked in Nashville for the last five days. He had been working at the Hickory Hollow Mall for Olan Mills. They send him all over the Southeast to sell prepaid photo packages for people. Evidently you just go up to Marcus and order a photo package that you can redeem at a time that's convenient. It's a hustle job, and Marcus was probably pretty good at it. He was engaging and affable.

Marcus rides the Greyhound often. He says he prefers it to putting the miles on his car. While the company offers him mileage reimbursement, he chooses to take the bus because his car is on its last leg. "So, do you enjoy taking the bus?" I asked him.

"Not really. But, it ain't bad. Man, I've seen it all. You're gonna see some crazy shit out there on the bus," he offered. "Oh, God. I've seen drug sniffin' dogs find an entire bag of cocaine in Memphis. People are gettin' arrested all the time. One night, there were like five of us on a bus down in Mississippi. It was raining real bad and the driver wasn't paying attention to what was going on. I saw these two dudes and two chicks head to the back of the bus and they started doin' it. Right there on the damn bus."

"What did the driver do?" I asked.

"He didn't give a shit. He was payin' attention to the road cause of the rain," Marcus explained.

We shot the breeze for about an hour before my bus finally arrived. I was taking the eastbound bus that had come from Memphis. It was the first, but definitely not the last, bus that I would have to wait for. That's part of the deal on Greyhound—you just have to wait. Delays are more the rule than the exception. And it does no good to complain. Aside from chartered buses that church groups take on mission trips or a group of seniors might take on their way to Branson, Missouri, Greyhounds are the only bus line in town. In the Northeast there are a host of other bus companies that take people to Boston or Atlantic City, but for the rest of the country, Greyhound is it, and since they have little to no competition, they don't seem to worry too much about customer satisfaction or on-time arrivals.

Since the purpose of my trip was to meet people and tell the story of the bus world, I didn't really care that there were delays. It was an odd experience. Had I been in a hurry to get somewhere, I would have undoubtedly felt the same sense of despair and urgency that the other passengers did. I was able to just objectively observe the frustrations and headaches imparted on other travelers without feeling too burdened myself. But what was interesting was how people responded to the repeated inconvenience and delays of bus travel. The seasoned rider would just shake his head and climb aboard or find a quiet nook in the terminal to wait out the storm. Another would pitch a fit at the counter, trying to find the ear of anyone who would listen or be sympathetic to her cause. Time and time again over this trip I would watch indignation lead to resignation. Once people realized that there was nothing anyone could do to fix their problems, they just gave up. Many passengers I met made that journey along the emotional spectrum, but almost everyone ended up in a place of peace after the resignation. It was as if once they realized they were not in control, a peace came about them and they would just accept whatever befell them. It appeared to be somewhat liberating. It's actually probably not a bad way to live.

Marcus shook my hand, posed for a picture, and told me to be careful and to have fun. I went over to door #2, where Marcus had instructed me to place my duffel bag on the floor to hold my place in line. I didn't really care what number I was in line. I just wanted to make sure that I didn't miss the bus.

"Re-boarders heading to Knoxville please report to door #2," barked the driver of our bus. "Re-boarders," I've learned, are the poor suckers who have been on the bus for God knows how long and have to get back on after they get done smoking. The driver repeated this message about four times and nobody came forward to re-board. This confused him and he started shuffling through the wad of papers on his clipboard.

"I know there are a bunch of people continuing on," he mumbled. "Where are they?"

A Good Samaritan came forward and said, "I think they're all out there smoking. I don't think they can hear you." So the dutiful but irritated driver began his slow stroll across the terminal floor, making his way out the eastern doors where the smokers pit was located. Soon, he returned with about a dozen passengers in tow. He started taking their re-board slips and they went back on to reclaim their prime seats that they had been occupying.

I turned and gave Marcus a last look and a thumbs up as the driver took my ticket. I placed my duffel bag by the side of the bus where the baggage guy was throwing everyone's suitcases under the bus with the ease of tossing a Thanksgiving turkey. I was apprehensive about just leaving my bag by the side of the bus, but I saw everyone else doing it and I figured that my bag would eventually end up in New York, my destination. With the same excitement I felt as a kid mounting a county fair tilt-a-whirl, I climbed aboard Greyhound bus #1510, ready to see America.

DAY TWO

Nashville, Tennessee to Richmond, Virginia

Nashville, TN-Cookeville-Crossville-Knoxville-Greeneville-Johnson City-Bristol-
Marion, VA-Wytheville-Roanoke, Lynchburg, Charlottesville, Richmond

My very first seat partner on the bus was a young African American woman named Denise. When I asked if I could sit next to her, she politely smiled and moved her bag off the seat. We didn't speak much at first; she was listening to music through her headphones. While I was eager to talk to people and learn about their stories, the last thing I wanted to do was immediately announce myself as a nuisance. Historically I've had pretty good luck being a nuisance without much effort, so I figured I would just let that evolve organically.

Our early afternoon ride through the plateau of Tennessee was bright and sunny. The mood on the bus was fairly relaxed. I saw a grandfather and his grandson sharing a package of Twinkies. There were several people curled up against their windows, somehow sleeping despite the bright sunlight. About thirty miles east of Nashville there was an accident in the westbound lanes that caused traffic to slow. Everyone on the bus leaned on their knees and peered out the window to catch a glimpse. An ambulance was loading an injured party on a gurney. I guess it's true what they say about car accidents–people can't help but look. The slowdown lasted no more than twenty minutes, but our driver announced that we would have to hustle at our upcoming stops. "If Cookeville or Crossville are not your final destinations, please remain on the bus." I got the feeling he didn't want to have to herd a group of smokers back onto the bus.

Denise and I finally started talking after we stopped in Crossville, about an hour and a half before we would arrive in Knoxville, which turned out to be Denise's destination. She had started her trip in her hometown, Memphis, and was heading back to Knoxville for the start of the fall semester of her junior year at the University of Tennessee.

"Why don't your parents bring you to school?" I asked her.

"Well, my mom passed away a few years ago and my dad doesn't like to make the drive. He brought me here for my freshman year and said, 'I'll see you at graduation.'"

Denise had a nervous giggle. She didn't seem to mind that her dad wasn't bringing her. She had loaded most of her possessions under the bus to be shipped with us to Knoxville, and was moving into an apartment with three other girls there. This would be a big improvement over dorm life, according to Denise.

I asked about her dad. "He's a manager of a Piggly Wiggly in Memphis. He's been doing that forever," she replied. She told me that she had three siblings that all went to Yale, but that didn't appeal to Denise. She wanted to stay closer to home. She was majoring in social work and wanted to return to Memphis when she was done. She and all of her siblings had gotten significant scholarships to attend college. We talked about Tennessee football and basketball. She told me how much fun the games are and how she didn't understand it when people started burning couches when Lane Kiffin announced his resignation. "These were grown adults, acting like that!" she exclaimed. When we got to Knoxville, I wished her luck and she lugged all of her belongings out onto the sidewalk and waited for a roommate to come pick her up.

The Knoxville terminal had a vaguely familiar feeling. It hadn't changed much in the twenty years since I had last spent a few hours there. I milled around the station for forty-five minutes waiting for my bus to continue on to Richmond, Virginia. I was too excited to sit down. I wanted to snoop around. Inside the terminal was a row of lockers that people can rent for an hour or a day. The restroom looked like it hadn't been cleaned since I was last there. Across from the restrooms was a "restaurant and gift shop" that consisted of a refrigerated shelving unit of cold sandwiches and drinks and two shelves that held Tennessee snow globes, decks of cards, and Greyhound trinkets, such as piggy banks in the shape of a bus. In the waiting area was a bank of vending machines where one could buy a Pepsi for $2.00 or a package of M&Ms for $1.25. One of the vending machines had an "out of order" sign taped to the front.

Suddenly I heard a voice come over the PA system: "All re-boarders heading to Richmond need to report to door #2." I looked in my ticket sleeve, found the re-boarding slip, and marched with purpose over to my door. There was something empowering about holding that slip and walking right by the twenty or so people who were waiting for the same bus. I felt like a VIP. A creature of habit, I went back to the same seat I had taken from Nashville to Knoxville, although I slid over next to the window now that Denise was gone. As people started filing on the bus, one by one, I saw that the bus was going to be full. Every Greyhound bus has a capacity of either 47 or 55 passengers, depending on the presence or absence of handicap seating. This bus held 55, and every seat was taken.

"Can I sit here?" asked a man who looked to be in his late fifties. "Of course," I replied as I moved all of my gear under the seat in front of me. I checked out the guy as he fiddled with his carry-on bag, trying to cram it into the overhead compartment, exhaling and cursing in frustration. He had on a black polo shirt and a mesh hat with a picture of an eagle on the front. His right forearm had a tattoo that I couldn't quite make out, but looked as though it had been there for a long time, maybe something he got in the military or in prison.

"My name's Mike," I said with an outstretched hand.

"Arthur," he replied, "but call me Art. Everyone calls me Art."

"So where are you headed?" I asked him.

"Some shithole town in New Jersey. I gotta go pick up a truck that's in impound," he answered. And with that, Art and I began a ten-hour conversation. Art was a talker, and funny as hell.

As our bus got off I-40, we started winding our way on state highways toward the little burg of Greenville, Tennessee. Greenville was well out of our way, but part of the Greyhound route nevertheless. There we picked up a woman who was having a tearful goodbye with her boyfriend in the parking lot of a gas station.

Larger cities have stand-alone, bustling Greyhound stations, but in most of the smaller towns the "stations" either look like little shacks or are attached to a gas station. You have to look hard for the Greyhound logo at these little stations, but at least the drivers know where they are. Luckily someone got off the bus in Greenville so this poor woman had a place to sit. She sobbed for the next hour or so.

"Her boyfriend probably went straight over to some other girl's house," Art mumbled cynically.

The out-of-the-way stop in Greenville is a perfect example of how the bus works. The Greyhound Bus is kind of like a progressive dinner, only the dinner guests change. You parade from place to place and say goodbye to someone who reaches their destination, hopeful for a new beginning, and you take on a cluster of passengers who are trying to get the hell out of wherever they are. The majority of the 1,775 buses in Greyhound's fleet are constantly in motion, mostly full of passengers on short trips. There's a lot of turnover on the bus. While the guests change frequently, the crowd usually looks the same.

We rolled into Johnson City, Tennessee, a little before midnight. The majority of the bus passengers stepped out to enjoy the ten-minute smoke break, including Art. He was holding court in the informal smoker's circle under the streetlight next to the Greyhound depot. "I think our driver's on somethin'. Did you see the way he was weavin' all over the place?" he asked the group, addressing no one in particular. Several people just nodded their heads while taking long, introspective drags on their cigarettes. "Same old shit," one guy offered up, to which Art said, "You ain't lyin'." It occurred to me that there is an unspoken bond among Greyhound travelers, especially within the community of smokers. Someone makes a blanket statement like, "Same old shit," and, while nobody knows exactly what the person is talking about, everyone just nods in agreement.

People want to belong to a group. It starts in grade school and never ends, I guess. It seems we all have an inherent desire to be a part of something bigger than ourselves. Gangs have thrived for decades, not out of the fun of robbing people or spray painting buildings or bridges, but because they give people a place to belong, a place where they can feel a sense of family. I remember begging my parents to let me join Webelos, an intermediate step between Cub Scouts and Boy Scouts, when I was in the fifth grade. I wanted to wear the uniform. I wanted to get badges and ribbons and make a little wooden car for the Pinewood Derby. But mostly it was about being with my buddies, about having a place to belong.

The people on the bus are no different. Groups form quickly on the trips, some people united by no other factor than their common leg of a bus journey. There were a few people here and there who never said a word to anyone and preferred to be silent, independent travelers, but it was clear that most passengers were looking for connection and community.

The A-list group of the bus world is the smokers. The bond of people huddling together in the rain to enjoy the short-term buzz of nicotine was amazing to watch. Even with the price of cigarettes skyrocketing, people would pass around a pack of Marlboros as if they were living in a commune. It seemed that ten-minute interlude gave people a chance to puff away and talk about anything and everything. It's reported that about one in five adult Americans still smoke,[1] a number that has stayed fairly constant for the last decade or so, but on the bus, I would say it's more like four out of five people who smoke. People looked so forward to that chance to run off the bus and immediately break out their Bic lighters that you would have thought they won the lottery.

Art quickly became the foreman of our bus's informal band of smokers. Just as he had talked my ear off for the past couple of hours, he commanded the same level of attention from the assortment of people in that temporary club as well. The driver, who also smoked, stood about twenty feet away from the cluster, a part of the group, but not really. His body language seemed to say, "I'm part of you, but I'm different from you. I *choose* to be on this bus; you *have* to be on this bus."

After stopping in Johnson City for a smoke break that lasted about fifteen minutes (smoke breaks tend to run long, especially if the driver's a smoker), we all got back on the bus for the very short jaunt to Bristol, Tennessee, where the same cycle would soon be repeated. The smokers would file back out and form a little group, lamenting things about life and about the bus ride.

As we were pulling out of the Bristol stop, I noticed a fifteen-foot-tall guitar statue on the town square that read, "Welcome to Bristol, Tennessee."

"Hey, Art! Check that out!" I said excitedly. He looked at the guitar and quipped, "That was Elvis Presley's guitar." We both laughed. That was the first time I noticed that the bottom half of Art's jaw was slightly skewed to the side. It gave him a mischievous look that was endearing.

"You know it's all bullshit about Elvis. His mom trained him to be a gospel singer. It was that jackass manager of his that made him do rock 'n' roll. It took a toll on Elvis. He never wanted to do that stuff. He became a puppet for those people," Art theorized. As I would learn during our conversation, Art had a theory about everything.

He continued on about Elvis: "You heard about that guy that got in big trouble for digging up his grave, right? He dug that sucker up, and, guess what? No body. But the media doesn't want you hearin' about that." While Art was professing his belief in this Easter morning miracle, I countered, "I heard he died in the bathroom." "Well, that's what everybody said—he died on the shitter. But that's a lie. He ain't dead at all. I'll bet you he just got sick of all the fame and pressure and they're gonna find him on an island somewhere."

As he rambled on I began to look forward to the rest of the ride through Virginia in the dead of night. It wasn't every day that I got to sit as a disciple at the feet of a creative historian like Art.

"Man, this world is just controlled by politicians and the media. I don't know why we don't just vote all those people out of office. They just sit there in Washington gettin' fat and happy. It pisses me off. We need somebody like Davy Crockett. He took care of the people." As Art ranted, I couldn't quite place Davy Crockett's accomplishments, other than making the coonskin cap famous, but Art informed me that he was a dutiful congressman from Tennessee who "didn't put up with any of that Washington bullshit."

He continued, "You know who followed Lincoln in office?" I thought for a minute and debated between Jackson and Johnson. I went with Jackson. "Nope, it was Johnson," Art corrected me. "And you know who followed Kennedy in office? Johnson. You see what I mean? It's just history repeating itself. But you know who's the worst of 'em all? Hillary Clinton. You know that building that got bombed in Oklahoma? Who do you think was behind that? She was. They were investigating her for all of that financial stuff and she blew the damn place up. She just didn't want them snoopin' around. And she's off, free as a bird . . .

"And I'll tell you somethin' else. They try to tell us that they don't know where Osama bin Laden is. That's a load of crap. They know exactly where he is. Hell, they've probably had him for the last ten years. It's because of the damn CIA. Bin Laden's their prodigal son. They taught him everything he knows in Saudi Arabia and then he bombs the shit out of us. They just don't know what to do with him. But they've got him. Don't believe any of that crap about him hiding out in a cave somewhere. We've got him . . .

"And another thing about them terrorists . . . you know how these guys just strap bombs to their bodies and blow their selves up? They've got some religious nut tellin' 'em that they're gonna get to heaven and they'll have a ton of virgins waitin' for 'em. That's a crock of shit. The only thing they're gonna get is the devil's pitchfork up their assholes. I'll tell you that right now."

Art was comfortable jumping from topic to topic.

"See what I mean about this driver? We need to check his cup. It says Wendy's on it but I'll bet you it's full of booze. He can't stay on the damn road." Art was referring to the periodic growling of the rumble strips on the shoulder of the highway. As somewhat of a Greyhound novice, I didn't know if this was something to be worried about or just the natural byproduct of a driver trying to keep a big steel vessel in the dead center of the highway for hundreds of miles.

"Yep, I'll bet he's drinking," I agreed with Art.

"You bet your ass he is," Art added for emphasis.

"So, where is home for you, Art?" I asked, trying to steer our conversation to a happier place.

"I've got a farm up in Michigan," he said, "but I ain't home that much. I only get home for between thirty-six hours and three days every three weeks. The rest of the time I'm drivin'," he lamented. "The truck I usually drive is messed up. It's brand new and under warranty, but this place can't figure it out. They're sending diagnostic tests up to Detroit to see if they can tell what's wrong. In the meantime, I gotta go pick up trucks here and there and make deliveries to keep paying the bills. I deadhead it on the bus. But I hate the damn bus. I'm too old for this shit. I mean look, it's two in the damn morning and we're stopping at every pisshole town from here to New Jersey. Look, it's rainin' out and we're stoppin' at this shithole town in Virginia and there ain't even no one gettin' on the bus. We probably just have to pick up a fuckin' postcard."

Art was referring to the fact that Greyhound not only hauls people around the country, but they make deliveries of packages too. It's kind of like a poor man's UPS. So, even though there might not be a soul waiting for the bus in Monroe, Virginia, at two in the morning, the driver still has to stop because there might be a parcel waiting to be delivered. It would seem that with the advent of cell phones much of this unnecessary stopping and starting could be avoided, but Greyhound hasn't seemed to adapt to the times all that much.

Art continued, "All the trucks nowadays have these snitch boxes, so you pretty much gotta play by the rules. I mean, there're ways around it, but they can tell when you're on the road, when you're sleepin', when you stop to take a dump . . . " Art was explaining the recent addition of GPS units on most eighteen wheelers. In the past drivers just kept a log book of their hours and their stops, but once the new technology was available most trucking companies jumped on it. It's obvious why. "The law says I can only drive eleven hours at a time and I can fiddle with my truck for three hours off the road, but then I gotta rest for ten hours. It's hard for a man to make a livin' anymore with all that stuff."

Art teetered back and forth between being a jovial storyteller and a disenfranchised Vietnam veteran and truck driver. I took in the whole package and was fascinated by this man. I've always wondered who was behind the wheel of the trucks that I see flying down the interstate. Art was a faithful driver. He was providing for his family, his wife and two teenage children on a farm outside of Ann Arbor, Michigan.

"Do you miss your family?" I pried.

"Yeah I miss 'em," he said. "But it's what I gotta do. I gotta earn a living. My dad was a truck driver and my brother's a truck driver. Well, he was until he had a bad car accident. He was going to visit my mom, who was recovering from brain surgery, and on his way to the hospital, he got nailed by somebody. It broke his back. He wasn't paralyzed, thank goodness, but he can't drive a truck anymore. He's on disability for the rest of his life. It's pretty sad. So I feel lucky that I can still drive. Plus, my wife drives me nuts with all her animals. She's got goats and ducks and chickens. What do you do with goats? I don't know what she's doin' with all those animals. I stay far away from it."

"So did you grow up in Michigan?" I asked him.

"No, we just settled up there because we got a good deal on that farm land. I grew up in Kentucky, right on the river. I loved it. Most of my family's still there in Greenup County," he explained.

"I went to school in Lexington," I offered, trying to establish a common bond. "It sure is beautiful there along the river. I'll bet you miss it."

"Yeah, it was a great place to grow up. My cousin and I got into all kinds of shit. One day we went ridin' our bikes and, you know how when the power lines are goin' up the mountain, they've mowed a patch so it's always clear?" I nodded, and Art continued without waiting for a response. "Well, one day we went ridin' our bikes up on the ridge line. We were probably fifteen or sixteen at the time. We were crossin' over by the power lines and we saw this other path that went along this other ridge. We looked down and saw this shiny barrel. Of course we were curious so we went over there and opened it. Would you believe what was inside it? A shit ton of dynamite. So, bein' kids, we took the dynamite and started blowin' shit up. We didn't do any real damage. We just blew up a ton of trees. One of us would stick the dynamite in the neck of a tree and then we'd run back and detonate it. BOOM! Those trees looked like toothpicks when we were done. We were runnin' all over that mountain blowin' shit up. It was so much fun."

"Did you get caught?" I asked him.

"I'm gettin' to that . . ." Art giggled. "We were up there for an hour or two and up some side road we hear a siren and it's the damn sheriff. We had the town police after our ass, the sheriff and, would you believe, the secret service? Well, we didn't have any idea, but President Nixon was planning on making a visit to our little town a few days later. So there were secret service guys all over the place to make sure it was safe. My cousin and I shit our pants. They called our dads and we got in so much trouble. But, the crazy part came when they started questioning us. They were asking if we were planning on blowing up the President. I told 'em no, we just found the dynamite and started blowin' trees up. We didn't mean any harm by it.

"Man, we were grounded forever. The President canceled his trip to Kentucky, and we had to get up at the crack of dawn and do extra chores for weeks. But, I'll tell you what, it was worth it." Art grinned. "We had a hell of a good time."

In Roanoke, Virginia, we switched drivers. Ken, the alleged drunk, surrendered control to an African American woman named J.M. She was no-nonsense. Thin but strong, J.M. looked to be in her early fifties. Immediately upon beginning her shift, she announced her presence with authority and started barking orders to everyone in earshot of the bus about needing to have your tickets out of the sleeve. "If you do not have your ticket ready to hand to me, I will not accept it! You, over there, what do you think you are doing?"

she yelled at a man who was fishing his suitcase out from underneath the bus. "You may not go under the bus. Baggage handlers will do that!" The man got in her face and started cussing at her and she gave it right back to him. Eventually both cooled off and new passengers joined us for the duration of our trip to Richmond.

"Great. We get rid of the drunk and now we've got Annie Fuckin' Oakley," Art complained. "What's her deal?"

"Yeah, it seems that some of the drivers aren't in too good of a mood," I agreed with Art.

"Nobody on the bus is in a good mood," he said. "I mean, look, I gotta ride this damn thing to Philadelphia, wait for three hours, and then get back on for a thirty-minute ride to New Jersey. Does that make any damn sense?"

"No, it doesn't," I offered. "Why don't you check and see if they have other buses or cabs or something so you don't have to sit around so long?"

"Yeah, I just might do that. I don't want to sit for three hours with my thumb up my ass and then get back on another one of these things to go like twenty miles. It's stupid. I'll tell you what, if I had a million bucks, I'd buy my own bus. I'd put a nice crapper in the back and I'd put in a full bar. And, on this side, I'd put a hot tub. I'd put it right up to the window so that when cars came by, I could get out of the hot tub, press my bare ass against the window, and moon everybody that drove by. That's what I'd do."

As our bus pulled out of Roanoke, Art started complaining again about all of the stops we were having to make and then started singing at the top of his lungs, "We're off the see the wizard . . ." That drew much laughter from the weary bus crowd.

"I'll bet you didn't think you'd get this much entertainment tonight, or that you would be sitting by some smart ass who made you laugh all night, " Art said.

We both settled down for a nap on our way into Richmond. Art and I had only known each other for a few hours, but we had developed a quick bond. It was comfortable. We didn't need to say anything to each other. It was like we had known each other for years. This wasn't a feeling I had anticipated on the bus, and it came rather quickly. It felt like I was right where I needed to be. While my trip was less than a day old, I was feeling that this was exactly why I had signed up for this adventure. I wanted to find out who was on the bus and what made them tick. Art set the bar pretty high.

DAY THREE

Richmond, Virginia to Wilmington, Delaware

Richmond, VA-Baltimore, MD-Newark, NJ-New York, NY-
Newark, NJ-Mt. Laurel, NJ-Wilmington, DE

A few miles outside Richmond, J.M. began a speech about us needing to participate in a process she referred to as "claim and transfer." "Claim and transfer" is fancy talk for "walk out beside the bus, trample anyone in your way like you're at a Who concert, grab your bags, and try not to let anyone steal anything for the next hour while you're waiting until you have to shove the bag into the bowels of another bus." "Claim and transfer" is Greyhound's way of saying, "You're pretty much on your own," but they make it sound like a sophisticated ritual. J.M. made it clear that we would each be responsible for our bags because this particular bus was done in Richmond. We would all be changing over to a different bus, no matter our destination. While she had aggressively reprimanded a passenger back in Roanoke for reaching in the luggage compartment and grabbing his own bag, she now informed us that we would have to do this very thing.

The rules appeared to be fluid, but we were expected to just follow along and take orders.

When we pulled into Richmond, I asked Art where he was going after picking up the truck in New Jersey.

"I've gotta drive it back to Knoxville and then pick up another load and head to Dallas," he said, " Then I've gotta take the damn bus back to Knoxville and see if they've got my truck fixed by then."

We shook hands good-bye. Art was heading to Philadelphia and I was on a different bus going to New York. "It's been a pleasure," I said.

My layover was brief, only thirty minutes, one of the benefits of consistently late buses. A little after six in the morning, I joined about thirty other passengers for the fairly straight shot up to New York. We would only make one stop, at a rest area in Baltimore.

I decided it would be a good time to try and talk to a driver. So I grabbed a seat in the front row. On every bus is a large Plexiglass shield between the driver and the passengers, a result of the stabbing death of a driver that took place shortly after 9/11. People were worried that there might be a terrorist connection, but it turned out to be a mentally unstable immigrant from Eastern Europe who attacked this poor driver somewhere around Manchester, Tennessee. As Art had earlier explained to me, "It used to be kind of cool . . . You could sit right behind the driver and bullshit with him all day, but those days are gone."

In 2008 there was another highly publicized crime on a Greyhound bus traveling to Winnipeg, Manitoba. A 22 year-old carnival worker, Tim McLean, was heading home after having worked in Edmonton, Alberta. A deranged Chinese immigrant named Vincent Li began stabbing the young man while he slept. As bus passengers started screaming and running off the bus, the attacker continued stabbing McLean, eventually decapitating him. At Li's trial, he was found to be not criminally responsible for the murder and continues to be held in a high-security mental facility in Canada.

There are a few other random stories about attacks and shootings, some at Greyhound stations and some on the bus, but bus travel does not appear to be any more prone to violent outbursts than you would find in any other part of society. The murders of the driver in Tennessee and the young Canadian man were certainly out of the ordinary, the byproducts of mentally ill people who could have carried out their attacks anywhere. They just happened to be on the bus. Greyhound buses are generally safe. While the stereotype exists that buses transport hardscrabble passengers who may be prone to lives of crime, the bus is probably every bit as safe, if not safer, than any other form of transportation.

Nonetheless, the Plexiglass barrier is a reminder of a corporate reaction to try and eliminate the possibility of a passenger harming a driver. For better or worse, the barrier was there. The drivers were set apart and protected. They could still communicate with passengers via the public address system that all of the buses had, but it also gave them the opportunity to just tune out the bus conversations and be in their own worlds as they steered the big bus down the road.

On this leg I was determined to get to know our new driver, who introduced himself as Henry. Henry was a thin African-American man, who wove his way through the streets of Richmond with great ease, looking for the ramp to I-95N. Once we got on the highway, I leaned my face forward, hoping my voice would carry through one of the cracks in the plastic.

Me: "Henry, can you hear me?"

Henry: Silence.

Me: "Henry, CAN YOU HEAR ME?"

Henry: "Yeah."

Me: "So, how long have you been driving?"

Henry: "Too long."

Me: "Do you live in Richmond?"

Henry: "No."

Me: "I'm riding the bus around the country and writing a book about it."

Henry: "Ok."

Me: "So do you like driving?"

Henry: Silence.

At this point I gave up and figured, *you can't win 'em all.* Henry did a great job of driving but he wasn't much of a conversationalist. I thought that there would be other opportunities over the next thirty days to pick the brain of a driver, so I gave up on Henry. I put in my own headphones and enjoyed the scenery around Washington D.C. and Baltimore.

I had decided to make New York my first overnight stop for a couple of reasons. First, I had never been there before and, at thirty-eight years old, that seemed to be a tragedy. Second, in my mind, New York seemed to be the epicenter of public transportation. I figured if I were writing a book on bus travel, I might as well go to the capital of the bus world.

I walked from the Port Authority to 35th Street in search of a comfortable bed and warm shower. I was tired, dirty, and smelly. Exploring this vast, noisy, smelly city for the first time, I feared that I looked like I was from Green Acres. I wandered around midtown Manhattan looking for a reasonably priced hotel room. This was a large task. One desk attendant said, "Our starting rate is $279 per night." She had a sing-songy voice that meant, "You look like you just got off a bus and there's no way in hell you can afford to stay here, but I'll humor you." I sulked out of the hotel like I had just been cut from my middle school basketball team and started walking the sidewalks again.

New York was pretty much what I expected. People moved around at a frantic clip. It smelled like sewage and there were just tons of people everywhere. Finally I bit the bullet and found a hotel in Chelsea for $179 a night. I immediately showered and put on clean clothing. When I opened the drapes I saw that I had a view of a parking garage and several apartment buildings that looked like they could have been in Warsaw, Poland. Horns and sirens were going off constantly. After enjoying a $16 sandwich and $6 Budweiser, I climbed into the cocoon of my room, cranked the air conditioning to dim the noise, and slept for twelve straight hours.

I woke up refreshed and ready to head back out on my journey. I decided I had spent almost twenty-four hours in New York City and that was plenty. But before I left town I wanted to at least snoop around and see a couple of landmarks, if only from a distance. So I walked over toward Madison Square Garden. As I walked I would occasionally stop and look skyward, noticing the enormous buildings and sights I had seen on TV for years. But this trip wasn't a sightseeing mission, so I resisted the urge to act like a tourist and go to the top of the Empire State Building or ferry out to the Statue of Liberty. I realized this was going to be one of the hardest parts of the trip. I was going to traipse across America and see a lot of cool stuff out the window of the bus. But, if I were to stop and see everything that I wanted to see, then it would feel like I had cheated on my family with my mistress, the bus. I didn't want to be sneaky. I would maybe catch a ball game or two, but the landmarks and great destinations of this country would be better left on a shelf for another trip at another time. I consoled myself with the thought that I'd rather share that with my family on a proper vacation anyway. So I took a leisurely stroll back toward the bus station, wondering who I would meet on the next leg of my trip.

After devouring some cheap, greasy, and delicious pizza, I headed back toward the bus station, bound for the Midwest. I had learned from Art that St. Louis had the crappiest bus station in the whole country. If that received Art's special distinction, I decided I had to check it out. My spirits soured a bit when I went to the ticket counter and saw about one hundred and fifty people in line with only four ticket agents handling the transactions. The New York Port Authority is enormous. In fact, New York ranks as the busiest

Greyhound station in the US and Canada.[1] The volume is twenty-fold more than any other bus station I visited. So I got in line and trusted that they knew what they were doing.

I stood right in front of a very attractive-looking couple. "Where are you all headed?" I asked them. They just smiled at me and said something about not speaking English very well. "Where are you from?" I continued. "Barcelona," they said. I started speaking to them in Spanish (finally, my Spanish minor in college was put to good use!) and they smiled radiantly at me.

They introduced themselves as Jose and Pepita and explained that they were here in the US on vacation for a couple of weeks with their teenage daughters. Their travel agent back in Barcelona had recommended that they take the Greyhound because it's a good way to see the United States. They were going to Washington D.C., and then up to Niagra Falls. I suspected that their smiles would soon fade as they lugged their suitcases from bus to bus, but I didn't have the heart to tell them what they were in for.

"Oh you guys are going to have such a great time!" I exclaimed.

Jose and Pepita were so excited to see the sights. They had previously traveled to the US but spent their time out west, seeing San Francisco and the Grand Canyon. I got my ticket to St. Louis and wished Jose and Pepita well.

I was told to report to gate 74. The terminal was a maze, but like most public transportation hubs, seemed to be full of people who knew what they were doing and where they were going. Everyone but me. I had to stop three times to get directions for gate 74. But I found it and got in line. It was a long line. I was sure this bus would be full. For all of the financial trouble I had heard that the bus company was having, it sure wasn't for a lack of passengers.

The driver summoned all riders to Baltimore. That would be my first stop and from there I would take another bus west. We loaded on the crowded bus and I chose a seat next to a young woman about four rows back on the driver's side. In front of us sat a man in a Panama hat who looked to be in his late forties, along with an oversized man in a tank top who was probably twenty-two. The young man had headphones on the entire time, but the man in the Panama hat was a talker.

"I can't believe how crowded it is here. They probably have twenty thousand people a day coming through here getting on buses," I began the conversation.

"I'd say your estimate is way too low," corrected the man. "There are four hundred bus slips at Port Authority and they run a bus out of each of them about every hour of the day. If you figure each bus holds between forty and fifty people, well, you do the math . . ."

Soon I learned that his name was Joe, and my seatmate introduced herself as Kate. For the next three and a half hours, we had a great conversation.

Kate was a college student traveling to Delaware for a friend's twenty-first birthday celebration. She began her trip in Albany and had to transfer buses in New York City to get her where she needed to go. "Why are you taking the bus to Delaware?" I asked her.

"My parents don't want me driving my Honda Accord down the Jersey Turnpike on a Friday afternoon. It's got 240,000 miles on it and they're worried something might happen to the car, or to me," she said.

I remember wondering if her parents had ever ridden a Greyhound bus. If they had, I was sure that they would have had bigger safety concerns about their beautiful daughter riding a bus full of strangers than piloting her trusty Accord down the turnpike. But, as I would learn, traveling by bus around the Northeast is different from bus travel in the rest of the country. There is far more socioeconomic diversity on the buses out of New York than in the rest of the country.

In most parts of the country, the bus is for poor people.

Almost everyone I encountered on the bus said that they would rather be flying, but they couldn't afford it. In New York, people take the bus because driving is a pain. People take the bus to and from work. They travel to the beach on the bus. They go to Atlantic City to gamble via the bus. It's not a move of desperation–rather, it's one of convenience. If you've grown up with buses, subways, trains, and cabs, you learn the game pretty quickly. It's easier to just plop on a subway or bus, pay the fare, and get where you're going than it would be to drive your car in a city of nearly ten million people, find a place to park, and deal with incessant traffic headaches. Of the top six busiest Greyhound terminals in the US, five are on the eastern seaboard: New York, Atlantic City, Philadelphia, Washington D.C., and Boston.[2]

Kate was excited to be going to Delaware. She was taking the bus to Wilmington and then a couple of her friends were picking her up to drive her the remaining twenty miles to Newark.

"I can't wait to see my friends. All of my roommates are getting together and we're going out. But I hope Tim's not there," she fretted. "He's my roommate's boyfriend. He's not a real bright guy to begin with and when he drinks he turns into a mess, and he drinks a lot. I don't know what she sees in him. But, what can I do? I remember last year, he was drunk after a party and he didn't know where he was. So I gave him the wrong directions back to his dorm. I sent him in the totally opposite direction and he didn't even know it. He's an idiot."

Kate was looking forward to the next semester when she and three roommates would share an apartment off campus. "We've already bought a blender and we're going to make margaritas!" she said enthusiastically. "I was pretty straight in high school. I never partied at all. But, I absolutely love college." I was a little bit jealous of Kate–she was me, twenty years ago. Her biggest responsibilities in life right now were to go to class and write some papers. Her world revolved around her friends, the Gamma Phi Beta sorority, and the college lifestyle. Kate had started out studying biology but she hated it. She had since switched majors to sociology and public health. She said she would love to get into Johns Hopkins in their public health program, but didn't know if she'd be able to pull the requisite grades.

"My parents wanted me to stay close to home and go to RPI–Rensselaer Polytechnic Institute, a school near Albany, but I wanted to get away. I've been there my whole life and wanted to try something new. Delaware is a good school and it's not too far away," she explained. Kate was a bright girl, full of youthful wonder. She loved and respected her family, but also wanted to get out there and carve her own way. "When I was a freshman in high school, I went to France for two weeks on an exchange program. It was so exciting to be in a different country. I would go back in a second. But everyone over there smoked and it smelled gross. Oh, and also, this one time, we went out to eat and I ordered a steak. All my friends ordered a steak. When they brought it to our table, though, the steaks were bloody. I haven't eaten a steak since."

She said that she would love to go to South Africa for the seven-week winter term. She wants to go to Honduras, Costa Rica, or Belize and help children with AIDS. I enjoyed sitting next to her and having her rapid-fire, broad-reaching dreams wash over me.

"You're lucky you started talking to me right away," she laughed. "I was about ten minutes away from plugging in my iPod, and then we never would have gotten to know each other. This kind of disproves my parents' whole 'don't talk to strangers' thing. This is fun."

Joe was leaning against the window so that he could listen to our conversation and offer his two cents when it was asked for, and even when it wasn't. Kate was explaining that she was really going to miss her summer nanny job in Albany. "I love kids. They have two boys, thirteen and nine, and they are the sweetest kids. It's been a great job. It's pretty much nine-to-five all summer and then on evenings and weekends I work at a place that does birthday parties for children. I can't wait to have children. I hope to have two little girls so I can dress them up really cute," she said.

"Kids are a lot of work. It's more than just dressing them up," Joe chimed in, totally missing the point. "I've got a thirteen-year-old and he's a big responsibility."

"So, what brings you to New York, Joe?" I asked.

"I dropped off a UPS truck here this morning. Now I'm riding home to Elkhart, Indiana. Most of the RVs in the country are made in Elkhart, but they also make ambulances, cherry pickers, and small trucks there. I work for a company that delivers all of these vehicles to their destinations. Then I take the Greyhound back to Elkhart. I bought a sixty-day pass for $569. It's a pretty good deal," he explained.

I was instantly interested in Joe's job since he constantly rides Greyhounds so often. Joe had an inviting way about him. While he was an expert on all things Greyhound, and many other things, for that matter, he enjoyed listening to Kate's story and weighing in from time to time. "What are those orange balls on the power lines for?" Kate asked, looking out the window. Joe jumped on that.

"Those are there so birds won't electrocute themselves."

When Joe wasn't looking, I raised my eyebrows at Kate and slowly shook my head from side to side. Joe was a subscriber to the mantra, "If you don't know the answer, just make it up and sound confident."

Kate unknowingly ingratiated herself to Joe by asking him questions and asking for his opinions on things, a tactic I've deliberately used many times myself. I figure people's favorite topic of conversation is themselves. If you're willing to ask questions and listen intently, you are able to show that you value that person and that what they have to say really matters. If you show you care, people will open up and share their stories. It was an approach that was already paying dividends for me on this trip. People want to feel that their opinions and experiences matter. For Joe, this was a welcome chance to be the king with his court seated nearby.

"I've seen it all on the bus," Joe said. Kate and I listened to him like a couple of kindergartners at storytime.

"What's the craziest thing you've seen on the bus?" I prodded.

"Well, one time I saw a bus driver make a U-turn in the middle of the street to kick a guy off the bus. The guy was pissed off that the driver was taking too long to leave Baltimore, and the driver had stopped the bus about a block from the station because some old guy in the back of his bus was washing his feet in vinegar. She went back there to tell him to knock it off, but the passenger was up in her face. He was saying, 'What's your problem, bitch? Hurry the bus up, bitch.' She did a U-turn on a dime and kicked his ass off the bus. She said, 'I'm not telling you that you can't ride a Greyhound bus. I'm telling you that you're not going to ride this Greyhound bus.' Everybody on the bus was quiet except this guy, but she wasn't gonna put up with his shit," Joe informed us. Kate and I just sat there wide-eyed, perhaps hoping for a similar dramatic moment on our bus.

I steered the conversation back to Kate. "So, are you dating anyone?" I asked.

"No. I've dated some guys, but nothing serious right now." Kate was really good-looking. She had long brown hair and soothing blue eyes. When she smiled, a dimple formed off the corner of her mouth. "My dad jokes around that he's always going to give guys the third degree when they come pick me up for a date. He's all bragging about how he's going to grill them and scare them off, but he usually just ends up talking to them about sports." Joe was positioning his head so that he could look back and join in the conversation but also keep an attentive eye forward. He was smiling as Kate talked about college, boys, and her future. You could tell Joe really enjoyed bus interactions.

"I don't know," Kate continued. "Guys are kind of jerks

sometimes. I mean they seem to only want one thing. I had this friend in high school who had to break up with her boyfriend a million times. They were on-again, off-again all the time. They were both on the cross country team and one time, on their way to a meet, he wanted her to have sex with him right there on the school bus. She told him he was crazy, but he got pissed and broke up with her. Can you believe that?" "Yeah, guys are pigs," I agreed.

As we pulled into Wilmington, Delaware, Kate got a text message. "God," she said. "Tim's going to pick me up. Ugghhh."

DAY THREE

Wilmington, Delaware to Pittsburgh, Pennsylvania

Wilmington, DE-Baltimore, MD-Breezewood, PA-Pittsburgh, PA

We were only in Wilmington for ten minutes or so. The driver ran a tight bus; he didn't even let the smokers off. On the way out of New York, he had introduced himself as "Officer Starling." I didn't know if he borrowed this from days spent in the military or if he had given himself this name.

Some drivers did tend to assume a military persona. In fact, as I later learned at the Greyhound Bus Museum, the founders of Greyhound originally insisted that bus drivers wear military-style clothing so that they would get the respect of the passengers. But that was eighty-five years ago. Today they all wear the same snazzy uniform consisting of black pants, short-sleeved royal blue shirt, maroon necktie, and gray vest. Most of the men wear a bus conductor's hat that looks just like a police officer's hat.

Officer Starling was tall and thin and no-nonsense. "Unless Wilmington is your destination, please sit tight," he said when we stopped.

As a new handful of passengers got on, they looked left and right, scanning the bus for open seats. A very large man plopped down next to me. He was huffing and puffing, exhaling loudly, cussing under his breath. He was wearing a navy-blue tank top and long royal-blue gym shorts.

"Can't believe this bullshit," he began. "I haven't ridden a bus in twenty years and here I sit."

"So what happened? Why are you on the bus?" I asked the man who introduced himself as Kevin. "I got in a fight with a business associate up in New York. I'm up there all the time, but this guy was trying to screw me. I had planned on spending most of the day up there, but when things went south, I decided to head back to Baltimore. My wife and I are flying up to the Vineyard this weekend on vacation. I went to Amtrak and asked how much it would cost to take the train from New York to Baltimore and they told me it would be $189. I thought that was nuts. I'm not that frugal, but that's way too much for a short train ride. So I take a commuter train down into Jersey, then I switch on another train that takes me to Philly. And I get on another one that brings me here to Wilmington. At this point, I'm still up like $125 compared to what Amtrak was going to charge me. But I find out that there are no other commuter trains from Wilmington to Baltimore. Can you believe that? It's just Amtrak. So I ask them how much it would be and they told me $89. I'm like 'fuck that.' I'm not giving Amtrak a cent. Greyhound's only $55. I'm riding the bus out of principle. But I hate it. The bus sucks."

Kevin was articulate, even with his salty language. He was wearing an outfit that was typical bus attire: baggy gym shorts and a muscle shirt, but I could tell there was more to this guy. I poked for more information.

"What do you do in New York?" I asked.

"I'm in construction. I do everything from residential to small commercial. I was just up there trying to get a project hammered out and this guy was trying to mess with me. I was like, 'I don't need this,' so I left. I've been in construction for over fifteen years."

Turns out that Kevin used to work on Wall Street, but he didn't like the pressure and stress, so he decided to get into something he enjoyed and could make a living in. Kevin was not the prototypical bus rider—he was one of the few passengers I met who had a college degree. A few of the people I spoke with on the bus had gone to college and dropped out. Many admitted to never having graduated from high school. Two-thirds of Greyhound's adult passengers have an annual income of less than $35,000.[1] Kevin certainly stood out with his high-paying job, assuming he was shooting straight with me.

"I've done really well. I make a lot of money. But I've changed what I'm doing. I used to go into Baltimore and flip houses. If you know what you're doing, you can buy a house for next to nothing and make a killing on it. But the neighborhoods sucked and we always had our shit stolen, so I decided to get out of there and get into more commercial stuff. I used to have a crew of forty-two, but I've gone down to eleven," he continued.

Kevin's phone was ringing constantly. Sometimes he'd let it go to voice mail; other times he would answer in an abrupt, rapid-fire, business-like manner. "That's the bad thing about this job. People are constantly calling. There's never a break. Nights, weekends, it doesn't matter. I've actually got one of the guys that does work for me picking me up at the bus station. They're good guys, for the most part. But some of them are tough to deal with. Like 75 percent of the people in construction don't have a high school degree. Of those, 40 percent are illiterate. They don't have formal training but they've been doing this kind of work so long that they just know how to do it. They know how to frame or hang drywall, but they couldn't explain to anyone else how to do it."

"That must be a pretty big challenge, staying on top of these guys and communicating with them," I weighed in.

"Yeah, exactly. Here's the thing. You can't trust these guys for shit, either. I don't tell these guys where I live anymore. I'm having this guy that's picking me up at the bus station just take me to a mall near my house and then my wife will pick me up from there. I quit trusting them after I threw a party at my house. You know, I'm a nice guy and I was trying to do something nice for my workers. But a few months later, my house got robbed. They stole all my shit. I know it's one of the subs [subcontractors] that did it. It was a tough lesson, but there's people like that out in this world.

"So what's up with you? What are you doing on the bus?" Kevin asked me.

When I told him the background story about my history with the bus and about this trip, he was intrigued. "No shit? That's wild. Really?" From that moment on, Kevin's mood improved and we started theorizing about the human condition. Instead of continuing with his irritated tone, he took a more diplomatic, detached approach. "Those dudes that ripped me off, it's just sad. It's sad that people feel like they've got to resort to that. I don't know what they're going through, but if they had just asked me for something, I would have given it to them. And the reason we got out of Baltimore wasn't just because we were getting our shit stolen. It's just depressing. There's no hope there. The people that live there feel like the only way they can survive is to rip each other off. I guess it doesn't really change no matter where you live. People step on each other all the time to get ahead."

Kevin had spent a lot of time thinking about what drives people to steal and why he and his family were lucky enough to be financially successful. He knew that he had a path for success, but I could tell that it gnawed at him that there were some who would never have the chance to be in his shoes. Like most of us, Kevin rationalized that he had made it successfully on his own. But really we all know that there's a lot of luck and access to opportunity involved in being successful.

Kevin eventually moved on from the ills of the construction world when he realized he had found someone who was generally interested in what he had to say. I discovered that Kevin was married, with two girls, one in college and one in high school. At this point Joe woke from a brief nap in the seat in front of us and chimed in.

"It's too bad Kate isn't here," he said. "She wants to have two girls so that she can dress them up and play with them."

"My oldest goes to the University of Virginia. You wouldn't believe how much that shit is costing me," Kevin countered. "Before that, she went to a private high school. When she's done there at UVA, she wants to go to law school. My youngest is still in the private high school, but she also wants to go to UVA next year. I thought it would get cheaper as the kids got older, but it's crazy. I told them I'd pay for it all the way. So I've got a lot of stress to keep making a lot of money. And then there's my wife. She's never worked a day in her life. She's never paid a bill. We've been married twenty-one years and she doesn't have a clue about bills. I'm the guy. I'm the one who knows how much all this shit costs. It never ends."

Wanting to pick his scab even more, I asked, "So . . . what are you going to do when your oldest comes to you and says, 'daddy, I want a big wedding'?" Kevin quickly jumped on that. "I've already told them no way. I'm not paying for a big wedding. We have these friends that paid like $250,000 for their daughter's wedding. It was obscene. You wouldn't believe how nice this thing was. Open bar. The best of everything. And guess what? Four and half months later, the marriage was over. The dude had this girl on the side that he had met at work and he was banging her and the wife found out. Her parents were so pissed. I'm not going through that. What a waste of money!"

"My wife and I got married in our living room," Joe weighed in. There were maybe fifteen people there. We didn't really even get dressed up. We kept it simple. We're divorced now. But at least we didn't piss away a ton of money on a wedding."

Kevin nodded. "That's the way to go. My wife and I had a huge wedding. There were like three hundred and fifty people there. Three hundred from her side and about fifty from mine. But I had to pay for the whole damn thing. It was like fifteen grand. I told her that I wanted to invite more people from my side because they would probably give better gifts than people from her side." He continued, "Sure enough, we got like $9,000 in cash gifts and most of it was from my side. So I was still in the hole like six grand on the wedding. I was hoping we would break even. I don't even understand why we had that big wedding instead of using that money to start out on our life. That would have made a nice down payment on a house." At this point, I was wondering if Kevin's wife would agree with anything that was coming out of his mouth. But, on this bus ride, Kevin was the solo historian.

"Big moments are important to women," I said. "Women like the fairy tale. That's just the way it is. And I'll bet when your daughter comes to you and wants that big wedding, you're going to cave."

"Hell no!" he exclaimed. "There's no way."

I said goodbye to Kevin at the travel plaza in Baltimore, hoping that his first bus ride in twenty years was one that he enjoyed, even if just a little.

Baltimore has two main Greyhound stops—one just north of the city, the travel plaza where I said goodbye to Kevin, and one downtown, which has only a handful of bus slips. Joe and I got off the bus together downtown and grabbed our bags. The circuitous route to St. Louis required this transfer in Baltimore. Joe traveled light, carrying only a backpack that held one change of clothes and his toiletries. He pretty much had this bus thing down to a science. He only took what he needed to be comfortable for his trip home.

Because of all of the traffic we'd encountered on the New Jersey Turnpike, we only had a short layover in Baltimore. Within minutes of getting to the terminal, we were summoned to gate 3. On that day, there were so many people heading west that Greyhound had ordered another bus. Over the PA system we heard, "If you are going to Frederick or Hagerstown, please head to gate 2. If you are going to Breezewood or Pittsburgh, please go to gate 3."

"That's good news," Joe informed me. "That means we're going to get an express bus to Pittsburgh and we won't have to stop in Frederick or Hagerstown. That will save us thirty minutes, at least. That means we'll have a longer dinner break in Breezewood."

Joe considered this a small victory. He couldn't believe his good fortune that we would have an extra half hour at dinner. Maybe he felt like after all the miles he had logged on Greyhound, it was his time to be rewarded. And, because it was a victory for Joe, it became a victory for me. Honestly, at first I didn't much care. Later in the trip, I would grow to care about these small victories, but for now I was still just about riding the bus, getting to know people. A smoke break in Frederick, Maryland, would hardly ruin my night.

We all like to have small victories. We like it when we find a parking spot close to the entrance of the store or are the first in line. We like it when the hostess at Applebee's tells us that it's going to be a forty-five-minute wait and it turns out to only be ten. I enjoy an unforeseen stroke of good fortune as much as the next guy. When I was in the sixth grade, I sat around all day listening to Z-104, waiting for the cue to be the tenth caller to win concert tickets for Michael Jackson's Victory Tour. I hurriedly dialed 663-8104 and, after getting busy signals for the first few times, I heard the phone ring. The DJ picked up and said, "You're caller 10!" I went bananas on the radio and was simultaneously ridiculed and celebrated by all of my friends. It felt good to win. I was special and set apart.

These undeserved victory moments feel good. None of us are owed, or "due" for an instance of good luck. It just happens. And, when it does, our spirits are buoyed. We feel that maybe there is something special about us, that maybe we are somehow just a cut above. For that moment, however fleeting, we feel grand. On the bus, especially, moments like that matter.

A burly, African American driver was standing by gate 3 collecting our boarding passes. I gave him my sleeve, which contained a handful of tickets. Greyhound gives passengers a series of tickets, based on where they are going. They are in sequence and fold up like an accordion. The driver tears off the ticket for the portion of the trip that he or she is driving. It is up to the passenger to keep the sleeve of tickets in a safe place, as Greyhound will not replace stolen or lost tickets. Some drivers are glad to take the passenger's sleeve, root around until they find the right ticket and tear it off. Other drivers bark out "Have your ticket out of its sleeve and ready to hand to me." This driver, whose nametag read "Kendrick," was one who didn't want to fool with searching for the right ticket.

For that reason, I purposely just handed Kendrick my entire sleeve of tickets and looked off in the distance. He didn't take the sleeve out of my hands. He just stared at me. It was a Western stand-off until I finally, slowly and deliberately, dropped my two bags and licked my fingers to flip through and find the proper ticket. Kendrick couldn't take it anymore. He spoke up "What did I just tell everyone? Have your ticket ready to give to me." And with that little reprimand, he slowly rocked back and forth and huffed and puffed until I gave him the ticket. He was shaking his head as I took my bag over to the handler to load on the bus.

Because we were getting on an overflow bus, there were seats aplenty. Since Joe and I had struck up a bus friendship, we weren't interested in spreading out. Instead, we sat next to each other the whole way to Pittsburgh. "I guess while I nodded off in Delaware, I got a phone call from the dispatcher in Elkhart. She assigned me to deliver another UPS truck down to Alpine, Texas," Joe began. We got out a map and discovered that Alpine was in the bend of Texas, close to the Mexican border. "I had hoped to spend a few days with my son in Elkhart, but now I've got to leave about twelve hours after I get there because the truck has to be in Alpine by Tuesday morning by 10:30," Joe lamented.

This was Joe's life. He had begun driving for this company about eight months earlier and he had the routine down: drive a truck to God-knows-where and take the Greyhound back to Elkhart. He said that he got paid by the mile, so it was in his best interest to grab as many runs as he could. This night he would ride through Pittsburgh, Cleveland, and Toledo and arrive sometime the next morning in Elkhart.

Kendrick got everyone loaded on the bus and started fiddling with his microphone. After a few minutes, he realized that the PA system on the bus was broken. This happened about 25 percent of the time during my trip. So he walked down the aisle, to about the halfway point, and with his booming voice, went through the drivers' spiel.

"My name is Kendrick. I will be taking you to Pittsburgh this evening. There is to be no drinking alcohol or using drugs on the bus or during any of our stops. There is no smoking on the coach. That includes the bathroom. If I catch you smoking, you will be put off the bus. It is a federal offense. If you need to speak with me, you can approach me, but do not cross the white line. We're going to be together for the next several hours, so why don't you introduce yourself to the person seated next to you. Maybe you will make some new friends."

"I'M MIKE," I announced at the top of my lungs. Kendrick quickly replied, "We're not in an A.A. meeting, Mike, but it's nice to meet you. Now if any of you have Walkmans, iPods, computers, any of that stuff, please use headphones. Keep your cell phones on silent and keep your conversations quiet. Now, enjoy your ride." With that, Kendrick got behind the wheel and started taking us west on I-70 through Maryland, a gorgeous ride, especially at sunset. Before we got on the ramp to get on the interstate, Joe pointed out the exact spot where the driver kicked the guy off the bus a few months earlier for calling her a bitch. He was proud to reconstruct the scene for me.

I was excited to have some time to really get to know Joe. I knew that I would have the chance to have his ear for a few hundred miles and, more importantly, to chronicle some of his tales. Some seemed apocryphal, but Joe told every story with factual conviction. He was a likeable dude.

"So, you mentioned that you're divorced. Does your wife live in Elkhart?" I asked.

"Yeah, that's why I moved up there back in January. I got a call from the counselor who said that our son was borderline suicidal. He had gotten into all that Goth stuff. My ex can't handle it all. So, I figured I would leave Florida and find a job up in Elkhart. I lucked out with this job. It pays pretty decent and I get to see my son a lot," Joe explained.

"I've only been up there for a little less than a year, but the counselor said that my son has done a complete 180. He dresses normal and he's a lot happier." Turns out that Joe had lived in Florida for over twenty years. "That's where I met my wife. I installed blinds, mostly at apartment complexes and sometimes in office buildings. She was in charge of billing for one of the companies that I worked for. We started dating and got married."

"So where did things go sideways with you guys?" I asked.

"Pretty much after our son was born, she didn't want to work and she didn't want to do anything around the house. She's the laziest person I've ever met. She wanted to put our son, plus her son from a previous relationship, in day care while I worked. It wasn't so she could work. It was so she could watch TV. That's all she did. That's still all she does. She Tivos an entire season of *Roseanne* or *ER* and watches every single episode, all day, every day.

"Then, one day while I was at work, she left me. She took the kids and headed off to Elkhart, where her family is from," Joe said.

"That's harsh. Were you broken up about it?" I tried to sympathize.

"Not really. We were both unhappy. But I wasn't thrilled that she took my son out of state." The divorce happened about twelve years ago and Joe says that he has dated a little bit but has never remarried. "She moved back up there to be with her parents but all they do is smoke pot together. That's how they deal with problems. They get stoned. She goes out behind the house with her dad and step mom and they smoke it up. She's even had the nerve to get on me about smoking cigarettes. My son knows that I smoke. But at least I'm not getting high.

"I guess it makes sense," he continued. "Her childhood was shitty. When she was twelve years old, her parents got a divorce and neither wanted her. It's kind of a reverse custody dispute. 'I don't want her. You can have her.' 'No *I* don't want her.' I mean, how do you think that made her feel? So her dad didn't want to raise her anymore and took her from Elkhart down to Sarasota to live with her grandma, his ex-wife's mom. Her grandma did as good of a job as she could, but that's a tough hole to climb out of, when your parents don't want you. So I understand where she gets her shitty parenting from."

Joe seemed to have some perspective, and perhaps a bit of sympathy surrounding his ex-wife, but his anger and disappointment seemed to trump that as he related the story to me.

"I mean, she's got four kids now from three different guys. I'm the only guy that married her. She just bounces around. She doesn't make time for the kids. She tells the counselor how busy she is, but I heard that one of the younger kids said 'Mommy, read me a bedtime story,' and she made one of the other kids do it. It's all so she can watch TV. She doesn't do anything active with the kids. Two of them are obese, and I mean *obese*. The oldest one is like 5'3" and 280 pounds. And he's only fourteen! It's crazy."

Joe seemed glad to be able to unload for a while. I'm sure there are two sides to the story, but I only had Joe's, and he was a sympathetic figure, in my mind, busting his butt driving a truck, leaving behind an occupation he had for a couple of decades so that he could be near his son that he loves. There's something admirable in that. There's a lot admirable in that.

"So, what do you guys do together when you hang out?" I asked about Joe and his son.

"We love to go to parks together and hike around. We like to go to the movies together. He loves roller coasters. So, from time to time, I'll take him to amusement parks. In fact, back in March, for his Spring Break, he went with me to Orlando on a run. He thought it was pretty cool. He got to ride up front in an ambulance with me. We stopped at every amusement park we could find and we rode roller coasters all day. It was great," Joe recalled. "I got us a cheap flight instead of riding the bus. If you know what you're doing, and if you know some of your runs pretty far in advance, you can sometimes find really cheap flights. I get on the Internet and do my best. But, for $569, I have this sixty-day bus pass. It has to be a really good deal for me to fly. I flew back from California one time instead of riding the bus for three days straight. I made that money up by being able to get another run instead of sitting on the bus," Joe reasoned.

As Joe was explaining all of this, I started to smell something odd. I looked to my right, where two Indian gentlemen were unpacking Tupperware containers of food from their backpacks. As soon as they took the lids off, the smell became overwhelming. I had no idea what they were eating. It was something kind of orangeish, with a soupy consistency. They had picked up the bus with me in Baltimore and we hadn't stopped in the last few hours, so they must have brought it with them. They were digging their plastic forks in and thoroughly enjoying their meal. But it stunk up the bus. I worried that they would be headed back to the nasty bathroom in a matter of minutes after having finished their meals. After they were done, they took out a plastic bag of hard candies and started offering them to people seated nearby.

"Where are you guys headed?" I asked them. The shorter of the two men, the one seated nearest said, "Chicago. We gamble in Atlantic City." I've heard before that Atlantic City is kind of a poor man's Las Vegas. But I can't imagine taking a bus from Chicago to Atlantic City to play poker or slots when there are now count-less nearby casino riverboats and Native American reservations that offer the same entertainment. Maybe they had family in New Jersey. Who knows? "The bus cold," he said. At that point, he got up and walked up toward Kendrick.

"Excuse me," he said. Kendrick ignored him. Again, "Excuse me." Not a word from Kendrick. The man walked back to his seat, shaking his head.

Joe was excited about our approaching visit to Breezewood, a sleepy Pennsylvania town at the junction of a couple of inter-states. Joe knew what restaurant was at every potential stop. For a man who had been riding the bus like this for only eight months, he had an incredible memory. "Oh, I've got to tell you about this one time we were coming through Pennsylvania. We stopped for a smoke break and I was out there smoking with two guys who were sitting behind me. They asked, 'Did you see that couple that's sit-ting back by us?' I told them I hadn't and they started explaining that there was this guy who had been on the bus for almost two straight days. He was coming up from Florida and joined my bus in Philly, for some reason. Anyway, the guys tell me that this guy started making out with the girl sitting next to him. At the next stop, we actually had a little time. So, I go in and use the pisser and I see this guy that they're talking about. I guess he had told this woman that he had been on the bus for a couple of days and before this went any farther, he wanted to wash up. So there he was stripped down to his skivvies in some truck stop bathroom. He's washing all over, probably getting ready to wash his dick. I'm sure he's thinking, 'Cha-ching! I'm gettin' lucky tonight.'

"Well, I go out to the bus and the driver gets on board and asks: 'Do we have everybody? Is the person who was sitting next to you still there?' Nobody says a damn word. So the driver starts driving away. The damn bus left the guy. And the girl that was sitting next to him didn't do a thing about it. She didn't say anything to the driver. He's back there washing himself so that he can consummate their relationship and she leaves him out in the cold. When we get to Pittsburgh, the driver gets a phone call just before we get to the station and he starts ripping everyone on the bus. 'Why didn't anyone say anything? I've got a pissed-off passenger back at the rest stop, and now he's got to wait eight hours until the next bus comes rolling through to pick him up!' Can you imagine? Can you imagine how pissed off that guy must have been? He comes out of the bathroom and not only is there no girl, there's no bus."

Joe is on a roll as bus historian. "Then, another time, there was this guy who had worked in the carnival for years. He was like forty-nine years old. He was an odd dude to begin with, but at a rest stop he sits next to me on a bench. He pulls out a bag lunch that his mom had packed for him. After he gets done eating, he decides to smoke and shoot the shit with me. Then he needs to go to the bathroom. He walks up to the building and holds the door for the driver who's exiting the building to get back on the bus. But the guy was clueless. He goes in and uses the bathroom. He didn't pay attention at all to what time the driver said the bus was leaving. I mean these guys are on a schedule.

"So the bus driver leaves. It's one of those rest stops where it loops back around. So he drives on the over pass and then loops around on the ramp to get back on the highway. At that point, the lady who was sitting next to the carnival worker alerts the driver that he left him. The driver pulls over on the shoulder of the road. We're all looking out the window back at the rest stop and we see the guy coming out of the building with his hands cupping his eyes looking around for the bus. He sees that we're pulled over, a few hundred yards away and he takes off running. But as he's running up beside the highway, he doesn't realize that the ground underneath him is marsh, and BOOM. Down he goes. His feet are sticking in the muck. Everyone on the bus is losing it, but the guy keeps running. A trucker sees what's going on and picks the guy up and lets him ride on the running board for the last hundred yards. So the guy gets on the bus and apologizes to all of us as a group. He's standing up there soaking wet and muddy. He then goes to each individual person on the bus and shakes their hand and offers a personal apology. It was the craziest thing I've ever seen."

As we pulled into Breezewood, Kendrick parked the bus at the back end of the parking lot of a Pilot truck stop. As everyone was filing off the bus, an Asian woman in front of me asked Kendrick in broken English: "This have bathroom here?"

Kendrick raised his eyebrows and immediately shot back to her, "Lady, it's a fucking truck stop. What do you think? Is there a bathroom here? Come on." The Asian woman didn't really understand what Kendrick was saying, but she sensed his tone. She nervously giggled and started walking toward the building.

Everyone barreled into the truck stop, which featured a sitdown restaurant with a menu and waitresses, a convenience store, a Subway, a pizza restaurant, and a gift shop. I wandered around the gift shop looking for a stray outlet to plug in my cell phone. Behind a rack of sweatshirts that said, "Pennsylvania: The Keystone State," I found an outlet. I stood guard until another passenger saw me and came over to plug in her cell phone. She was an attractive woman, but looked a bit hard, with many tattoos and piercings. I asked her if she could watch our phones while I ran to get a burrito and use the bathroom. In retrospect, I should have just dumped the burrito straight into the toilet and cut out the middle man.

When I came back to my phone, next to the snow globes, Kendrick was talking up the attractive passenger. They were making small talk and she was laughing at all of his comments, throwing her head back and flashing him a big smile. I felt like a third wheel, so I grabbed my phone and headed out to the parking lot. As it turned out, Kendrick was not far behind. He stood next to me and pulled a Newport from his pack. As soon as he lit it up, the Indian man who had been trying to get Kendrick's attention one hundred miles ago marched toward us with short, bow-legged steps and announced: "The bus too much cold." Kendrick, using the same facial expression he had with the Asian woman looking for the bathroom, shot back in a cartoonish Indian accent: "What do you mean, 'the bus too much cold'?" The Indian man said, "Yes, the bus too much cold." Kendrick just nodded at him and smiled. This caused the Indian man to smile and return to the bus. As he was walking away, Kendrick says to me, "What the fuck's he talkin' about? The bus too much cold. They're from Pakistan or some shit. They're used to it being 110 degrees. I'm a black guy from Philadelphia. I like it cold."

"I'll bet you've seen it all," I said, trying to bait Kendrick into a tell-all conversation about bus tales.

"You know it. I've had to call the cops. People gettin' drunk, smokin' in the bathroom, everything. I've seen fights. Boyfriend-girlfriend fights. Girl on girl fights. But I hate that shit. When I gotta call the cops, it messes up my schedule. It takes like an hour to fill out all the paperwork. It's a pain in the ass. I like to get there, man. I like my hotel time," Kendrick said.

He went on to complain about this particular route. "I hate going to Pittsburgh. There's a lady that works there that I can't stand. They'll probably make me sleep on a cot in the break room. Fuck that. I'm going to a hotel. I'm not even supposed to make this run, but they needed me. The union usually does a good job of keeping us in districts. But sometimes you gotta do what you gotta do. When you're union, you gotta play ball." With a final puff on his cigarette, he said, "Alright, let's go!"

For the remaining few hours to Pittsburgh, Joe continued to share a few more pearls from the road. "Did I tell you about the crazy singer?" "No," I said, wanting to glean the last few gems from Joe before we split. "Yeah, he almost got kicked off the bus. I knew we were in trouble when I saw him in D.C., waiting to get on the bus. He was walking around with his guitar and he would come up and get like six inches from your face and say: 'What do you want to hear? I can play anything.' He had a metal Band-aid container with a slit in the top hung around his neck. That's where he stuffed his tips, if he ever got any. He was driving everyone nuts. Something was wrong with him. So, at like two in the morning, he breaks out his guitar on the bus and starts singing some Elvis song. Everybody started screaming at him to shut up. But he kept going. The driver pulled the bus over and took the guy outside. I went out there to smoke and overheard what he was saying to the guy. 'Look, I'm responsible for what happens on that bus. But I'm not on the bus right now. So you can either stop playing and singing or I can wait out here and send you back on the bus and let all of the passengers deal with you.' The guy seemed to get the threat and he got back on the bus and didn't make a peep. But you see that kind of shit all the time. There are crazy people on the bus.

"Like the one lady that had a priority pass," Joe transitioned into another story. (I had learned earlier that a priority pass can be purchased for an additional $5, a luxury that most passengers cannot afford. It allows you to be the first ones on the bus so that you are guaranteed a seat and can choose where you sit.) "Well, this lady gets on the bus and goes up to a blind guy and says, 'I want your seat.' The driver was like, 'What the hell are you doing?' She said, 'I've got a priority seating pass.' That lady thought that the pass allowed her to just take any seat she wanted, even if someone was already sitting there. The driver told her to get lost."

After that modern-day Rosa Parks story, the conversation between Joe and me dwindled and we started to nod off. It's not easy to sleep on the bus, especially when it's full and the seat next to you is occupied. But before we drifted off, Joe gave me a brief workshop on the proper way to sleep on the bus.

"Most people don't sleep on their backs, right? They sleep on their sides. So, what I do is just try and put my back against the window, roll my jacket up and use it as a pillow and try to imitate my natural sleeping position."

Joe really thinks everything through. He knows that cigarettes in Manahattan are $11 a pack. In Virginia, they're only $3.80. He knows how to sleep, where to eat, where to get coupons for the Days Inn. Joe loves riding the bus. While I was just on a thirty-day trip around the country, this was life for Joe, and he loved it. We parted ways in Pittsburgh. Joe was headed home to see his son.

I also said goodbye to Kendrick, whose spirits had seemed to improve drastically. I looked over and saw the same woman with whom he was chatting and flirting at the truck stop in Breezewood waiting for him. "You ready?" he asked her. She just smiled and started walking with Kendrick. Where they were headed was any-one's guess. I hope, for Kendrick's sake, it was somewhere better than the break room.

DAYS FOUR–FIVE

Pittsburgh, Pennsylvania to St. Louis, Missouri

Pittsburgh, PA-Cambridge, OH-Columbus-Dayton-Indianapolis,
IN-Terre Haute-Effingham, IL-St. Louis, MO

I tried to sleep between Pittsburgh and Columbus, Ohio, our next stop.

It is not easy to sleep on the bus. You're constantly jostled around and the seats are small. Eventually I turned to Benadryl for help. I was able to employ Joe's "sideways in the seat" method of getting comfortable and was finally able to nod off for a few hours in the wee hours of the morning, when the bus is fairly quiet.

We arrived in Columbus at 3:30 in the morning. We picked up a new driver who would take us all the way to St. Louis. She was a very pleasant woman named Donna. Her voice was sweet and encouraging as she took our re-board slips; there was no barking or unnecessary attitude. Though I had only been on the bus for a few days, I was amazed at the variety of approaches from the different drivers. Many were stern and business-like. Some bordered on sounding like prison guards. Others were disengaged, just trying to corral the madness and get to the next stop. Donna was different. From the first moment we met she had a very welcoming attitude, like an elementary school teacher on the first day of school. She made us feel at home. It was refreshing, even at 4 a.m.

Our first stop was in Dayton. The station was in a strip mall, four or five miles south of I-70. Most stations are in urban centers, but in smaller towns they seem to just be wherever Greyhound could plop a station. Dayton is a pretty good-sized city but its station didn't make much sense. It was a newer terminal, but I can't imagine it being very convenient, especially for the many Greyhound passengers who rely on public transportation everywhere they go. We wound up picking up only two or three passengers and returned to the road, continuing our early morning pilgrimage.

As the sun rose, the chatter level elevated and people started stirring as we approached Indianapolis. It was a beautiful morning as the sunshine beamed off of the Indianapolis skyline. Donna informed us that we would have a full hour break, plenty of time to grab some breakfast. The bus station in Indianapolis is right downtown, close to shopping and all of the sports stadiums. But it was seven in the morning and everything still looked pretty sleepy.

The perimeter of the bus station was a standard scene. People were milling about, smoking, with seemingly nowhere to go and nothing to do. I went in to use the restroom and immediately noticed that the bus station looked dated, like an old-time train station. There were dark colors and arching doorways. Back in the day, it was probably a centerpiece of the city. But, that was generations ago. There were some homeless people sleeping on the floor in the hallways. The bathroom was nasty. I brushed my teeth while trying not to breathe through my nose, not an easy task. Rather than eating a package of Twinkies from the vending machine, I made the three-block walk down to Steak 'n Shake. I ordered some biscuits and gravy, hash browns, and a cup of coffee.

We hit the road a little after eight. I moved up to the seat right behind Donna. In the seat to my right, also in the front row, was an older woman who was traveling alone. She was dressed well and was dripping with jewelry. She began a conversation with Donna, asking her how long she'd been driving. I was still tired but tried to eavesdrop the best I could. I heard Donna say, "Well, women weren't permitted to drive until 1978. That's the year they made the change. I think they started with only twenty-five women drivers." That surprised me—1978 seemed awfully late to fling wide the bus doors for female drivers.

The well-dressed woman exited the bus in Terre Haute and I took her seat. I liked the way Donna handled herself and I wanted to get to know her story. The brief stop in Terre Haute was enough for us to say goodbye to the woman and for Donna to take stock of prospective new passengers. She gently approached a man sleeping on the sidewalk with his bag next to him. She tapped him on the shoulder and asked if he was waiting for our bus. He mumbled something to her and she left him alone. I found it odd that he wasn't waiting for our bus, as small towns like Terre Haute don't have the volume of through traffic that other hub cities have. He would likely be continuing his nap for another four hours until his eastbound bus came for him.

Donna got back on with a smile and announced on the PA that our next stop would be in Effingham, Illinois. We would have sufficient time for a meal break there. I remember Joe remarking to me earlier: "Doesn't it seem like whoever named the town Effingham was in a bad mood?" He put extra emphasis on the *eff* in Effingham. That made me laugh. It is a strange name for a town. At times, I wondered if we would ever effing get to Effingham. For the last two states, we had seen nothing but cornfields, each looking exactly the same as the last.

"So, Donna, did you start driving back in '78?" I began, referencing the previous conversation.

"No, actually I had a career in the insurance industry before

I started driving. I've only been driving for eighteen years," she stated with great ease, as if she were still in the honeymoon phase of being a bus driver.

Donna was a breath of fresh air. She had big bangs and an even bigger smile. She wore her uniform with pride and just had an easy way about her. She was relaxed and looked like the type of woman who would say "Oh, dear!" or "Goodness gracious!" rather than ever letting an ugly word depart from her lips. I decided to find out what was behind that smile.

"I'm riding around the country for a month and I've met quite a few drivers so far. You're really different than other drivers I've had on the bus. I really appreciate that you are friendly and open. I can tell a difference in the mood on the bus."

Upon hearing this, Donna perked up even more. She flashed a large but humble smile and said, "I know what these people are going through. It's not easy to ride the bus. A lot of them are going through some serious stuff. Some of them are on the bus for days at a time. If I can help make their day a little better, then that makes me feel good."

I countered, "But don't you have people that give you grief or act ugly?"

"You know, you'd be surprised. I've been driving for eighteen years and I can probably count on two hands the number of times I've actually had to call the police or had a problem that I couldn't handle. I've found that if you treat people with compassion and understanding, they respond really well. I know that if something happened to me, these people behind me would have my back," she explained.

Donna is on to something. In short time on the bus, I'd realized that there is clearly a culture of distrust between Greyhound and its passengers. How much of this is based on actual experience or maybe just self-fulfilling prophecy, I don't know. It seems to me that when drivers treat passengers like potential thieves or troublemakers, passengers are more apt to behave like thieves or troublemakers. I wonder what would happen if the entire bus line adopted Donna's attitude. I would bet that they would see immediate benefits.

It's not just drivers' attitudes, though; it's everywhere: from the buses, to the drivers, to the terminals. The whole scene rarely feels welcoming. Greyhound terminals are dated. They look like the company just doesn't care anymore. Vending machines and bathrooms consistently have "out of order signs" taped to them. There are warning signs up by cell phone charging stations and in waiting areas about "lost and stolen property" being "your responsibility." It is emotionally exhausting to have to constantly worry about somebody stealing your stuff. When layovers can range from thirty minutes to five hours, it's draining to carry your bags to the bathroom stall and worry about someone stealing your cell phone that is charging at a charging dock. It's defeating to have to spend hours in a terminal, trying to scrape together enough quarters to buy a $2 bottle of Mountain Dew and worrying about who is going to abscond with your belongings as you pound on the machine, hoping your drink will pop out. In one station, a maintenance woman kept walking back and forth in front of a group of huddled passengers, telling them that their bags were sticking six inches out in the hallway, which is a violation of a fire code. Every five minutes she would walk by and tell someone to move or to move his or her bags. The message sent was, "We don't really want you here. Keep moving."

So, not only do travelers have pressing issues in their lives that have forced them to choose this low-cost, inconvenient form of travel, but they are also treated like nuisances by employees of the station. It's a bad combination, and frankly, it's bad business. But Greyhound has no national competition, so it's clear that customer service isn't exactly a top priority for them.

Donna was a refreshing change to the culture of distrust and apathy that seemed to permeate Greyhound's stations and buses. Donna told me how she has people that just open up and share their life stories with her. I can see why. Whether we admit it or not, all of us are hungry for someone to care about us, what we're going through. And, when it's someone who is approachable, like Donna, it provides for a perfect situation for impromptu relationships and community building. Donna mentioned that being a bus driver is far more than a job for her. She referred to it as a "calling." I wonder how many people consider their jobs as their "calling"? Where there is intersection of ability and opportunity, great things can happen. For Donna, her calling was driving the bus.

"I was working in the insurance industry," she explained. "I was a professional–I'm not just some country bumpkin. I chose to do this. I got trained down in Dallas and Greyhound has been a great company to work for. I get great benefits and I've got some seniority now so I get priority when I bid on runs." Donna was referring to the fact that drivers can "bid" on certain routes. For her, she wants the St. Louis to Columbus run. She lives in St. Louis and gets to sleep in her own bed far more often than many other drivers.

Perhaps the most surprising thing about Donna is that she is married to another Greyhound driver, Tom. "Tom was in charge of the training in Dallas. They still call him down there sometimes to train new drivers. He's a great driver and a good teacher," Donna gushed. "I'll bet you guys have some stories to tell when you get together after work," I solicited. "Oh yeah. I've got a brother who loves to come at Thanksgiving and hear all of our war stories. He asked me one time if I'd ever had a baby born on the bus. I told him 'no, but I've seen a couple of babies conceived on the bus!'"

When we got to Effingham, we pulled into a Pilot truck stop. Donna was excited because she had a scratch-off lottery ticket that she had bought during her last stop there. It was worth $3, the price she had originally paid for the ticket. While the passengers sauntered about, smoking, using the restroom and, likely, shoplifting beef jerky from the convenience mart, Donna redeemed her $3 and bought another ticket. She scratched it off immediately and realized she had won another $3. She walked right back up and got another ticket. This one busted. But she got a good four minutes of entertainment out of the exchange.

Many of the truck drivers and cashiers knew Donna by name and struck up conversations with her. Donna has acquaintances and friends dotted at truck stops in four different states. They talk about their family and their jobs, sipping coffee, until it's time to hit the road again.

As we got back on the bus, Donna and I continued chatting for the next few hours. Donna was a religious person. She talked at length about her Pentecostal upbringing. She explained that there are different varieties of Pentecostals. There are some that don't allow their women to wear makeup or jewelry, but Donna is part of a slightly more relaxed group. They have definite, strong opinions about theological matters, but they don't take the Bible as literally so as to prohibit women from wearing slacks. Donna said that she has never received the gift of being able to speak in tongues, but the gift has fallen on her husband, Tom. He's only done it a few times, she said.

"I've had a hard time with my job, reconciling it with my faith. The Bible says that you shouldn't work on Sundays and often I'm on the road then. I can't go to church and it just eats away at me. I was feeling really guilty about it and went to speak with my pastor. He really helped me put it in perspective. He said that Jesus did things on the Sabbath and that it doesn't make me less of a Christian. I was even thinking about quitting my job, but he helped me to see that I was doing ministry by driving the bus. If I can be a little bit of light for the people that I'm driving, then I'm being faithful," Donna explained.

Donna has still found ways to be a part of her church group, even if she can't be there every Sunday morning. "My Bible study group is great. We read *The Purpose Driven Life* and it was wonderful. In fact, I gave a copy to my mother to read and I got her a journal to write in. She was harboring a lot of anger toward one of her sisters. My mom was in declining health back in Louisiana, but I was able to visit with her. I told her to write in that journal and to make peace with her sister. After she died a couple years later, I was going through her stuff and I saw that she had written in her journal every day. She finally forgave her sister and they were in a good place when she died. That made me so happy. I was really proud of her."

Donna mentioned that she has a son, and she wishes they were closer. Tom is her second husband and it's clear that they are very much in love. "It's hard being on the road so much. It would be nice to spend more time together, but we talk every day on the phone and our schedules make it so that we really can be together a fair amount. He does the St. Louis to Nashville run. So we try to time it so that we're back home at the same time," she explained.

"I'll bet you're one of the few 'driver couples' in the country," I said.

"I think there are a few of us, but not that many. It's a hard life," Donna stated.

"Have you ever been to the Greyhound museum?" I asked Donna. I had learned in preparing for the trip that Greyhound has a museum in northern Minnesota, where the bus line started. I was planning on heading north toward the museum after my stay in St. Louis.

"Oh, yes. A few years ago, Tom and I took a vacation up there. It's really neat. They've got all of the old buses there." Donna told me that she and Tom had taken some of their old driver's uniforms up to the museum. "You know, the kind with the legs that flared out and the boots that come up to your knees," she described. "You mean like astronaut uniforms?" I inquired. "No, more like German soldier outfits," she quipped.

"Someone donated a brick in our names. It was really nice. We got to go up there and see our brick. And, would you believe, they had an old poster on the wall of me? Back in the mid 90s, I was one of the models for Greyhound. I couldn't believe it when they asked me, but they had me come to Dallas for the photo shoot. They had me, a ticket agent, a maintenance guy, and a baggage handler. The four of us were standing there in a line for the picture. That poster wound up going up everywhere. For the next two years, every stop I'd make, I'd go into the station and there would be the poster. It was kind of embarrassing, but kind of flattering that they would pick me. Anyone who says modeling isn't hard work doesn't know what they're talking about. We stood there for like eight hours, smiling. It was tiring, but a lot of fun."

"Does the Greyhound run up to the museum?" I inquired.

"No. Isn't that crazy? It's in a little town called Hibbing, Minnesota. The bus doesn't go all the way up there. You should just take the bus to Minneapolis and then rent a car. It's not a bad drive, maybe three . . . four . . . five hours? It's really pretty. You've got to do it if you're writing a book about Greyhounds," Donna opined. In the world of the bus driver, three to five hours is considered a nice afternoon drive. For the rest of us, it's a grueling distance we might only travel to visit grandma.

"So what do you love most about driving?" I asked Donna.

"I love the people. I get to meet so many different people every day. Even though it's the same route that I'm running, it's the passengers that make it interesting," she explained. When I asked about the craziest thing she'd ever seen on the bus, she said, "Well, one time we were stuck on the bus in a really bad snowstorm. It was a few years ago and I was doing the Nashville route. We got into Indiana and they had chosen not to plow the roads. The government just didn't want to spend the money. We got about fifty miles north of Evansville and traffic just came to a stop. It was backed up for miles. This was on December 23, and people were trying to get home for the holidays. I was going down and then going to come back to St. Louis so I could be home for Christmas. But we weren't going anywhere. It turned into hours and hours.

"It started getting dark and people were worried. We had a baby on the bus who didn't have formula. But then, these really nice farmers started showing up. They had ATVs and offered to run to the store to get us supplies. It was really neat to watch. Everyone on the bus pooled their money together. Altogether, we raised about $150 and these guys went to the store and came back with formula and snacks for everyone to tide us over. It was kind of like a Christmas miracle. There were people in cars ahead and behind that wanted to come on the bus. We were pretty full but I let the women come on the bus to use the bathroom. I mean, what are you going to do? Guys can just go in the snow, but I had to open the bathroom up for these women.

"We wound up spending the whole night in the bus. As it turns out, the guy in the car behind us had some connections. He was stuck in his car with his wife and kids, but he knew somebody at CNN. So, he used his cell phone and we wound up being on CNN on Christmas Eve. They interviewed me and everything. I guess with all the publicity and pressure, the governor of Indiana ordered the National Guard to come out and plow the roads. So we were stuck for a whole day, but we made it. I got everyone where they needed to go in time for Christmas. I'll never forget that. I still get a Christmas card from the guy that was in the car behind us."

Donna's voice was excited as she rattled off that story. She said it was beautiful to watch everyone come together. That pretty much sums it up about Donna—she chooses to focus on the good in everyone. That's how she approaches her job. Donna serves Greyhound well.

"I'd really like to meet Tom," I told Donna. "Well, let me call him on his cell phone. His bus is supposed to get in about a half hour before ours." Tom was making his run back from Nashville.

"Hi, honey. I've got someone on the bus that wants to meet you. His name is Mike and he's writing a book about the bus. You could? Oh that would be great!" Donna said before hanging up. "Tom will wait for us at the station. You'll really like him. He's a great guy."

I was nervous about arriving at the station in St. Louis because of what Art had told me a few days earlier about it being the worst station ever. "Hey Donna, I heard the bus station in St. Louis is bad news. Is that true?" "Oh, you're thinking of the old one," Donna explained. "Nineteen years ago the local government eminent domained the land where the bus station used to be. They said that they would build a new bus station, but it took them forever. So, they stuck the bus station out in a not so nice part of town. That was pretty bad. But you'll love the new station. It's clean and bright. It hasn't been open very long." With this, I didn't know whether to be excited or disappointed that I couldn't prove or disprove Art's "nastiest station in the country" claim.

As we pulled into the station, Donna was looking for her husband. It was a steamy hot August afternoon in St. Louis. The air almost felt wet as we walked out into the parking lot. It felt as if a large dog was breathing in my face. "Oh, there's Tom!" Donna exclaimed. As the baggage handler was unloading the bus, Donna and I walked over to meet her husband, stationed in front of the bus he had just brought in. Tom was leaning against the grill of the bus when he extended his hand. Tom had a flat top and was about the same height as Donna, maybe 5'8.

"How was your trip?" she asked him. "Not too bad. I had this drunk in Paducah that was a bit of a pain. I could tell he'd been drinking all day. He asked me if I knew of a convenience store where he could get some cigarettes. I told him, 'Yeah, about four blocks that way,'" Tom said, gesturing with his finger. "The thing is, if I kick him off the bus for being drunk, then I've got to fill out an incident report. But if he *misses* the bus, it's his fault. So, he starts walking off to find cigarettes and I loaded everyone on the bus and off we went," Tom chuckled. Donna playfully slapped his arm at this anecdote.

As much as I wanted to continue the conversation in the smoldering parking lot, I needed to get a shower and a soft hotel bed. I thanked Donna profusely for her attitude and conversation. She wished me luck on my book and I headed inside the terminal. Donna was right. It was nice, but I wasn't in the mood to explore all of the nuances of the new station. I marched directly over to the Sheraton across the street.

The lobby was bustling with Chicago Cubs fans. There was an afternoon game at Busch stadium against the Cardinals, their biggest rival. As I approached the front desk, I was a bit self-conscious. I smelled pretty ripe. I was also worried I would have a Manhattan-like experience and need to refinance my home to pay for my hotel room. "Do you have any rooms available tonight?" I asked of the desk clerk.

He looked at me for a couple of seconds and asked, "Do you have a reservation?" "No, that's why I just asked if you had any rooms available," I replied sarcastically. That turned the conversation south in a hurry. An insincere, condescending smile broke out and he giggled, "Good luck finding a room anywhere in St. Louis. The Cubs are in town, the Rams have a game tonight, and the Black Eyed Peas are playing across the street," he said smugly.

"Listen, I just got off the bus. I came all the way from New York. Don't you maybe have a cancellation or something?" Trying to break the ice, I continued, "I recognize that I look and smell like a contestant on *Survivor*, but I could really use a shower and a bed." This did little to change the trajectory of our discussion.

"If I were you, I would just go get back on that bus," he said in a feminine, motherly voice, pointing back toward the Greyhound station. With that, I slinked off like a chastised dog, with my tail between my legs.

I began to feel like Jerry Lewis on Labor Day; not the funny, young Jerry Lewis, but the old, tired, heavy, messy Jerry Lewis. In a sleep-deprived, out-of-my-element stupor, I wandered around downtown looking for a vacancy. Eventually I found a room out by the airport, where I proceeded to spend two days sleeping, grooming, eating, and writing. I even went to the Cubs game the next day. It was a welcome break from several days of hot, stinky bus travel.

The first week of my bus trip had been all I had hoped for. I had met some incredibly interesting people and my fear of people not being willing to open up to me had been assuaged. I was missing my family, but the unanticipated phenomenon of making friends every step of the way never made me feel all that lonely. St. Louis, known as the "Gateway to the West," had been the perfect place to rest, regroup, and begin the next leg of my journey.

DAY SIX

St. Louis, Missouri to Kansas City, Missouri

St. Louis, MO-Columbia-Boonville-Kansas City

I woke up early on the morning I left St. Louis, feeling rested, refreshed, and ready to head up to Minnesota to check out the Greyhound Museum. From St. Louis I would go to Kansas City, then straight up I-35 into Minneapolis. I had mapped the trip out and figured I would get there later that night. It was a long drive, but bearable for a one-day trip. The beauty of the discovery pass is that you don't have to be rigid in your planning. I knew that I wanted to ride all over the country, but I didn't have strong opinions about needing to go to certain cities.

I enjoyed a standard, hotel room-brewed cup of coffee and hopped on St. Louis's public rail line to take me from the airport area back downtown to the bus station. Greyhound encourages passengers to arrive an hour before their bus is scheduled to depart. During my trip I tried to abide by that suggestion, but it didn't always work out. This morning was one of those occasions. I severely underestimated the length of the train ride back to the station, and arrived about twenty minutes before my bus was scheduled to leave for Kansas City. The line at the ticket counter was not horribly long, but long enough to stress me out. Then I saw a laminated sign on one of the posts in front of the ticket counter that read "Sold Out" in large, block letters above "7:30 Kansas City."

Immediately I worried that my non-refundable hotel reservation for that night in Minneapolis was in serious jeopardy. "May I help you?" asked the uninterested woman at the ticket counter. Pretending that I hadn't seen the sign, I said, "I'd like to get on the 7:30 bus to take me to Minneapolis." "It's sold out," answered the woman robotically.

"Isn't it possible you have an extra seat on there? I have a hotel reservation tonight in Minneapolis that is non-refundable," I countered.

"It's sold out," she repeated, this time more tersely. "There's a 1:30 bus you can take," she offered.

"That does me no good. It doesn't get to Minneapolis until 5 in the morning. I need to get on that 7:30 bus," I repeated.

"Sir, the bus is sold out. I need to help the next customer. Do you want the 1:30 bus or not?" she asked, clearly agitated. "No, I don't want the 1:30 bus. I want to get on the bus that leaves in five minutes. In fact, I'll bet you guys knew this bus was sold out last night. Why don't you have another bus? This is ridiculous," I stood firmly. I had yet to throw a fit in the bus station, but this seemed like the perfect time to do so. She ignored me and said, "Next," summoning the next person in line.

"Wait, I'll take the 1:30," I said.

Unlike airline tickets, there is more wiggle room with bus tickets. If you miss a bus, you can use your same ticket to just get on a later bus. You just need proof that you paid for the ticket. Sometimes they don't even ask for that. Greyhound has not invested their profits in technology, so they don't really have sophisticated ways of checking on who is on the bus or where they're going. Donna's foremothers probably used the same ticket system in 1978 that they employ today.

I took my ticket and ran quickly down to gate 10. There was no one there, but I could see the bus out the window. I ran out into the parking lot and located the driver who was doing some last-minute paperwork before he got on.

"Sir, is there any way I can get on this bus?" I asked him.

"Let me see your ticket," he said callously. "This ticket says 1:30."

"I understand, but the woman at the ticket counter told me to come down here and see if you had space," I fibbed.

"Yeah, you can get on."

As I climbed the steps to get on the bus, I felt relief, the kind of relief I felt when I skipped out on study hall senior year and didn't get caught. Once on the bus, I looked around and, to my surprise, saw about fifteen open seats. That laminated "Sold Out" sign was a load of crap. The fact that they even have a laminated sign says it all. It appears that it's easier and more cost effective for Greyhound to put a sign out that, in effect, says: "You can take the next bus six hours from now," than it is to dispatch another bus to handle the potential demand. It was irritating.

I sat in the third row and looked out the window only to see another potential passenger running like OJ Simpson across the parking lot, but the bus started backing out. "Ha ha, sucker!" yelled out a very, very large man with many tattoos. "We gotta get movin'." The bus driver didn't stop. I didn't really feel guilty that I made it on and this poor guy didn't. *Life isn't always fair,* I thought.

I felt the need to process what had happened over the last twenty minutes with someone, so I turned to the guy with the tattoos and said, "Man, I had to move heaven and earth to get on this bus. I don't normally get worked up, but that lady at the ticket counter was terrible."

"Dude, you have to be an asshole or you'll end up at the back of the line every time," he stated.

I got the feeling he wasn't just referring to bus etiquette, but that this might have been an axiom that he leaned on for life. I've never felt like I have needed to be an "asshole" to get where I needed to go in life. I'm sure I have been an asshole plenty of times, but rarely intentionally so, just to get my way with things. In fact, I've always been turned off by people who raise a stink. I don't like it. I don't like being around it. I've seen people dress down a cashier at the grocery store for not redeeming a coupon. I can remember a man bringing a girl to tears at Circuit City because he wanted his money back for a computer that he had purchased even though the return date had long ago passed. She held her ground but was rattled to the core. I wanted to defend that poor girl and punch the guy. I hate watching stuff like that. But, on this day, I stepped inside the world of intentionally being an asshole. Perhaps the bus was wearing off on me.

Tattooed Tyler was probably 6'5, an intimidating looking guy in every regard. He had tattoos on his neck, a large tattoo of a marijuana leaf on his forearm, and his head shaved bald. He was headed out to Oregon. "I started in Michigan," he said. "I hate the damn bus. I've counted—this is my thirty-eighth trip across the country on this thing. I take the bus all the time, dude," he said.

Tyler was fond of the word *dude*. I took it as a term of affection. I explained that I was riding the bus for a month, writing a book. He smiled and said, "You're crazy, dude. You know what, dude? I should write a book. I've seen it all on the bus. It's nuts. You'll see it all, man." Tyler was animated when he spoke. He had been awake for several days, but had an amazing amount of energy.

"So what's going on out in Oregon?" I inquired.

"My brother lives out there. He's a caregiver. I'm gonna go out there and stay with him for a while and probably become a caregiver too."

Wow, I thought. *You can't always judge a book by its cover. Tyler looks scary, but he's going out to become a caregiver.* I was assuming that "caregiver" was something like a hospice consultant or senior citizen helper. I learned moments later that "caregiver" is code for "pot grower."

"Oregon's awesome, dude. It's soooooo easy to get your medical card out there. My brother got his license to be a caregiver without any problem. I'm gonna learn from him and hopefully get some plants of my own. He's got two patients already. I'm gonna be his third," he stated.

"Do you have some medical issues?" I asked ignorantly.

"Oh, hell yeah. Dude, my back is so messed up. I've had two surgeries already and I'm not having any more. I've got all my medical records with me so it shouldn't be a problem to get my card. Plus, they pretty much give out cards for anything out there. I mean, you can't get it if you've got itchy skin or something, but they give it out for the big stuff like AIDS and cancer but they also give 'em out for headaches and arthritis. I even heard of one dude getting his card for having a fucked up childhood or some shit. Like post-stress or something."

Tyler had put a lot of thought into this. He planned on going out to get high for a while and hopefully to start a lucrative pot farming business with his brother. I had my doubts that this would be a viable long-term goal, but Tyler seemed enthused and willing to put the work into becoming the best "caregiver" he could be.

"You married?" I asked him.

"No. I've been married, but not right now. I've got six kids though, dude," he said. Tyler looked awfully young to have that many children. He was perhaps in his early thirties. "I've told my kids to stay away from drugs. I've told 'em that drugs will mess up their lives. Dude, I was hooked on meth for two years. Now, I just take pain killers. I'm taking Suboxin. It helps with the pain and also the withdrawals from the pain meds I was taking. I've seen it all, man. I've been in jail. I was in college up in Saginaw, but it wasn't for me," he lamented. Clearly, Tyler had taken more than a few wrong turns in his life, but, he was a really personable guy, which had probably gotten him out of a lot of trouble along the way. It probably could have been worse.

Seated in front of Tyler was a man in his late fifties named Gale. Gale was wearing a short-sleeved, blue button-down shirt and a pair of jeans. His prematurely snow-white hair looked wind-blown. His Fu Manchu moustache framed his smile, which featured a notable gap between his front two teeth. He wore large glasses and spoke in a low voice, almost in secretive fashion. Gale merged gently into our conversation, introducing himself. Tyler took to him immediately as kind of a mentor/wild uncle.

"Where are you headed, Gale?" I asked him.

"I'm going down toward Dallas. I've got to change buses in Kansas City and then head down to get a truck," he explained. "I'm a contractor. I go to repossess trucks that have been abandoned or stolen. In the eyes of the law there's really no difference," he said.

"So, you're a repo man!" exclaimed Tyler. "That is so cool, dude!"

"Yeah, it's a great job," Gale agreed. "I only work from like April to November. Then I go to the Philippines. I spend the winter down there with this great girl. We may be getting married in a year or two. Those women really know how to treat their men. I come in the house and she's waiting for me. She meets me at the door and takes off my shoes and socks and starts massaging my feet. She gives me a full body massage every day," Gale said, wistfully. It was a bit uncomfortable picturing that encounter, but that Tyler got excited.

"I've heard the women down there are beautiful, dude."

Tyler was really interested in Gale's job. "Does that pay pretty well?" he asked. "Oh, yeah. I get between $4,500 and $6,500 a run, depending on what's in the truck. If it's got stuff in it, they usually pay me more so they can get it back," Gale explained.

I jumped in, "Who in the world just abandons a truck?"

"You'd be surprised," Gale said. "It happens all the time. Guys are out on the road and they get pissed off or homesick or something and they just pull into a truck stop, put the keys on the counter and call their family to come pick them up. Sometimes, they drive the truck all the way to their house and I find out it's sitting there and have to go pick it up. Once in a while it gets testy. I've had a few guns pulled on me, but when that happens or if they give me shit, I just call the sheriff. I still get paid no matter what. So, I either get the truck or the police get involved. It's a pretty nice gig."

"That sounds awesome. I'd like to get in on that. Is it pretty hard to get in?" Tyler inquired. "Are there lots of background checks and stuff?"

"Yeah, they're pretty strict about it. You have to get a license from the government to do what I do," Gale replied. They check into you pretty deep."

"Man, that sucks. I've got some things on my record that might be a problem. Do they care about felonies?" Tyler continued.

"Yeah, but it's not a deal breaker. I've been to jail too," Gale commented.

"Yeah, but do you have any *felonies*?" Tyler probed.

Gale grew more uncomfortable with the questioning and simply replied, "I've been to jail. I'll leave it at that."

Gale eventually opened up about his six-month stint in the penitentiary. He had stolen some 33 Corvettes back in the early 70s. "It was so easy, man. You could go to Texas and they wouldn't ask for the paperwork at all. You'd just unscrew the license plate, put a new one on, hotwire it and take it to somebody who would buy it. I did it all the time, man. I was good at it. I'd steal a car on my *way* to steal a car," Gale proudly recalled. "But, I got out of that. I was a truck driver for a lot of years before I landed this job. I make so much money. I'm probably going to retire in a few years. But, then again, I don't know if I'll be able to walk away from it. I've gone everywhere to pick up trucks. I even went up to Nome, Alaska, once. It took about two weeks to bring the truck back. The roads up there are mostly privately owned and it's a major pain."

Gale informed us that he was being paid $1 per mile to ride the bus to get to his destination. By this point, Gale had become the wise sage and was controlling the conversation. He was an authority on many, many subjects. I wondered why I had bothered taking so many history classes in high school and college—I could have gotten a more thorough and colorful education at the feet of Gale the repo man. "You know most people think the Germans invaded Poland unprovoked. Hitler knew what he was doing. He locked a bunch of his own people in a building and set it on fire. Then he told everyone it was the Polish that did it. That got everyone fired up and off they went," he hypothesized. Gale had a string of rapid-fire nuggets that he threw our way, including: "You know John Kay? The guy from Steppenwolf? He was a Soviet activist. The government got pissed off at him and kicked him out of the country. He came over here and started Iron Butterfly. Great band . . ."

The Vietnam era and all of the surrounding cultural phenomena were instrumental in shaping Gale's view of the world. "I was in the very first smoke-in. It was in Normal, Illinois. Politicians have changed it now. They still have it but it's a 'smoke out.' Can you believe that shit? We used to protest and it felt like it made a difference, but the government was corrupt as hell. They knew everything. They tapped John Lennon's phone. Nixon did. He was an asshole. And, the way they gave those soldiers LSD . . . you ever seen somebody that's climbed the ladder?" Gale asked in my direction. I shrugged. "Jacob's Ladder, man. They used to give that shit to the soldiers and they'd be fucked up for thirty-five days. You can tell when you're looking at someone who's climbed the ladder. It's their eyes, man. They can just stare into your soul.

Straight into your soul. I mean they had those guys so messed up they would do anything. You couldn't kill those dudes. They were killing machines. You could shoot 'em right there in the shoulder and their minds could will their bodies not to bleed. They would shove a stick right in the hole where they were shot and they would snap it off and just keep moving. You've never heard of Jacob's ladder? There was a great movie about it, man."

Gale was amazed that Tyler had never heard of Howard Hughes. "Oh, there's a great movie about that guy too. You gotta watch it. He was the richest man in the world, but he flipped out. He sat in his hotel room in Vegas for like the last ten years of his life. He didn't trust anyone or let anyone in. He was crazy. He sat in his own shit. But, back in the day, he controlled every island in the Caribbean. He had George Bush, the first one, in his back pocket. Man, they were oil and airplane buddies. Nobody knew anything about it, but it's the truth. Howard Hughes pretty much ran this country." Gale was not dissimilar to Art in that he had many theories about "the real truth," although his were more nuanced, intricate, and drawn out. Art would just blurt out some theory and he didn't really care if you believed him or not. Gale wove these stories in Forest Gump-like fashion that made you feel like he was really there in the cockpit with Howard Hughes. "You know there are bridges in the Philippines that are like twenty thousand years old? Yeah, man, they've carbon dated that shit. There have been God knows how many people over there. The Spanish, the British, us. They've got hieroglyphic drawings on the underside of these wooden bridges that are from civilizations long ago. It's amazing."

By this time, Tyler was fidgeting. "Man, when are we gonna stop for a cigarette? I'm about to die over here."

A few miles later we arrived in Columbia, Missouri. The bus station was a ramshackle excuse for a building. There were large potholes in the parking lot that the driver navigated his way through like he knew just where they were. As soon as the bus stopped, people bum rushed the front door to run out and enjoy their smoke break to the fullest. I saw Gale pull a pack of Marlboros out of his shirt pocket, but Tyler was gone. It was a beautiful day and everyone was pretty relaxed once they had some nicotine in their systems. Tyler finally reappeared right before the bus was to depart. As he climbed aboard, he announced without reservation, in an outside voice, to no one in particular: "Dude, I just smoked a joint and my mouth tastes like I just licked somebody's asshole. Does anyone have a piece of gum?" Some kind traveler a couple rows back passed up a stick of gum, which Tyler put in his mouth and then made noises like he was having an orgasm.

After we left Columbia, the conversation turned back to marijuana. Gale and Tyler went back and forth on all things horti-culture. "Dude, I can't wait to get to Oregon. I heard the weed out there is AMAZING," Tyler enthused with bloodshot eyes. Gale started a brief lecture about fertilization. "Here's the thing, man. You don't want to use Miracle Grow. That shit's too expensive. You want to go to a pet store or, better yet, go online. Get a bunch of the cheapest dog food they've got. I think you can get a whole pallet of it for like $60. Then, you just want to trench out a hole around your plant. Not real deep, just use your foot. Trench you out a circle around twenty-four inches away from the plant and put some of this Bow Wow dog food in there. Then right before winter, just cover the dog food with dirt and leaves and sticks. That will decompose all winter and you'll have amazing plants the next spring," Gale espoused.

"This is awesome, dude. I'm learnin' how to grow some good shit, prison-style," Tyler responded. Gale added, "The other thing you want to get is some of that Bo Peep ammonia. Just make a ring around the plant, right on the ground. Don't let any of that shit hit the stem or it will burn it. Just put it in the ground and it will fertilize your pot like you wouldn't believe."

"Dude, I can't wait to go try that. These are great tips," Tyler complimented. "I mean, I'm fucked up right now but I can't wait to grow my own shit and have it all the time."

Gale just flashed his toothy grin. "I love it too. I don't smoke it as much as I used to, but I used to smoke a lot. One time, my girlfriend and I were out in Stockton, California, stoned as can be. We were sitting on a bench in this town square area. I was playing my Jew's harp and we were just watching cars go by. We see this guy come up in a car in front of the red light. He's got his finger buried up his nose, like two knuckles deep, trying to dig one out. Well, he's not paying attention and he rear ends the car in front him. He hits it fairly hard and his finger's still up there. It ripped his nose clean apart. There was blood everywhere. It was nasty. But, the cops came and we had to give a statement. I mean we had been smoking earlier, but this was years ago. Cops didn't give you shit back then." Gale had a story for all occasions. Most of them were enjoyable, if not totally believable.

Gale seemed to enjoy his job as a trucker, but he got frustrated by all the rules. "Man, they make it harder and harder for a trucker to earn a living. There's those damn log books. I mean you can cheat your way around that, but they've gotten more strict about it with the snitch boxes and all that. But, it's always the trucker's fault. There was this one guy in Nebraska or Iowa or some place. He had pulled into a truck stop, gotten something to eat and was just chilling out in his cab in the parking lot. Some dude comes barreling in the parking lot in his car. He was tired and had fallen asleep at the wheel. He plows into this guy's truck and can you believe this? They blamed the trucker. Even though this idiot was at fault, they had the lawyers do their thing and they checked out his log book. They found out that he shouldn't have already been at the truck stop. If he were following the rules, he still would have been eighty miles back up the road. So, they sued him and won. It's bullshit, man."

I asked Gale, "Who is behind all of the rule changes? I mean are there lobbyists or something? It doesn't seem like something people would get that fired up about, putting driving restrictions on truckers."

Gale answered immediately. "It's those groups like MADD and MAFD. They get in bed with the congressmen and next thing you know they're saying we can only drive eleven hours at a time. I've heard they're trying to cut it down to eight hours in a twenty-four-hour period. They'll lose a lot of truckers with that bullshit."

"What is MAFD?" I asked.

"Mothers Against Fatigued Drivers," Gale responded.

As Gale was going on about the injustices of the trucking world, Tyler was sleeping like a baby. His head was tilted straight back on his headrest and his long legs were splayed open. I didn't know if it was the marijuana or Tyler having been awake for several days straight, or a combination of the two, but he was spent. It wasn't until our next stop in Booneville that Tyler woke up. After his power nap, he lobbied unsuccessfully with the driver to let him off to smoke. In Booneville, we picked up only one passenger. He was a small, thin man with salt and pepper hair. He looked to be in his late forties. He was wearing khaki shorts and a blue button-down shirt with black shoes and white socks. He boarded the bus carrying a brown grocery sack with his belongings. He found a vacant seat next to Gale and sat down without saying a word.

Tyler accepted defeat on his quest to smoke and sat back down and started picking Gale's brain again. This time they moved on from marijuana to methamphetamines. Of course, Gale had good advice on how to manufacture meth cheaply and effectively. Tyler was grateful. Our new passenger didn't chime in on this discussion, but he did lean over to me and say, "I heard you say you're writing a book. I just got out of prison today. Do you think that could make it in your book?"

"Sure," I responded. "How long were you in?"

"Eight months," he answered. "Prison was rough enough that I don't want to cook dope anymore," he stated.

Tyler and Gale weren't the most sensitive men in the world and continued an hour-long discussion on how to get high on meth. " . . . But you gotta be careful with that shit. My nephew is doing fifteen to twenty for cooking meth," Gale warned. The recently released prisoner just tuned them out. I'm sure he was looking forward to putting that all behind him.

When we arrived in Kansas City, Tyler and Gale gathered in the smokers' area before they parted ways. I shook their hands and wished them well. As I entered the terminal, the freed prisoner followed me in and meekly asked if he could borrow my cell phone. His family was in St. Joseph, Missouri, about an hour away. Greyhound runs through St. Joe, but the next bus wasn't going through there for a long time. I handed him my phone and eavesdropped.

"Mom, can you have dad come pick me up? I'm at the Greyhound station in Kansas City . . . well, can you find him? . . . Mom, I don't wanna wait twelve fuckin' hours for the next bus to take me home . . ." He said goodbye to his mother and handed me back the phone, shaking his head. "I just want to get home. I've been in prison for eight months and they can't drive an hour to come get me?"

DAYS SIX—EIGHT

Kansas City, Missouri to Minneapolis, Minnesota

Kansas City, MO-Des Moines, IA-Ames-Mason City-Albert Lea, MN-Burnsville-Minneapolis

After a delightful morning of conversation with Tyler and Gale, I prepared to catch my afternoon bus that would take me up I-35 through Des Moines and into Minneapolis. It was a gorgeous sunny day. As I boarded the bus heading north, I was surprised to see how empty it was. This was a first. Most of the buses I had been on to this point had been fairly close to capacity. This bus was carrying maybe only twenty passengers, so we each had our own row. It was luxurious. And, for the first time, I was on a bus that actually had power outlets and Internet service. Greyhound says they are innovating the future of bus travel, but most of the buses I had been on were a long way from meeting the future.

I spent the next six hours writing, playing around on the Internet, and talking on the phone. It was a welcome change of pace. Just before sundown we stopped in Mason City, Iowa, to pick up some passengers on their way to Minneapolis. The terminal in Mason City was small but looked relatively new. I saw a decent-sized pack of passengers waiting with their luggage on the sidewalk. When the driver opened the doors, they started coming on, one by one. It seemed endless. A woman with three kids under the age of five took the seats behind me. The kids were crying. The mother was cussing at them. My peaceful, relaxing ride had come to an end. The last man to get on the bus in Mason City looked as if he was carrying every earthly possession he had in his hands. He had wild, crazy eyes and a ponytail sticking out the back of his baseball cap. He appeared to be well into his sixties. As he struggled to carry all of his stuff up the stairs of the bus, he dropped his sleeping bag, which immediately unraveled. He unleashed a string of profanities directed at no one in particular. He started shoving his sleeping bag, backpack, and bongo drums into the overhead compartment. The bongo drums would not fit despite his efforts of trying to cram them in at every possible angle. He passed my row and just stopped and stared at me. It was a long, uncomfortable stare. I looked down, and after a few moments, he continued back and took a seat about three rows behind me. He kept swearing in a loud, abrupt way. Nobody paid any attention to him, and within ten miles, he stopped talking altogether and fell asleep. The bus was full, but mostly quiet for the rest of our journey into Minneapolis.

I checked into my hotel and went directly to bed. I needed to rest up for my big trip up to Hibbing to visit the Greyhound museum. The next morning, after renting a small, red, foreign economy car, I headed north, toward Duluth on the interstate before cutting over to Hibbing on state highways. I had never seen northern Minnesota before. It was beautiful, but flat. Minnesota is called "The Land of 10,000 Lakes" for a reason. As I passed many placid lakes, I envisioned burly men wearing flannel, burrowing a hole in the ice, fishing for walleye. I'm not a big fisherman but I had a strong urge to pull over, dig up some night crawlers and cast a line. The air was crisp, even for late August. I was glad I was doing my bus tour in the summer instead of in February.

I felt like a teenager again. My windows were down and I had the radio cranked up. The local classic rock station there was celebrating the twenty-fifth anniversary of the release of John Cougar Mellencamp's *Scarecrow* album. Randy McIntosh was the ninth caller and won a copy of the CD. He had to stop his tractor so that the DJ could hear him when they talked. He went nuts.

"You guys are the best! I can't believe I won! I had this cassette a long time ago but I lost it."

I was jealous of Randy. As I sang along to the words, "I was born in a small town," I felt a pang of nostalgia about a life that I never had, that of a Minnesota farmer.

Hibbing, Minnesota, is in the middle of nowhere. I fully understand the decision made by Greyhound's corporate offices to suspend bus service to this area. I passed through many small towns on my way up there, but none of them had more than a gas station and a stoplight. It felt like nobody lived up there. I imagine it's because it's miserably cold for seven months out of the year. I expected Hibbing to be as sleepy as all the other towns I passed through, but that wasn't the case. The sign going into town listed its population as being over 18,000. In the middle of nowhere sat this decent-sized town that looked as if it was a peaceful place. I had imagined the Greyhound museum to be the focal point of the town, but I had to look hard to find the signs that directed me there. There was one billboard for the museum on the outskirts of town that looked as if it was painted by a junior high art class. It had an arrow pointing me when and where to turn. As I got near the museum, there were small signs affixed to telephone polls that read, "Greyhound museum straight ahead." The signs were white with red and blue trim, matching the color scheme of the bus line, with cartoonish-looking greyhound dogs that made it look like this place might be a joke.

I pulled into the museum parking lot and saw a building that was newer and larger than I had expected. My car was one of two in the parking lot. Out in front was a brick walkway. I immediately walked over and started staring at the hundreds of bricks, trying to find the one that was given in honor of Tom and Donna. After about ten minutes of searching, I found it. I thought it was nice that someone did this for them, but it wasn't as satisfying as I had hoped. It was an engraved brick, after all. Most of the bricks were named after drivers or had the name of some local business that was sponsoring the museum.

Upon entering the museum, I was greeted by a woman in her forties who asked me to sign the visitors' book. It was a spiral notebook that listed the names of people who had passed through all summer. I leafed through the names and noticed that most of the people were from towns in Minnesota. They weren't drawing a lot of travelers from far away, it didn't appear. After I introduced myself and told her what I was doing, she said, "Oh, you need to come back this afternoon around 2 or 3 and meet Gino. He's the owner of the museum. He can tell you lots of interesting things about Greyhound."

"How long have you worked here?" I asked her.

"I've been here for two years, but I'm a volunteer. We're all volunteers. Hibbing is my hometown and I moved back here not too long ago and was looking for something to do," she explained. "We get a lot of tourists, but we also have a ton of drivers and people who have worked for Greyhound over the years who come. They want to look around and learn about the history of the bus line. We've got a lot of memorabilia. That's pretty fun for them to see."

"Do you get to hear a lot of crazy stories?" I prompted her.

"Oh yeah. You wouldn't believe some of the stuff I've heard. We've had package handlers that have come up here and told some pretty outrageous things. One woman said that she went under the bus to get a package and saw some red liquid leaking out of the box. So she called the cops. When they opened it, they found a dismembered body," she reported. I cringed. Why would somebody ship a body on a bus? Why would someone dismember a body? Was this story even true? She continued, "There was another package handler that found a shipment of weapons. It was up here in Minnesota. They called in the FBI and everything. It was a huge box full of machine guns. They were able to catch the people when the guy showed up at the station to pick up the box."

I decided to come back later and meet Gino. In the meantime I went for lunch at a place called Zimmy's. It's a tribute to Bob Dylan, whose real last name was Zimmerman. Dylan grew up in Hibbing, and this restaurant seemed to have every photo, guitar, press clipping, and memento from his career. The menu items were even named after his songs. I was tempted to order the "Love and Theft" Coconut Chicken, but instead went with the "Positively" All You Can Eat Fish Fry.

"Does Bob Dylan come in here often?" I asked the seventeen-year-old waitress.

"I don't know," she replied. She wasn't too interested in conversation.

When I returned to the museum, Gino was nowhere to be found. Instead I found Mike, Gino's sidekick and museum curator. Mike was wearing blue jeans, a black-and-red flannel shirt, and a mesh trucker's cap that read, "Greyhound Bus Museum." He was in his sixties and had a beard that looked as if it kept his face protected from the harsh Minnesota weather. Mike was apologetic that Gino wasn't back from lunch yet. "Gino is eighty-five years old. He still comes in here every day, but he takes long lunch breaks. Sometimes he says he'll be back at 2 or 3, but that really may mean 4," he explained. I told Mike about my bus trip and that I felt that I needed to come up to Hibbing to learn all I could about the bus line.

Mike invited me back to his office for a conversation about

the museum. He said that Greyhound used to pitch a little money in the museum's direction, but that they stopped doing so about five years ago when the company fell on hard financial times. So now the museum is funded by private donations and memberships. I had noticed the sign in the lobby that listed the admission price as $5 but you could buy a family membership for $40. I imagined that most people who were buying memberships were more interested in supporting this local attraction than they were in making a weekly pilgrimage to see if the mannequins or display cases had changed. Mike started walking me around the museum. We started in the gift shop. He suggested that I purchase a recently written book about the history of the Greyhound Bus. It was $35, and appeared to focus more on things like the types of engines in the buses. I explained to Mike that my project was a little more anthropological in nature, but that I might pick it up later.

The first display in the museum was a re-creation of a ticket counter from a bus station in 1930. The mannequins were dressed in old-time clothes and looked like they were stolen from Sears. We then proceeded to the display that explained how the bus line was started in 1914 by Carl Wickman. It told the whole story with pictures and descriptions about the "good ol' days" with Mr. Wickman and his good friend, Andy "Bus Andy" Anderson. As I surveyed these black-and-white photographs and mannequins on display, I wondered if Carl Wickman or Bus Andy could have had any idea that, some ten decades later, their buses would be hauling "caregivers," released prisoners, and carnival workers all around this great country.

The name "Greyhound" allegedly came when a bus driver was passing through town and noticed the reflection of the bus in a store window. He remarked that it looked sleek, "like a greyhound." As we continued around the museum looking at old photos and discussing the early prosperity of iron mines, my mind started to wander. I confess that I wasn't as engaged as I should have been. Maybe it was a belly full of fish, or a warm museum building, but I was ready for a nap. It reminded me of a grade-school field trip to an old farming settlement where we learned how people used to make brooms and churn butter. It was boring. I had driven three and a half hours in a rental car to hopefully hear some stories that might aid my project, but instead I was itching to get back in my car and head back to Minneapolis. I looked for the uniforms that Donna said that she and Tom had donated, but I couldn't find them.

"Look at these old uniforms!" Mike continued with excitement that made it seem like he was seeing this for the first time. "Wickman wanted them to be dressed like military people so that they would have the respect of their passengers. In fact, people used to salute them when they drove through town." I had seen a few people salute the drivers on my trip, but it was a salute of a different variety, one that involved only one finger. I was also hoping to see the poster of Donna from her modeling days, but Mike explained that, "it's probably in storage." As we passed by a little theater room, Mike commented, "You don't want to go in there. It looks like a movie, but it's pretty much a twenty-minute commercial for Greyhound." He shook his head as he said this. There seemed to be a disconnect between the Greyhound of yesteryear and the Greyhound of today. I didn't know if I should feel sad about this. I tried to make myself care. I said, "That's a shame," and shook my head along with Mike.

Outside the museum was an impressive collection of old buses. Mike said that they were all still in working order, which is incredible due to the fact that they rarely get driven and have to endure months of sub-zero weather. Some of the buses looked like old mobile homes and campers. Originally built for and used by Greyhound, they had been purchased by individuals and converted into vehicles that look like they would be fun to take all of your college buddies to a football game. They have couches, beds, kitchens, and bathrooms. Other buses looked rickety. For as much complaining as I'd done about the small seats and difficult sleeping conditions on my bus trip, I saw that it could have been much worse. The old buses were a little more spacious but were certainly not built for comfort.

"My grandkids love to come up here to the museum. They just climb on the buses and play until they're beat. They came up here three days in a row last summer," Mike recounted.

"How long do you think Gino will keep running this place?" I asked him.

"This place is his life. He's up here every day of the year. We're only open during the summer months, but he's here in the cold of winter. Every day. He's always reading something or fiddling with the displays. The people in town asked me if I would come up here and help him because they're worried that once Gino's gone, nobody will know the story."

"So, you're kind of the heir apparent," I proposed.

Mike chuckled. "I like that. Yeah, I guess I'm the heir apparent."

We continued out into the gravel parking lot where they had about eight other buses on display. There was one with Arabic writing on the side. Mike explained that this bus was used in Saudi Arabia to take workers back and forth to the oil wells. "It's kind of like history repeating itself because that's how the whole thing started," he reasoned. "And look over here. Gino loves to do wood working. So, he built this whole thing himself." Mike pointed behind the Arab Greyhound bus and there was what looked like a nativity scene. He said that Gino had spent a long time putting this display together. I studied it for a few moments. There was a man and woman in Arab headwear pulling a camel on a leash. It was only missing a manger and the baby Jesus. What it had to do with the bus, I wasn't sure. But it was a nice display.

Mike posed for a few photos with me and I told him that I

really needed to get back to Minneapolis. On the drive back, I felt like I had accomplished a mission, checked something off my list, but the museum wasn't what I had hoped it would be. It looked old and tired. It served a purpose, that of preserving the history of the origin of the bus line, but that topic probably interests as many people as those interested in the history of butter churning. I did purchase some T-shirts and postcards to send to my boys. I was sure that they would proudly wear their Greyhound Bus Museum T-shirts around school and would be the envy of all of their friends.

The drive home was interminable. I wanted to pull over and have a beer at the Thirsty Moose but I kept driving. I felt like I had just spent a day of my life that I would never get back, though I was glad to have accomplished my task. How many people can say that they've visited the Greyhound Bus Museum?

DAYS NINE—TEN

Minneapolis, Minnesota to Denver, Colorado

Minneapolis, MN-St. Cloud-Willmar-Granite Falls-Marshall-Ruthton-Pipestone-
Luverne-Sioux Falls, SD-Vermillion-Sioux City, IA-Omaha, NE-Lincoln-Grand Island-
Kearney-Lexington-North Platte-Ogallala-Sterling, CO-Brush-Ft. Morgan-Denver

I decided to leave Minnesota and go somewhere out west. I had my eyes on the Pacific Northwest, but thought I would break the trip up a bit, so, I bought a ticket to Reno, Nevada. I had only heard about Reno in sad country songs and thought it might be interesting to see who is headed out there.

The line for getting on the bus wasn't too long. There was one man in line who caught my eye. He was a mountain of a man, wearing blue jeans and a denim short-sleeved shirt. He had brown hair and a matching moustache that drew down beyond the corners of his mouth. His arms were heavily tattooed and he had three or four teardrops tattooed to the left of his left eye. We made eye contact and he nodded his head at me. His blue eyes seemed sure to be hiding some serious stories of a hard life. Maybe he had been one of the men who had "climbed the ladder" because it was as Gale described. He was staring into my soul.

I picked a seat about two-thirds of the way back on the left. Seated behind me was an African American man named Ordell. Ordell was going back to Omaha, where he lived. "I gotta get out of here. What do you know about Minneapolis?" he asked me.

"Not much. I just spent two nights here. Never been here before," I replied.

"I'll tell you about Minneapolis. It's the land of lesbians. And gay dudes. I ain't never seen so many gay people in all my life. I'm trying to sleep on a park bench and these gay dudes come up to me and say, 'You're kinda cute.' Can you believe that? I was up here lookin' for work. I heard there were lots of jobs up here, but there ain't. I couldn't find nothin.' I got in a fight with my old lady"–Ordell was now about the twentieth person I had met who referred to a girlfriend or wife as their 'old lady'–"and Minneapolis didn't seem that far from Omaha, so I came up here. I spent three weeks in a homeless shelter. But, there weren't nothin' but bipolar and schizophrenic people in there. One dude took a shit in his hand and smeared it on the wall of the shower. Do you see what I'm dealing with? . . . Hey, man, I'd love to keep talking but I'm gonna get some sleep." And with that, our conversation ended. Ordell leaned back against the window, occupying both seats in his row, trying to get some rest.

The leisurely ride to Omaha was mainly on state highways instead of the interstate. We stopped in the towns of St. Cloud and Granite Falls. On a smoke break in Granite Falls, I decided to chat up the guy with the teardrop tattoos.

"So where you headed?" I began.

"Next town over," he answered curtly.

"What's going on there?" I continued.

"I'm preaching in a church there. I'm an evangelist," he offered.

"Wow, that's got to be a tough job. How long have you been an evangelist?" I asked.

"Just about two years. It's a hard living, but God always provides for me. There really ain't no money in it."

Before he was an evangelist, Robert was a brick mason, and before that, he was in prison in Ohio, in Mansfield and Lucasville.

"Lucasville? Isn't that where the prison riots were?" I asked.

"Yeah, I was there. I got caught up in that. The Aryan brotherhood had said they were coming in to the prison and I knew there was going to be trouble. I was already doing 22 to life. They came in and started attacking the guards. There were bodies everywhere. I tried to make a run for it back to my cell. I stepped over a body, but they caught me before I could get there. They added five years onto my sentence," Robert lamented. "But I found the Lord there in prison and I was able to get out early. So now I just go around preaching and telling my story. I pretty much preach whatever God lays on my heart. Someday I'd like to get a church of my own back in Cleveland. But, I've got to pay my dues," he explained. The driver informed all of the smokers that it was time to load up. I shook Robert's hand and wished him well.

A few towns later, Ordell perked up and started conversing with me. I learned that he loves to sing and play the guitar. He said, "I like white people music: Christopher Cross, James Taylor, that kind of stuff." He started singing "Fire and Rain" to the fairly empty bus. A couple of guys sitting behind us told him to shut up, but Ordell didn't hear them and just kept going, "Suzanne the plans they made put an end to you . . ."

Ordell's story is long and sordid. He has a grown daughter he rarely sees. His daughter's mother is a lesbian in a relationship with another woman. "One day I came home and my girl was watching *Soul Train*. Do you remember that show *Soul Train*? Anyways, she made some comment about how one of the girl dancers on the show was 'hot.' I said, 'What did you just say?' And she repeated herself. 'That girl is *fine*.' I asked her, 'Are you into women?' Sure enough, she turned into a lesbian, too, just like her momma. I can't go along with that stuff. The Bible says it's wrong. I don't want that goin' on under my roof. So she wound up movin' in with her momma and her momma's girlfriend. I don't see her that much anymore."

"So you divorced your girl's mother?" I asked.

"Naw, man. We never got married. We were young. I left her and started dating this girl who was a freak, and I mean a freak. She was a nym-pho-maniac," Ordell stated in a low but incredulous voice. "She wanted me to do everything. She wanted me to take the elevator down to the basement, if you know what I mean. But get a load of this. She decides she don't wanna be with me no more. And she starts making up stuff. She goes to the police and says that I did something that I did not do."

"You mean rape?" I asked.

"Bingo," he responded. "I wound up doin' twelve and a half years in the pen up in Michigan for that shit. It's all because she had rich parents and got a real good lawyer. I couldn't do nothin' about it."

Ordell is originally from Detroit but says he had to get out of there because, "It ain't nothin' but crackhead whores there now." After his stint in prison, when he was forty-seven, he married a sixty-three-year-old woman named Dorotha. They moved to Chicago, but only lived there for four days because "it ain't nothin' but crackhead whores there now." Dorotha and Ordell moved to Houston where she had family. But he says that her children were insane gang bangers and, after four years, he needed to get out. I asked him why he was living in Omaha. "Do you have family there? That's a long way from Detroit."

"Nah, man. Here's the story. Do you remember that TV show *Mutual of Omaha's Wild Kingdom*? I loved the theme song from that show and always thought Omaha would be a cool place to live."

I think Ordell was hoping to find zebras and lions in Omaha, but instead he found work housekeeping in the hospital. That's where he met Carolyn. She's a nurse. One night, he was cleaning the hospital and they started a conversation only to learn that they shared the same exact birthday: March 6, 1959. That was much more than coincidence, Ordell believed, and they began a relationship.

It wasn't easy because Carolyn's children were a bit of a mess. She had one son in prison. At sixteen he was involved in a drive-by shooting. He will get out for good when he's twenty-two, but he was furloughed on the weekends and came to the apartment where Carolyn and Ordell lived. "That boy's out of his head. He brings all of his homeboys over and they're smoking weed. I told him he's stupid 'cause if they catch him doin' that stuff, he'll go away for a long time. They kicked in the door of the apartment one night. I don't want any part of that."

I didn't get to the heart of the argument that sent Ordell to Minneapolis, but he was ready to make things right with Carolyn. Part of her problem with Ordell was that he hadn't started official divorce proceedings with Dorotha. So that was first on his list when he got back to Omaha. He also said he was going to try and get a driver's license and then hopefully find a job.

Before long we stopped in Marshall, Minnesota. That's where we picked up Becky. Becky was twenty-nine years old and the oldest of nine children from near Fort Worth, Texas. A Pentecostal, Becky said that she didn't even own a pair of pants until just a few years ago. Her mother always insisted she wear skirts and dresses. Becky was a very large woman. She was getting out of a four-year relationship with a guy named Tyson and moving back to Fort Worth to be close to her parents. She said Tyson was a deadbeat. "In the four years we were together he worked maybe a total of two months. My dad trained him on how to repair washing machines and other appliances. But he's lazy. He spends every penny he has on video games and clothes." Becky finally had enough and left him. She went on a week-long tequila bender and hooked up with a co-worker before she got out of Marshall.

"Did you feel bad about cheating on him?" I asked her.

"Not really," she said.

Becky married when she was nineteen, and that marriage ended when she caught her thirty-year-old husband writing love letters to her seventeen-year-old sister.

"How did you find out?" I asked.

"My sister finally told me. It had been going on for a while. She was living with us and I guess my husband was trying to screw around with her. So I kicked his ass out and we got a divorce. He tried to say he was sorry and that he didn't mean anything by it, but she showed me the letters."

I felt bad for Becky. She was rudderless and seemed to be an easy target for a succession of men that didn't treat her very well. Tyson, her boyfriend in Marshall, impregnated another woman while he was with Becky. But she stuck with him and helped raise the baby. She even proudly showed me a picture of the three of them together. The last straw came when she caught him cheating again.

Ordell joined in the conversation. "Did he ever rough you up?" he prodded.

"Yeah, one time. He pushed me and tried to choke me. But I told my dad about it and my dad went and beat the crap out of him. He never laid a hand on me again."

Ordell continued with personal, inappropriate questions: "Did your boyfriend ever give you a hard time because of your weight?"

"No," Becky replied.

"That's good, because there's nothing worse that a guy can do than call his old lady 'fat.' You are a very sexy woman, Becky." Becky didn't know whether to be flattered or put off by this line of commentary from Ordell.

Becky had nine tattoos. She got them all in the course of a week's time. Her mother flipped out, but Becky didn't care. Ordell asked her, "What's the most provocative place you have a tattoo?"

"Well, I've got one on my stomach that's a butterfly. The body of the butterfly is a penis," she told him.

Ordell was very interested in this. He continued to ask questions that made Becky—and me—uncomfortable. "Have you ever been with a woman?" "If your boyfriend wanted you to be a stripper, would you do it?" "You have a very sexy voice. Have you ever considered being a phone sex operator?" Becky tired of Ordell's shenanigans before long and started to feign sleep. He woke her up and asked, "Hey, have you ever been on the *Jerry Springer Show*? You look like this girl I saw on there one time." Then he started chanting, "Go to the pole! Go to the pole!", a common refrain on the Springer show where women are encouraged to strip.

Becky ignored him and leaned her head against the window, perhaps dreaming of greener pastures in Texas.

When we arrived in Omaha, Ordell set off to try and patch things up with his old lady. He said he was going to just go to a homeless shelter because it was 2:00 in the morning and he didn't want to piss her off right off the bat by coming home and waking everyone up. "She's gotta get up at 5:00 for work and the last thing I want to do is have her in my face about waking all them up. So I'm gonna just crash there and start walking home tomorrow. It's like three miles from the station to Carolyn's house. I don't want to put anyone out." That seemed mighty selfless of Ordell, but part of me wondered if he had any intention of moving back in with Carolyn or finding a job. He might have just been spinning a tale. Ordell left the station with no bags or belongings, just himself. Smoking a cigarette, he shook my hand and said goodbye.

The Greyhound station in Omaha, Nebraska, could be the worst place on earth. The awful experience began when we were told to claim our luggage and then find our connecting bus. I went

down by the luggage compartment and saw my duffel bag. So, I
reached in to pull it out. A security guard grabbed me by the col-
lar of my shirt and yanked me backwards.

"What the hell?" I exclaimed.

"Sir, step away from the bus. You are not allowed under
there. A baggage handler will get your bag." This was the first
time I had been told this. It was also the first time in my life I had
been in a physical confrontation with a security guard at two in
the morning. I figured this loading area was his kingdom and I
had somehow offended him, although almost every other passenger was doing the exact same thing. I guess I was an easy target.

This brief scuffle made me uncomfortable. I have always
avoided physical confrontation. In the third grade, Aaron Koenig
threw a kickball at my face at recess. It hit me square in the nose and
I was stunned. One of the girls in my class said, "Are you gonna let
him get away with that?" I paused, then unleashed an uncoordinated
violent attack on him. I was swinging wildly, punching and kicking
him until he apologized and started crying. I can even remember
at that age how unpleasant rage felt. I had lost control. And I had
to spend the next week's worth of recess with my back against the
brick wall by the kickball field. That was the pits. I quickly decided I
wanted no part of this security guard in Omaha, so I let it go.

The bus station was stinky, a mixture of body odor, human
waste, and cigarette smoke. It was also severely overcrowded.
There were people like Becky, heading south to Kansas City, and
folks heading east to Chicago. I was waiting for the bus to take me
west to Denver. I waded through the sea of people in this small,
smelly, dirty space and walked over to the vending machine/video
game area to try and find an outlet to charge my phone. Behind
a Donkey Kong machine that was probably still there from 1982,
I found a spare plug. A bus from Chicago rolled in and added
another fifty-five or so bodies to our waiting area.

A heavy-set African American man in dirty overalls

approached me and said, "Look at this place! Richest man in the world, Warren Buffet, lives here in Omaha and we got this raggedy-ass bus station . . ."

"Do you think Warren Buffet rides the Greyhound?" I teasingly asked him.

"Hell no. He probably don't even know it's here. Maybe he rode a bus one time back in college or somethin' but he ain't never been here. This place is a fuckin' wreck."

Then one of the two men seated behind Ordell, who had told him to shut up while he was singing James Taylor songs, approached me. Chris had an un-kept look about him. He had a tuft of post-pubescent facial hair below his sideburns and a sad excuse for a moustache. He was wearing oversized gym shorts and a white tank top.

"Hey dude, where are you going?" he asked me.

"I'm off to Reno," I replied. "How about you?"

"I'm heading out to Oregon . . . Portland. There's this chick I met on the Internet who asked me to come out and be with her. Look, I've got her picture here on my iPhone." Chris's potential girlfriend was very good looking. Chris was twenty-one and said that this girl was twenty. He had never met her in person before, but they knew some mutual friends and they had vouched that she would be worth his while. "She works out there as an escort," Chris explained. "Guys pay her to go out with them and act like she's their girlfriend. She gets paid really well."

"So, she just goes on dates with them? Nothing else happens?" I asked in a purposefully suspicious tone.

"Oh, she knows. She knows that if she messes around with any of these guys and I find out, it's over. She wouldn't do that. She pretty much just goes out to dinner and movies and stuff like that," Chris hypothesized. I had my doubts about that whole set-up, but Chris was excited to ride the bus for the next two days to go see her, so I kept my suspicions to myself.

"Are you from Omaha?" I asked Chris.

"No. I'm from Sioux City, Iowa. I needed to get out of there. I just got done with the Job Corps program. I came home and my mom was like, 'I'll give you one week to get a job.' She pretty much kicked me out of the house. I haven't seen my dad since I was thirteen. He beat the crap out of me, so I don't give a shit about him. My mom doesn't want me around, so I'm gonna see what I can do in Portland."

It seemed like the longest of long shots that things were going to work out for Chris in Portland, and I feared that he might be setting himself up for more heartache. But, for him, the fear of the unknown was better than the fear of the known. Chris's attitude toward change was born more out of desperation than calculation. For anyone who has faced a career change, the fear of the unknown can be terrifying. We might say, "My job sucks, but at least I have one." We don't want to risk making a change because of what might happen, so we just suck it up and stick it out. That emotional incarceration is a place that many of us know well.

Once we have mustered up the courage to make a significant change in life, it can be simultaneously freeing and frightening. But the in-between time is when we do a lot of soul searching. I've heard it referred to as being a "refugee in waiting." There are people in refugee camps who fear that they'll never get out and find a new homeland. But, once their number is called, they are excited because they know that something better is waiting. Even if the refugee is told, "Your number has been drawn out of a hat and it will happen sometime in the next nine months, but we don't know exactly when", that statement alone makes the next nine months somehow bearable. The promise of the unknown sustains hope. Many people on the bus seem to cling to this kind of hope.

So many people refuse to take a chance or risk leaving what they know, even when what they know is miserable or unsatisfying. I admire folks who are willing to step out and make a bold move, even at the risk of falling flat on their face. I think it shows a certain amount of courage and trust that it will all be okay. Chris was probably too young to have intentionally developed that mindset. Instead, it was given to him. His dad beat him up. His mom viewed him as a burden and didn't want him around. So he made a decision to forge out on his own, trusting that the unknown was better than what he knew. He was someone who had enough emotional equipment to realize that he was in a destructive environment. Maybe the Job Corps gave him a brief glimpse of what else was out there, and that was all he needed. Unfortunately, he was chasing an escort he'd met on the Internet.

"Did you see that guy that was sitting with me?" Chris asked. "His name was Justin. He's from Sioux City too. But, get this: in the daytime, he works as kind of like a nurse for old people. I don't think he's really a nurse, but he drives them around in a van so that they can get to their doctors' appointments and stuff. I think he gives them baths too. But, at night, he's got his own business. He makes porno movies. That's what he was showing me on the computer. He uses local people from Sioux City to be in his movies. He offered for me to do a movie. Said he'd pay me like eighty bucks. But I told him no."

"Wow. He actually gets people to do that?" I asked.

"Yeah, the chicks in the movies are smokin' hot. He says he makes pretty good money with people subscribing to his site on the Internet. He was coming here to Omaha to meet with some people. It's crazy, man."

After milling around in the nasty terminal for an hour or so, we were called to get on our bus headed for Denver. There were re-boarders that were called back on who had originated in Chicago. I was considered a "new board" on the Denver bus and thus, was one of the last ones to be able to get on. I found a vacant seat next to a young man who looked to be in his late twenties. He introduced himself as Jake.

"Pretty full bus, man," Jake commented in my direction with a slow country drawl.

"Sure is. "Where are you headed?" I asked.

"I'm going out to live on my buddy's farm out near Colorado Springs," he replied. "I'm from Lincoln County, West Virginia. I grew up there but I can't take it anymore. My parents are always fighting with each other. So, I called up a buddy from high school that I haven't talked to in like ten years. I asked him if I could come stay with him and if he could help me find some work. So, he says 'sure' and told me I can take care of his farm while he's in the service. He's in Hawaii until sometime after Christmas. He's got a wife there. I don't know if he's got any kids. I guess he moved out there and got a good deal on some land. He's got like fifty acres. He said it's beautiful. They've got rams and mountain lions and stuff. Hey, I've heard they've got gold out there. Wouldn't it be cool if I found a bunch of gold?" Jake reflected.

Jake–like Chris, like most of the people I met on the bus– had bought one-way bus tickets to Somewhere Else. The excitement that I heard in the voices of people who were just checking out of their old lives was fascinating. I had my doubts that their patterns of poor decisions and self-destructive relationship choices would be altered by a change of location, but a change of scenery seemed to be all the elixir these travelers needed.

Jake had had a host of odd jobs since he graduated from high school. He still lived with his parents, even though he was twenty-nine years old. He had two half brothers that live near Huntington, but he never saw them. He didn't know where they lived or where they worked. Jake had mowed grass at the lake for the West Virginia county parks department. "It was pretty easy work. Just sat on a mower all day," Jake described in his endearing, syrupy accent. "I also worked as a mover for a few years. Now that was wild. You wouldn't believe the shit people have in their homes, especially under the beds. One time, I was moving this couple and they had a rubber ass under their bed. No lie. I called my boss and said, 'I ain't movin' this thing. I ain't even touchin' it. But, I just got a plastic trash bag and moved it. They looked like a normal couple. Who has a rubber ass, dude? Then, this other time, I was movin' this Chinese family and we was down in their basement and found a bunch of stuff that looked like they were making a pipe bomb or some shit. My boss wound up movin' that shit. I didn't want to mess with it. It was pretty fun. We just mostly moved rich people. They're the only ones that can afford to pay movers," Jake explained.

"So, are you nervous about going and staying in a place you don't know?" I asked.

"Yeah, a little bit. I ain't never met his wife. Her name's Lisa. She's gonna be picking me up in Colorado Springs. I ain't never been out to Colorado and I ain't never taken care of a farm. I'm a little nervous but it should be pretty fun. But, I get in to Denver and then have to wait like six hours to get on the bus to Colorado Springs. It's only eighty miles away. Do you think I should call Lisa and see if she would drive to Denver to get me?" he asked.

"No, I wouldn't put her out right off the bat. I'd just wait for the bus to Colorado Springs if I were you," I counseled.

Jake was one of the few passengers I met who was genuinely happy to be traveling. He had never been on a Greyhound bus. He got to travel all over the Southeast when he worked for the moving company, but he had never been west of the Mississippi. For him, this was a great adventure. Jake had an enthusiasm about him that trumped the fear and apprehension he might have harbored about heading into uncharted territory. It was refreshing. He had never been married and had no children. He hadn't done any time in prison. I asked him all of these things. I asked him because, on the bus, pretty much any question is fair game. That might seem like an unreasonable and uncouth question at a dinner party: "Have you ever done time?" But on the bus, it elicited the same, nonplussed reaction as, "Do you root for the Yankees?"

Jake didn't seem to have a train of baggage that he was pulling behind him on the way to Colorado. He was excited to spend the better part of three days on the bus. He was excited to have had a two-hour layover in Chicago. He was excited at the possibility of finding huge amounts of gold on his buddy's property. Jake was a simple man with a childlike outlook on the world. It seemed that somehow Jake had made it through twenty-nine years of tumultuous living without having his spirit broken.

So many people I met on the bus just looked tired, and not just from bus travel. Many had a different, permanent kind of tired that you could just see on their faces, as if they were tired of being tossed around by life. Addictions, broken relationships, abuse, and loneliness are realities of life that transcend socioeconomic barriers, but people with strong support systems and financial resources can often find help more effectively than the poor. The problems of bus people were more visible and acute. That made them look tired and defeated, like they were on the verge of just giving up and waiting for whatever shit storm was getting ready rain down on them. Jake hadn't been hardened, and it was nice to talk with him.

The layover in Denver was brief. I learned that Greyhound runs two different buses from Denver to Salt Lake City. Chris, who was going to meet his escort girlfriend out in Oregon, was also going through Salt Lake, but he was on the bus that was going up through Wyoming. His bus would travel the entire way on interstate highways. I was booked on a bus that would weave and wind through the ski resort towns of Central and Western Colorado. I didn't figure it mattered which bus I took because they were scheduled to arrive in Salt Lake within forty minutes of each other.

"I'll see you in Utah!" said Chris.

I waved goodbye. I have no idea what happened to Chris, but I didn't see him again.

DAY TEN

Denver, Colorado to Granby, Colorado

Denver, CO-Idaho Springs-Winter Park-Granby-Hot Sulphur Springs-
Kremmling-Steamboat Springs-Milner-Hayden-Craig-Dinosaur

Ray was our driver on the scenic route out west. Ray was of medium build, in his mid-fifties. His hair was brownish-grey, thinning, and combed over to the top of his head. He wore tinted glasses and had a moustache. The black cowboy boots that accompanied his standard driver's uniform were a nice, original change of pace. Ray had a laid-back attitude and a matching Texas accent that he used to summon all the passengers on the bus. We were barely over half of capacity as we started heading west out of Denver.

I had never seen this part of the country and it was breathtaking. As we passed through little towns, we would periodically discharge a person or two from our care and pick up another passenger here and there. While we were traveling in the summer, it was apparent that these little towns had a lot to offer, especially in snowier months. There were signs for rental properties and ski clothing all over the place. Cottages and chalets dotted the mountainsides and subsequent comments from passengers on the bus ensued: "Those rich bastards up on the hill probably haven't ever had to ride the bus." The landscape was beautiful, although there must have been some beetle or something chewing the hell out of the evergreens. Many of them looked sickly. Most of the little towns we passed through looked like they were sparsely populated with full-time residents. It had an odd feeling about it, kind of like we were walking through a high school building on a Sunday. You could tell there was life in these places, but we were just there at the wrong time.

About two hours out of Denver, we stopped at a little town called Granby, Colorado. It was a dinky place with a few gas stations and restaurants, a bank, and a liquor store. Ray told everyone that we would stop for about ten minutes and that we were welcome to go out and have a cigarette or use the restroom. We stopped at a BP station right on the main drag. We all got off the bus and communed in the parking lot of this gas station. It looked as if a storm was brewing in the skies, and the temperature had plummeted into the fifties as we had climbed into the mountains.

Gas stations are odd places. While many of them carry the name of a big oil company: BP, Shell, etc., it is amazing how variable the look and feel of the gas station can be. Most of them are cookie-cutter stations with a dozen pumps, bright fluorescent lighting, beer coolers, and a cashier standing guard over mountains of cigarettes and lottery tickets. They have also gotten a lot cleaner through the years. But, occasionally, when you're off the beaten path, you find a gas station that time forgot. The BP in Granby was one of these. They had a bunch of cheap, plastic shelving out in front of the station that made it look like a third-rate yard sale. They sold everything from hair dryers to hula hoops. It made no sense. It was in disarray and looked like it hadn't been tended to in years.

There was barely enough room for the bus to park in the lot, but this was a regular stop, so our driver knew how to wedge our vessel onto a small patch of pavement away from the gas pumps. Unfortunately one would have no idea that this was a Greyhound station because the plastic red, white, and blue sign with the logo of the dog had fallen down from its casing and was barely visible behind the mountain of crap that they were selling out in front of the store. I went in to use the restroom. It was no surprise that this gas station had no bathrooms on the inside of the facility. It was one of those that required you to get a key, attached to a big block of wood, to carry around to the side of the building. Bathroom key theft must still be a big problem. I opened the door and noticed it was a one-hole bathroom with a filthy toilet. However, there was a chrome vending machine where, for 75 cents, I could choose between glow-in-the-dark condoms or condoms that promised to "tickle" my partner, if I were so inclined. I finished quickly and went to wash my hands, but, alas, there were no soap or paper towels.

As I made my way back to the bus, it had started drizzling. It was a cold, Chinese-water-torture kind of rain. I noticed that Ray was crouched down with a passenger by the right rear tires. Ray was shaking his head and then stood up and announced, "I ain't taking this thing down the hill." Granby is a town that sits at some 7,000 feet above sea level. The passenger had drawn it to Ray's attention that there was fluid leaking by the tire. It turned out that it was hydraulic fluid that had something to do with the brakes. Ray didn't want to roll the dice, so he called the Denver station and alerted them to the leak. They told Ray that they would send another bus and driver our way and that Ray could take our bus to be serviced. Ray informed our crowd of passengers that the replacement bus would be here "in a few hours."

Upon hearing this news, five or six passengers, who were in their early twenties, acted as if they had just gotten news that there would be a snow day at school. They made a beeline across the street and walked the three hundred yards over to the town's liquor store. They pooled their resources and came back with an assortment of supplies: a bottle of Jägermeister, several bottles of Jack Daniels, and some no-name vodka. One industrious fellow walked across to the 7-11, stole a plastic Big Gulp cup, and filled it with one of the two cheap bottles of Chardonnay he bought at the liquor store. Ray was just sitting on a bench in the parking lot, chewing on a toothpick. He saw this mad rush to the liquor store, but turned a blind eye. The drivers all make the announcement at the beginning of every ride that there is to be no smoking or consuming alcohol on the bus or at any of our stops. Ray had made that announcement, but in a moment of discretion and sympathy, chose to let it go.

The merry band of drinkers gathered under an overhang next to the bathrooms to pass the bottles around to each other. This was not a social drinking group. They were all bent on getting bent. And they did. Over the next several hours, they polished off three bottles of liquor and some wine for good measure. The plumes of cigarette smoke lingered in the heavy, damp air. This was a group that hadn't seemed to know each other when we left Denver, but suddenly had the comradery of the Phi Tau house.

I saw a guy walk into the parking lot. He was carrying a shoulder bag, and started to chat with the driver and some of the passengers. He was not on our bus out of Denver. He made his way over to the side of the building where the party was happening. "Are you getting on our bus?" I asked.

"Yeah. I came through here yesterday," he said. "I'm on my way out to Reno, but I had to get off the bus here and go to the hospital. The altitude was messing me up. I was worried I was having a heart attack. It turns out I was okay. They were really nice over there at the hospital. They even put me up for a night in a local hotel when I told them that I was going to have to wait a whole day for another bus," he explained to me.

Scott was an average-looking guy. He had on a gray T-shirt

that read "Las Vegas" in black lettering. He had blue jeans and sneakers on, and looked like any average Joe that you might meet at the grocery store. His hair was black-and-gray and wavy. He had a large nose, and gestured often with his hands when he spoke.

"Hey, I'm going to walk over to the hospital and see what's going on over there," Scott said. Next to the BP was a large parking lot and a medium-sized brick building, which, evidently, was the hospital in Granby. There was a police car and an ambulance parked in the lot and a couple of officers and a paramedic were having a conversation. Scott spent several minutes talking with them before returning with his report. "I guess some hiker fell and is hurt pretty bad. They're bringing in a med-flight from Denver," he said. Within five minutes a helicopter descended on the parking lot. All of the bus passengers lined up at the edge of the BP parking lot to watch this entertainment. It looked like a felonious group of onlookers at a Fourth of July parade. In short order, a bloodied hiker was loaded from his gurney onto the helicopter and lifted back to the civilization of Denver.

Scott quickly became part of the party group. He was offered a shot of Jäger, which he gladly accepted. I resisted the urge to join in, but I still wanted to be a part of the group and watch how this would unfold. The scene had an unsettled feel. These guys were likely no strangers to drinking, but they looked like the kind of guys that couldn't hold their liquor and would go to a bar looking for a fight. But, for the first few hours at least, they're usually pretty fun.

The life of the party was a young man in a green John Deere T-shirt. His name was Slone. He was from Chattanooga, Tennessee. He had a short, blond buzz cut and was covered with an assortment of tattoos, including something written in cursive around his neck.

His teeth were brown and crooked and he had a high-pitched, cartoonish country accent. In front of the assembled group, he took a swig of booze and said, "Man, you guys ain't gonna believe this! I left Chattanooga a couple days ago on the bus and I was sittin' next to this girl who was goin' to Indianapolis. She was hotter than shit, man. We started talkin' and she was comin' on to me. I wound up fingerin' the shit out of that girl." Slone, for emphasis, swung his arms around and cocked his head as he told this story.

Scott looked at him and furrowed his brow, saying, "You're full of shit, dude."

"Naw, man, for real," Slone countered. "If I wasn't goin' out to Oakland to see my mom, I would've just jumped on her bus to Indianapolis." I had my doubts about the veracity of Slone's claims, but he was insistent that he had found love. Then, in an outburst he said, "Wait! I got her number, dude!" He pulled a card out of his wallet. "Here it is! In your faaaaaaaaaace!" he said to convince any would-be doubters among us.

Scott took the card from Slone's greasy hand and examined it. "Holy shit! You're not going to believe this!" Scott exclaimed as he brought the card over to me. It was a business card with "Hamilton County Probation Officer" across the top and the name and phone number underneath. At the top of the card, in blue ink, was written "Wendy. 804-1968."

"Slone, she wrote her phone number on her probation officer's card!" Scott informed him. Slone hadn't looked carefully enough yet at the card. But he was non-judgmental.

"Well, that's the only thing she had to write it on." Slone seemed to miss the point that it might be a relationship fraught with obstacles if she not only had a probation officer, but was willing to get rid of her officer's card that dismissively. "Well, whatever dude. She was hot as shit!" Slone concluded.

A rough customer named Jason was also in the small gathering by the bathroom. He was tall and strong, likely in his mid-twenties.

He was wearing jeans and a navy blue T-shirt. He, too, had tattoos banding his arms at various places. He spoke up, "Slone, you probably didn't even touch her. What would she want with your ugly ass?"

Slone grew defiant. "Dude, I've nailed more chicks than you can count. Last year I went camping with my buddy and his old lady. He got drunk and passed out. I fucked his old lady *four times!* He found out and got all pissed off at me, but she wanted to fuck. What was I supposed to do? Plus, he doesn't want to mess with me. I've got a gun. I'd pop a cap in his ass real quick if he tried to fuck with me." Slone's bravado was falling on deaf ears and not having quite the impact he was hoping for.

Jason drew a long drag off his Marlboro Red. "I still say you're full of shit."

Ray, the driver, meandered over and stood on the periphery of the group. He was still chewing on his toothpick and had a subtle grin emerging from under his moustache, likely from Slone's tales. Slone had no filter. His voice was loud and piercing. "Any word from Greyhound yet?" Scott asked in Ray's direction.

"They said maybe by 4:00," Ray stated in his slow drawl.

"I hate ridin' the fuckin' bus," Jason threw out to the group. Several heads nodded as the cloud of smoke thickened.

"It's not that bad," Scott said. "It's always interesting. I was on the bus a few weeks ago coming out of Reno. We had this huge, crazy black lady. I was sitting the front row and she was right behind me. I started smelling the nastiest thing I've ever smelled. Everybody around us was gagging. This huge lady shit herself. She was literally just sitting there in her own shit. So, we stopped in Lovelock and I told the driver: 'The lady right behind me has had an accident.' The driver was like, 'What do you mean "an accident"?' I told him, 'I don't know how to delicately say this, but the lady lost control of herself. She shit herself.' The driver just looked at me. We were all getting off the bus in Lovelock, but the lady just sat there in her seat, staring straight ahead. She was clearly nuts. The driver told me to call the cops and report it, so that's what I did. I called 9-1-1 and explained that there was an accident on the bus. But, I didn't go into detail with the operator. So, they sent a fire truck, an ambulance, and a cop car. They didn't know if there was a fire or if someone was hurt, so they sent the whole cavalry. The lady hadn't moved. The paramedics climbed up on the bus and literally had to lift this lady off the bus and put her in the ambulance. I don't know where they took her. Hopefully, they put her in a mental hospital."

That story drew great laughter from the group and then Ray spoke up. "I've seen it all, man. I had a crippled lady shit herself one time. I had to put her off the bus. We couldn't stand the smell. But then this one time, I was driving across New Mexico and we stopped at some gas station. This cowboy comes hopping off the bus and he's mad as hell. He's screaming at me, hopping around on one foot. He's wearing cowboy boots and he says, 'Look, do you see this? I've got shit on my boots.' I asked him, 'How'd you get shit on your boots?' He said, 'Some dude just dropped his pants and took a shit right in the aisle of the bus. I stepped right in it.' So, I had to find out who that motherfucker was and I kicked him off the bus and I had to clean the aisle up. But that cowboy was mad as hell."

It was story time at happy hour. Everyone was trying to outdo the next with tales of hooking up with a woman or somebody shitting themselves. We didn't talk about politics or religion or sports. It was bus tales of woe for the next hour. I moved in and out of the party circle. I was wondering what the other twenty passengers were doing. I walked back by our broken bus and stepped on board. In the second row there was a couple making out. I just ignored them and walked back to my seat to make sure nothing had been stolen. There were some people sleeping and a couple of others listening to music on their headphones. After realizing that all of my gear was intact, I walked back out to the other side of gas station. Next to the dumpster were two abandoned bench seats that had previously been in someone's van. The red velour-like fabric had dark stains and had likely been rained and snowed on countless times. But they provided some auxiliary seating for stranded bus passengers.

Both benches were being occupied. One was by the guy who was now on his second bottle of Chardonnay, sipping on the straw of his Big Gulp cup. His attention was focused on the man seated on the bench to the left of him. There sat a man in his early sixties named Burt. Burt was wearing blue jeans, a white dress shirt, a navy blazer, and a fedora. He was strumming on an old guitar, singing a song. The guitar case was at his feet as he sang some beautiful melody about a woman who had run away with some guy's heart. Mr. Chardonnay was struggling to keep his eyes open and was nodding his head and tapping his feet, out of rhythm with Burt's strumming.

"What kind of guitar is that?" I asked when Burt wrapped up his song.

"I don't really know. It's from the 1930s. It's my baby. It was some offshoot company of Gibson that made it, but I can't quite date it. The guy that sold it to me forty years ago said it was from the Depression Era. She's seen a lot."

Turns out Burt was a folk singer who went around and sang at various festivals. "But it doesn't pay very well," he said. "I'm going out to Reno to try and look for steady work." Burt was a gentle, soft-spoken man. His face was weathered and he was missing a front tooth. His gray hair and moustache were distinguished looking, but the wrinkles on his face hinted at a hard life with many stories.

"What other kind of work have you done?" I asked him.

"I've done some teaching. I've worked with the homeless. I've done mostly social work-type stuff. I wish I could make some money singing. That's what I love. I write songs and love to share them with people." Burt was a throwback. He was clearly a product of the 60s and had lived through an era when things like folk music really mattered. The music was an anthem for things like justice and social change. I had the feeling that Burt was still trying to sing a tune that no one wanted to hear anymore.

Surprisingly, around 4:30, a new bus actually showed up. Burt and the party crowd made their way toward the replacement bus. In a moment of community spirit and togetherness, everyone gathered at the luggage doors underneath the bus. We began an assembly line-like transfer of belongings from the old bus to the new. The rain was now more steady and the air even cooler. Within five minutes, everything was loaded on our new bus, and we bid farewell to Ray. Our new driver was Curt. I don't know if Ray had informed Curt that a sizeable percentage of his passengers were now legally drunk, but I'm sure Curt could smell the fumes as we boarded the bus.

The mood was festive as we passed through the Colorado towns of Dinosaur and Craig. The roads were windy and steep. I was concerned that I would witness a repeat of twenty years ago with people vomiting in the bathroom, but that didn't happen. Slone was now in the row in front of me. Scott was directly across from me. Jason was behind me, diagonally, and Burt and Mr. Chardonnay sat in the seat right behind me. The drinking did continue on the bus as Jason had smuggled on a few more travelers' bottles of Jack Daniels. The bottle was being passed around like communion wine. Within a short time, the inevitable happened.

"Slone, watch your fucking mouth!" Jason burst out.

Slone stood up. "What did you say?"

Jason was out of his seat like a shot and immediately puffed out his chest. His face was now three inches from Slone's face. "I told you to watch your fucking mouth, motherfucker. There's a fucking kid sitting right in front of you. You've said *fuck* twenty times in the last two minutes. You need to chill out. I know you're drunk, but what the fuck, dude. You've got to keep it down." Jason was the voice of reason, although every F-bomb he was dropping was being heard every bit as much as all of Slone's by the eleven-year-old boy in the row in front of Slone. The boy's dad had not entered into the fray, probably for good reason.

These two guys were rough as corncobs and were about to come to blows with each other.

"Just chill the fuck out," Jason lobbied. He stuck out his fist and did a fist bump with Slone who was much thinner and weaker. It wasn't quite the same as the Middle East peace talks at Camp David, but it was a successful diffusion nonetheless. With that, Slone lay down in his seat and, within five minutes, was sleeping like an end-of-life patient in the ICU.

Jason kept ranting to Scott and me about Slone. "Some people just can't handle their liquor. I mean, how would he feel if his fuckin' kid was on the bus? He wouldn't want them hearin' that kind of shit." Scott and I just looked at each other and raised our eyebrows. Jason would have blown a large number on a Breathalyzer at that moment, but he was the diplomat of the drunks. Every few minutes Jason would walk back to the bathroom. We would soon smell the strong odor of cigarette smoke. Jason wasn't trying to hide it. He needed to smoke and the bathroom was convenient. Everyone on the bus who hadn't yet passed out could smell the smoke, including our driver, Curt. But Curt, either from a wave of sympathy or a fear of having to kick someone off the bus, let it go. Within a half hour, Jason had his sunglasses on and was passed out on his seat. He was lying down and his legs were fanned open, extending into the aisle.

The sun had set and the bus was getting quieter and calmer, especially with the two loudest and drunkest riders having called it a night. Our driver informed us that we were going to be very late into Salt Lake City. We were supposed to have a brief layover around midnight and then hop on a bus for Reno, which would have put us in Reno about nine the next morning. Our driver said that wasn't going to happen. He informed us that he would be checking with Greyhound to see if they could run another bus for us into Reno.

Strangely enough, that seemed to appease the fifteen to twenty people who were planning on going that way. Everyone was remarkably patient. On the bus, shit happens. And you have to accept that. It seems to me that people who have less stable lives are able to adapt more easily. They've long ago learned a lesson that it does very little good to complain. Authority figures have been complicit in their instability, in their minds, so, they are usually viewed as the enemy, uninterested in being an ally. So they just go with the flow. I don't know if it's a product of resiliency or resignation, but it's the truth. The bus broke down. We were going to be late. There was nothing anyone could do about it. We were all in the same situation. Life would go on.

I've always been a person who likes to be in control of my life and the situations around me. Growing up, my family life was pretty stable. I knew that my family would have dinner together. I knew that there were expectations and a curfew. There were consequences and rewards. The rules were usually pretty clear. I've tried to replicate that, for better or worse, with my own kids. We have a routine: dinner at 6:00; kids in bed by 9:00. We stick to that as much as we can. But rigidity also comes with a price. Rigid scheduling and expectations can send us in a tizzy when things don't work out the way we plan or hope. I'll still take schedule and routine over chaos, but I also recognize that those things give me a false sense of control. The truth is that we can't script and orchestrate everything in life. We can try and plan and prepare for every eventuality, but we set ourselves up for heartache and frustration when we fool ourselves into thinking that we need to control everything. My month on the bus was a not-so-gentle reminder that a lot of what happens is beyond our sway.

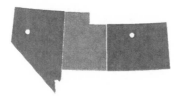

DAYS TEN–ELEVEN

Granby, Colorado to Lovelock, Nevada

Dinosaur, CO-Vernal, UT-Ft. Duchesne-Roosevelt-Myton-Duchesne-Heber City-Park
City-Salt Lake City-Wendover, NV-Elko-Battle Mountain-Winnemucca-Lovelock

As we neared the border of Utah, I was feeling a sense of adventure that I hadn't had on the trip so far. While the bus had broken down and our travel plans were in disarray, I relaxed in my seat, feeling as if these fellow nomads were now part of my world and I was a part of theirs. Our union of inconvenience gave us a bond, even temporarily, that we would remember forever.

The bus was quieting down and I thought it would be nice to hear some music. "Hey Burt, could you get your guitar out and play us a tune?" I asked. His eyes brightened and he flashed a grin that featured his missing tooth. It gave him a loveable look. He reached up in the compartment above his seat and pulled down his guitar case. He opened it and proceeded to fiddle with his guitar, tuning it for the next five minutes. The remaining drinkers who were awake settled down and joined in with the more solitary, sober passengers in giving Burt a captive audience.

He played two or three songs that he had written. His sad, wistful, melodic voice made us forget that we were on a bus for a while. It was peaceful and beautiful. Burt was in his element. He had a bus full of people giving him their undivided attention. I couldn't help but think about the last few days. I had met Ordell and Becky. I had gotten yanked out of the bottom of a bus by an overzealous security guard in Omaha, and I had an impromptu frat party in Granby, Colorado. Now I was on a bus full of people who had been united by all of this inconvenience, being serenaded by a tired, gentle, unemployed folk singer. This was a slice of Americana that I couldn't have created in my mind, but I was glad to be a part of it.

When I set out on this journey, I had wanted to observe the world of the bus people. But I think, deep down, I was also longing for community. And here we were, a group of strangers plopped into an unfamiliar culture. Aside from a few couples and a father and son, the bus was a collection of individuals. The spider web of travel routes had caused us all to intersect at this moment in time and a community was born. No one would have chosen the string of inconvenient circumstances that resulted in the confluence of dozens of personal journeys, but that's what happened. While our paths will most likely never cross again, we will all be united in some way by our common experience. It was our story, our time together. I suddenly felt like I've been a part of something organic and beautiful, something bigger than myself. It was a beautiful moment I wouldn't have necessarily anticipated on this bus adventure.

As a father, I have learned that you can't plan memories. They just happen. I have spent hours researching and preparing for family vacations. I have tried to orchestrate memorable trips to Disney World and the beach. I can map out a full itinerary of where we're going to eat and what activities we'll be doing. But nobody remembers much of that. Instead, it's the accidental encounter with a colorful character or a funny conversation in the car that everyone remembers. It's the stuff out of left field that usually makes for the best memories. Vacations are usually a fine manifestation of some of my control issues and I enjoy planning things out, but my fondest recollections are of times when everything wasn't prescribed. I've learned the value of placing myself and my family in situations where we can be open to random events and encounters. If I spend my life trying to sequester myself and keep things as orderly, sterile and void of mistakes and heartache, I've missed the boat, so to speak. This bus trip reminded me of that.

Scott and I began a long conversation. There was something about Scott that intrigued me. He was well spoken and witty. It didn't make sense on the surface—why was this guy on a bus headed for Reno? Was he running away from something? I wanted to get to know him and hear his story. I had a strong feeling that it would be worth my while to dig a little bit with him.

"So, what's going on out in Reno?" I asked Scott as the majority of the bus had slipped off to the land of slumber.

"I've been out there a few times and I really like it," he began. "I'm out of work right now, so I'm going to see if I can find something." Scott was engaging, but mildly evasive. "I was in sales. I enjoyed it. But the economy turned south and they had to make cutbacks. I was selling things like tasers and personal protection devices." Again, this sounded a bit cloudy, but I just nodded and went along with it.

I remembered seeing Scott show up in Granby when the bus was broken down. He wasn't toting a substantial amount of luggage. I wondered how bad things must have been that he would just pick up and try to move out to Reno with very few belongings. "Where were you living before this?" I asked.

"I've moved around a little bit, trying to find things here and there," Scott responded. "My last job in sales was in New York.

But I went to college in Akron. I was a non-traditional student. I went later in life."

Scott was fairly brief and non-descript with his answers. He deflected the focus from himself and started peppering me with questions about the nature of my travel. I explained that I was riding the bus around the country and writing a book about the people I met and the experiences I had. He was very interested and offered insightful commentary when I mentioned the story of Ordell, the homeless man I had met on the way to Omaha from Minneapolis.

"I've ridden the bus a lot in my life, and I've met a lot of Ordells along the way," Scott expressed. "He's probably part of 'Greyhound therapy,'" Scott commented.

"What's Greyhound therapy?" I asked.

"It's when the police, or churches, or social workers don't want to deal with someone's problems so they just buy them a bus ticket and stick 'em on a Greyhound to get them out of town," he responded.

I hadn't heard of this before, but it made sense. If there were people being shuttled from town to town, it wasn't something that they openly admitted, but some of the people I met on the bus looked like they might definitely fit the mold—a few were clearly mentally ill, mumbling to themselves; others looked hard, weathered, unshaven, or drunk.

"I'm kind of jealous. I would love to do something like what you're doing. How much did the thirty-day pass cost you?" Scott inquired.

"It was $439," I answered.

"Wow, that's not bad. I'd love to ride along with you. I could help you write!" he enthused in a half-joking, half-serious way.

We chatted about the bus and Scott was eager to share some of his stories. I had already heard about the mentally ill woman who had soiled herself in Nevada. But he offered up another nugget that sounded apocryphal, but was told with such conviction that

I was soon a believer. "There are some real nut jobs on the bus. This one time, I was riding through Kansas, actually coming out to Reno. The driver at a stop in the middle of nowhere told me, 'You know this bus isn't permitted to stop in Colby, Kansas anymore?' He went on to say that, evidently, at a rest stop next to a McDonald's, some drunk flicked his cigarette into some dry grass and it ignited a farmer's entire field. The fire department came out and all hell broke loose. They said the flames were licking at the windows of the McDonald's. Could you imagine being there with your girlfriend eating a Big Mac and seeing some bus load of hooligans pouring out and some guy starts a fire that looks like Dante's Inferno?" Scott gestured with his hands and raised eyebrows as he told the story. He had me laughing, thinking about that scene.

He continued, "You know, nobody on this bus has two cents to rub together. They shoplift stuff all the time. Hell, I just stole an egg roll from the Kum & Go back in Colorado. People are stealing beef jerky and sodas all the time. You know Greyhound negotiates contracts with particular stores and gas stations? You ever notice that? We don't just stop wherever the driver wants. They have to stop at these exact places. Can you imagine that conversation with the negotiator from Greyhound? 'Listen, we've got a proposal for you. Every day we're going to bring six different buses full of fifty people each into your store. There may be a little bit of inventory loss, but it will still make economic sense . . .' I'm guessing they don't mention the rampant shoplifting."

I confirmed this with a representative from Greyhound. They do indeed negotiate the rest stops for their buses. Many of the bus stops are just little ten-minute deals where they dump somebody off and pick up a person or two, but every three or four hours the bus stops for an extended period of time, a half hour or more. For those stops, the regional manager for Greyhound will seek out the best deal. Each individual stop is negotiated with the owner of the truck stop or restaurant. Greyhound gets a percentage of the estimated amount of money that a busload of passengers will spend. That varies, roughly, between 3 percent and 10 percent although the representative would not divulge the exact numbers because, the representative told me, "It's all about business. I wouldn't even tell my brother what we get from these places."

I didn't make much of the stolen egg roll. I thought Scott was just being a little rebellious. He mentioned that he had tucked the egg roll under the two hot dogs that he actually did purchase. He just wanted to see if he could do it. It was a small thrill. We shared a few more stories and then the conversation quelled and we drifted off for the last hundred miles into Salt Lake City.

As we exited the highway and pulled into the terminal in Salt Lake, Driver Curt grabbed the microphone and addressed the bus crowd. Slone and Jason slowly sat up, having slept off their buzz. "Ladies and gentlemen, as you might have guessed, we missed the midnight bus to Reno. It's now 2:00 in the morning and I learned that the next bus doesn't leave for Reno until 11 a.m. I spoke with Greyhound and asked if they could put you all up for the night since it was the result of a bus breakdown. They declined to do that. But what I'm willing to do is leave the bus unlocked and you can sleep in here instead of on the floor of the terminal. I know that isn't much, but it's better than nothing. I'm really sorry about all this, but things like this can happen." Curt's pseudo-apology was met with some mild groaning and moaning, but most of the passengers were too tired to argue. We just sat there absorbing the news that we would spend the next nine hours together in Salt Lake City. Two foreign exchange students, who we had picked up somewhere in Colorado and who spoke very little English, looked at each other and with raised eyebrows shook their heads as if to say, "I don't know what's happening." A friendly passenger seated behind them and said in slow, loud English, "WE ARE STUCK HERE UNTIL 11." The exchange students just nodded their heads.

The groggy throng of passengers slowly filed off the bus and milled around the terminal, some going to the bathroom, some just pacing. Slone and Jason looked rough. They didn't speak to each other as they returned from the bathroom and headed back toward the bus. Curt vanished quickly. His run was finished and he had no desire to be the point person for the complaints department. Scott and I stayed close and decided that we would go back to sleep on the bus. About twenty people chose to bunk down on the bus and another dozen or so built a nest with luggage and clothing and did their best to find a quiet corner of the terminal to sleep in for a few hours. After coming all the way from Minneapolis with no sleep for two days, I was on fumes. I was actually able to sleep until almost 7 a.m., when people started rustling about. Scott rose about the same time I did and we wandered into the terminal to use the bathroom, brush our teeth, and figure out our next steps.

We spotted Burt and Daniel, a passenger that we had picked up in Colorado, sitting on the hard floor in the corridor between the gates and the exit. They were sipping on coffee and sitting with their backs against the wall. The bus station in Salt Lake, thankfully, was one of the nicer ones that I had seen. It was newer looking and fairly bright and clean. This was a good thing, as it would be our home for the rest of the morning. Scott and I had a seat with Burt and Daniel, forming a small circle.

"This has been an interesting trip," remarked Burt.

"Yes, it has. Look at us sitting here. We look like a hobo version of the Breakfast Club," Scott chimed in. We all laughed, glad to have found each other. It was a good arrangement for the next few hours. When one guy had to get up and go to the bathroom or get a drink, the other three would vigilantly guard his gear. It's surprising how liberating that felt after having spent a taxing couple of weeks not wanting to let my stuff get out of my sight.

As we were sitting in the hallway, three uniformed police officers made a brisk pass in front of us. They were obviously scurrying to find someone or something. Scott was unable to let this pass by without being in the know. He followed the cops out the door onto the sidewalk and had a brief conversation. He came back and reported, "They got a call that a deranged woman was here in the Greyhound station. They also said that we should stay away from this neighborhood. They said there is a homeless shelter and a bunch of hookers hanging around." Scott seemed to find joy in this. It dawned on me that maybe Scott should be the one writing this book. He was just as passionate about finding and reporting the news of the bus world as I was, perhaps even more so.

Scott was unable to sit still. He was surveying the entire bus station, wanting to know where everyone was and what they were doing. He pointed out the window and said, "Look at those jack-asses." Slone and another passenger were walking on the sidewalk with orange construction cones on their heads, passing the time. Scott shook his head as if to say, "I'm above all that." Scott seemed to be really glad to be holding court with our foursome in the hall-way. But he sensed that he had a higher purpose. Scott walked over to the service counter and came back a few minutes later with a huge grin on his face. "I've got good news. I convinced Greyhound that they should compensate us for our inconvenience. Look what I've got," he said, holding out his hand. Scott had procured break-fast vouchers for everyone on the Granby bus. He was so proud of himself. He was kind of like a modern-day Robin Hood who had just given our little Nottingham Village his bounty of microwavable chili dogs, bags of chips, and Mountain Dew. Slone was thrilled. He had pissed away his last two cents on liquor some eighteen hours ago. This sustenance was a welcome sight.

For the next few hours, we just sat around and told stories. I learned that Burt had spent the last several years in Arkansas tend-ing to an ailing mother and brother. They had both died within the last fifteen months. He was going back to Reno, where he had lived for most of his adult life. Burt was proud of how he had been sober for the past three years. He said that his missing front tooth is a reminder of a drunken night in Arkansas when he tripped and smashed his face on some concrete steps. He's never had the financial resources to arrange for reconstructive dental work.

Daniel complained that he was accosted by campus police officers in Reno and arrested on public intoxication charges. "I can't believe that, man. I was just walking back to my apartment after spending a few hours at a bar after class. I told them I was a student, but they said, 'You don't look like a student.' That's profiling, man. That place is fucked up." Daniel's ponytail and beard, combined with shorts and flip-flops, made him look like a homeless Jimmy Buffet fan. He was a perpetual student. He studied geology but had struggled to maintain steady employment over the years. He said that he had two sons. His ex-wife was always on his case about contributing money for the kids' education. But Daniel explained, "they're adults now. They've got to figure it out just like I did". The fact that Daniel was riding a Greyhound bus, heading back to Reno, unemployed, suggested to me that maybe Daniel hadn't "figured it out" yet. It was no surprise when he revealed that his youngest son was in jail for multiple DUI offenses.

Scott also opened up in a significant way for the first time. He revealed that his mother had kicked him out of the house when he was fifteen because she "didn't want to deal with me." Scott moved in with his father, who was a raging alcoholic. His dad drank every night, and often throughout the day, but was able to hold onto a job working in a mill in New York. The drinking and smoking caught up to him, and he died a few years ago. "Was the funeral sad?" I asked Scott. "I don't know. I wasn't there. I regret not going. My dad was hard on me, and we had a tough relationship, but I'll have to take that to my grave. I wish I would have gone to his funeral." Scott drew pensive as he recalled this chapter of his life. After a few seconds of uncomfortable silence, he offered another layer to their relationship. "After high school,

I didn't have my shit together. I stole my dad's checkbook and started writing hot checks all over the place. I was young. I was like nineteen. I didn't know any better. Well, they caught me and I wound up doing ninety days in jail for it. My dad just let me sit there in jail. He was pissed at me, and I was pissed at him for just letting me sit in jail. and we never really patched things up."

Scott shared that he had straightened up in his twenties and wound up enrolling at the University of Akron. He studied political science and criminal studies. Scott knew a lot about the law and weighed in on Daniel's situation with his son and his earlier experience with the University of Nevada police. He was the uncredentialed, pro-bono lawyer figure for our small bus crew. Again, I had the feeling that there was more to this guy than met the eye. I couldn't figure out why he was on the bus and how he was unemployed. He was bright, witty, and engaging.

The hours passed and we boarded the bus to Reno together. We picked up a few regularly scheduled passengers in Salt Lake that filled our bus. It was a bright, beautiful day in the Rocky Mountains. We left the crappy neighborhood that housed the Greyhound station for the promise of neon lights and new beginnings in Reno.

I was excited to get to Reno, and not just because of the mayhem of the last few days. I'm a sucker for neon. The bright lights and jingling and clinking of slot machines can be magical. It's like when I was a kid going to the town carnival—it wasn't just the thrill of riding the rides. It was everything about it: the smell of the corn dogs, the noisy music, the hustle of the crowds, and the neon lights. Burt, Daniel, and Scott all were hoping that this magical oasis would afford them a new start on life. They had bared their souls to each other, and to me, and the one common thread was that there was hope in a new day. Reno seemed like as good of a place as any to start over.

We stopped at an Arby's in Wendover, Nevada. This was our first stop in Nevada, and I was immediately drawn to the sign for the Red Garter Hotel and Casino.

"Scott, you ever been to the Red Garter?" I asked.

"Yeah, it's not bad. They have a nice steak there," he replied. Scott seemed to have been everywhere and done everything. People like that usually annoy me. I have had a few friends and a larger number of acquaintances over the years whom my wife and I refer to as "one uppers." They will listen to your story and then trump it with a story of their own. They usually have no idea that they're doing it, and that they come across as arrogant and unaware. But Scott fascinated me.

"Hey, I've got good news. Look at this," he said, drawing an envelope from his back pocket. The envelope was secured with a rubber band, and as he opened it, I saw a stack of cards and coupons that were the size of a thick wallet. "I've got six coupons for free junior roast beef sandwiches. It's a nice sandwich. All I had to do was fill out an online survey and print off these coupons."

"Sounds good. Do you mind sharing?" I asked.

"Not at all," he said.

We walked up to the counter at the Arby's, and a teenager wearing a visor examined Scott's coupons. "I'm going to have to check with my manager. I haven't seen these before," she stated. Scott was beside himself. "That's a perfectly good coupon. I don't know what the problem is."

"I'm sorry. We don't accept these," said the girl when she returned. Scott just shook his head and withdrew two dollars and some change from his pockets. He ordered two items from the value menu and a glass of water to wash it down. I ordered a roast beef melt, some curly fries, and a coke and handed them my credit card. As we sat down, Scott said, "Look at this, we're the only two people from the bus actually sitting in here eating. Everyone else is totally busted out. I'll bet you're the only one on the bus with solvent credit." I was glad that Scott had paid for his meal and not stolen another egg roll from the Pilot station that housed the Arby's.

As we walked back to the bus, we passed a room that held about a dozen slot machines. Our driver was in there gambling. Scott said, "I love to play video poker. I'm pretty good at it. I've got Diamond status at Harrah's." He went on to explain as he withdrew his Diamond card from the envelope in his back pocket. "They've got a rewards system set up. If you cycle through $5,000 on their slot or table games, you qualify for Diamond status. It's not as good as the Seven Stars, but it has a lot of benefits."

"What's Seven Stars?" I asked.

"That's for their high rollers. I'm not sure what the amount is, but those folks are serious gamblers. They get comped rooms, free food, tickets to shows, the whole nine yards. But Diamond status gets me into the players' lounge. It's nice. They have a buffet set out and you can sit in there all day." Scott seemed to have the system figured out. He had a card and coupon for everything.

I couldn't resist telling him, "If you'd put as much effort into a career as you did into your coupon gathering, you'd be a millionaire by now."

"I know, right?" Scott responded, well aware that he was an expert in working the system.

Back on the bus we passed through the desolate terrain in Northern Nevada, going for hours without seeing many towns. Daniel gave an unsolicited lecture on the salt and rock formations and about how the train line started. Scott humored him by asking questions and feigning interest in the importation of natural resources. We passed by the prison that O.J. Simpson calls home. It was visible from the highway, but was likely a few miles off the road. A little farther down the road, we stopped in the town of Lovelock,

Nevada. This was our last major stop before we got to Reno. "This is where the crazy lady shit herself," Scott reminded me.

We pulled into a gas station and most of the passengers exited the bus to smoke, standing on the grass embankment that buffered the station from the highway. Scott and I were just soaking up the sunshine and clean, mountain air when we spotted a well-dressed woman walking her dogs. She was a block away, coming toward the gas station. Scott approached her and asked, "Are those Standards?" He was referring to her Standard Poodles. These dogs were striking and well groomed, just like their owner.

"Yes. This one here is Max and this one here is Zoe."

Scott bent down to pet the dogs. "They're beautiful," he remarked.

"Thank you," said the woman. "We're on our way to our place in Tahoe and my little angels needed some exercise," she explained.

At this point the majority of the bus passengers who were out smoking descended on this woman and her dogs, all wanting to pet them. It was like an out-of-control third grade field trip, without chaperones. The dog owner was courteous, but clearly uncomfortable with this gaggle of smokers touching her prized pets. In a matter of seconds, a Lexus SUV pulled up and rolled down the window. "Peggy, what are you doing? Get in the car!" shouted the driver.

"Oh, that's Ted," said Peggy. "I'd better get going." It was an uncomfortable collision of socioeconomic worlds.

Scott said, "Did you see that guy? He looked at this bus full of criminals and thought, 'oh man they're going to rape my wife.'" The bus passengers finished their cigarettes and made some snide comments about the rich people not wanting to associate with them. I can only imagine what the conversation was like in the Lexus between Ted and Peggy.

DAYS ELEVEN–THIRTEEN

Lovelock, Nevada to Reno, Nevada

Lovelock, NV-Reno

We were about thirty miles out of Reno when I asked Scott where he was going to stay in Reno. "You gonna crash with friends, or do you already have an apartment set up?"

"No, not yet. That's my plan. I'm just going to get some minimum-wage job and save up some money to get a place. I'll do anything until I get on my feet. Reno's got a ton of unemployment, so it's going to be rough for a while. But, I'm gonna get it together."

I wondered why Scott would choose to start anew in a city that sported an astronomical unemployment rate. I was starting to think he was headed to Reno because he might have some gambling issues.

"Well, where are you staying *tonight?*" I pressed.

"I'm probably going to just head to Wal-Mart and pick up a sleeping bag and sleep by the Truckee River. It's actually pretty nice there. It's safe. I can do that for a week or so until I get a paycheck and can put a deposit down on an apartment."

This was unsettling to me. I felt bad for Scott. He was a smart guy. It sounded like he had had a rough upbringing, but he had gotten a college degree, for goodness' sakes. What was he doing sleeping by a river?

"That's silly, man," I told him. "I've already booked a room for two nights at the Sands. Why don't you just crash with me there? I'll just get a room with two beds," I offered.

"Wow. That's generous. But I can't really contribute to the cost of the room," Scott replied.

"Don't worry about it," I said. "I was going to pay for the room anyway. It's not a big deal. You'll at least have two nights that you don't have to sleep by the river."

I felt like this was the right thing to do. Scott had seemingly run into a string of bad luck, but when I looked at him, I didn't think he was unlike me. I was fortunate in life. My parents both loved and wanted me. I went off to college and got a good job, met my wife and had kids. I've had some bumps along the way, but I've been pretty darn lucky. Scott clearly had the skills to have a great career in sales or something that would require him dealing with people. He had an ease about him and an approachability that I felt could and would open some doors for him in the future. I wanted to help him. Besides, I thought it might be fun to hang out with this guy for a couple more days.

"Ok, man. I really appreciate it. But, here's the deal: when we get to Reno, I'm going to treat you to everything. I've got this Diamond card and we can go into the lounge at Harrah's. We can sit in there all day and eat and drink. I mean, whatever you want. If you like tequila, and you want a shot of Patron, done. They've got it all. High-end martinis. I'm talking Grey Goose, buddy. I'm gonna take good care of you." Scott was getting more and more excited as he crafted this scenario for me.

As we descended into Reno, a beautiful scene lay before us. The city sits in a bowl, its beacon of neon lights beckoning travelers off the highway. In the early evening, a soft orange blanket of light reflects off the mountainsides. Invisible to the outsider is the layer of filth on the streets, or the scores of people wandering aimlessly, victims of Reno's false lure of quick and easy wealth. For us, it was a welcome oasis of rest. It was a city I had never visited, but I felt like I was coming home—a mirage in the desert. A three-day bus voyage will make you feel that way.

Scott warned me about the bus station in Reno. "It's the worst, man. There are some bad apples. Tons of prostitutes, druggies, you name it. Let's just get our stuff and get out of there." We entered the small, darkish terminal. I quickly scanned the place and it fit Scott's description well. It was dank and dirty. It smelled of desperation. I retrieved my duffel bag and followed Scott's lead through a few parking lots, taking some dark back alleys to get to the Sands Hotel. I had noticed earlier in Granby that Scott was traveling exceedingly light. He only had a small black mesh tote bag, not a piece of luggage, but the type that you would use to haul your groceries in if you were environmentally conscious. I didn't make much of it. I figured he had left most of his possessions back east in storage. He was starting over and didn't want to haul a bunch of stuff across the country on a bus.

When we got to the check-in line at the Sands, Scott shadowed me closely to make sure that I was getting the best possible deal. I had booked a room online for $40 per night. I thought that was a bargain. But Scott tried to haggle them down even lower. He flashed some sort of card, AAA or a hotel gambling credential, but the man behind the counter informed us that $40 was the best that he could do. "It's fine, Scott. Really. $40 is a lot less than I've paid in other cities. It's within my budget." Scott let it go and the man handed us two room keys.

We dropped our stuff off in the room and headed straight back downstairs. I told Scott that I would cover the cost of dinner. But the Sands had an Arby's, and Scott wanted to treat me to that free junior roast beef sandwich. He presented his coupons yet again to a young woman behind the counter. "I'll need to check with my manager. I haven't seen this coupon before," she said. This familiar refrain didn't sit well with Scott.

"I don't know what you're talking about. I got those coupons straight from Arby's. There shouldn't be any problem with them," he lobbied. She hung up the phone and said, "I can't accept those." She offered no other explanation. Scott was livid. I quelled his anger by saying, "Let's just head over to the diner and get something and we'll try again tomorrow when the manager is here." Scott wasn't happy, but after a few more minutes of grousing, he relented and vowed to fight another day.

In the fifty-yard walk from Arby's to Mel's Diner (the in-house restaurant at the Sands), we had to pass by several dozen slot machines. The temptation was too great. Scott sat down and said, "Here, I'll just play a few hands." He inserted a $10 bill in the video poker machine and, within three minutes, it was gone. He pushed the buttons at lightning speed, somewhat recklessly, in my opinion.

"Don't you need to go slower so that you can see what the cards are?" I inquired.

"Man I've played this so much. I know what I'm doing. I'm a Diamond member, remember?" he replied, never taking his eyes off the screen. "Oh, can you believe that? I had a straight lined up two ways. Can't believe that shit. These machines have gotten a lot tighter. You would think with the recession, they'd loosen them up a little and encourage people to gamble. But they've made it impossible to win. It's a sucker's game." I consoled Scott and we continued the walk to Mel's Diner.

Our waitress introduced herself as Autumn. She was an attractive woman, in her late thirties. She had a nice figure, short bobbed hair, and stylish glasses. Scott was enamored by her. He tried six different ways to get her phone number, but she wasn't having it. She dutifully brought us some omelets smothered in gravy and a couple of Budweisers. Scott wouldn't let it go. "Autumn, you're a lovely woman. Would you care to accompany my friend Mike and me for the evening after you get off of work?" She just flashed us a pretty smile and briskly walked away, popping in now and then to check on us.

When I told her about my book project, she complained that Reno was a hellhole and she couldn't wait to get out of there. "You could write an entire book about Reno," she said. "This place sucks. It's run down. It used to be nice, but it's full of tweakers and crooks now. I've seen it all. It wears me out. I can't wait to leave." I found Autumn's words to be inconsistent with her bouncy walk and friendly smile. Maybe she was just putting up a good front.

Scott and I turned in before midnight. I was exhausted after all that time on the bus and was excited to peel back the turquoise comforter, draw the drapes closed, and slip into a coma. Scott rinsed off in the shower, but put on the same jeans and gray t-shirt he had been wearing for the last two days. "Do you not have any other clothes?" I asked him.

"No. I need to go do that tomorrow," he replied.

The sun fought its way through the crack in the drapes and Scott and I began to toss and turn around 9 a.m. We lay in our separate beds and began a conversation.

"What do you think Slone's doing right now?" Scott asked.

"God only knows. He's probably raiding his mom's piggy bank to go buy some more Jäger," I replied.

"God, that guy was a mess," Scott said. Somehow we ended up talking about where Scott was before he ended up on the bus to Reno. "I was down in Macon, Georgia. I met this girl on the Internet. We chatted online for a couple of months and she invited me down there. So, I took the bus. I show up and she picks me up at the bus station and she's loaded. She's a raging alcoholic. She's got a full eighteen-pack of Bud Light in the passenger seat and she's already ripped. She takes me back to her double-wide and introduces me to her kids. They're both potheads. They're teenagers. One is staying with his girlfriend and the other one lives at home. But this chick is funny. She won't let me stay in her trailer with her and her kids. So she takes me back to my motel and gets freaky. She was awesome in bed. But she's a wreck. I mean, she had a good job. She's forty-two years old and she's been a nurse forever. She makes a good living, but I could tell that the relationship wasn't going to go anywhere. She wanted me to stick around but she wouldn't let me stay with her in her trailer because it would set a bad example. I was thinking that her *excessive drinking* might be a bad example. I realized I couldn't deal with all of her drama, even though she was smoking hot. So I left town and decided to come out here to Reno." I wondered what had really happened in Macon.

"You want some coffee?" Scott asked.

"Yeah, man, that would be great. Here's a couple bucks. Hey, why don't they have a coffee maker here in the room? Every hotel I've ever stayed at has a coffee maker in the room," I ranted.

"It's a casino, man. They want you to leave your room. If you're in your room, you're not gambling. They make you walk down to the casino for everything. I'll go get the coffee and then I'll take your clothes to a Laundromat and you can do your writing. Then, this afternoon, we'll go over to the Diamond Club lounge at Harrah's," Scott said.

"Sounds like a plan," I replied.

Scott brought the coffee up and took my duffel bag to the nearest Laundromat. For the next few hours, I caught up on my blog and tried to recall all of the conversations of the past three days. Scott had programmed my cell phone number in his $3/day prepaid cell phone and agreed to call me when he was done with the laundry. That way I could shower and we would be ready for our afternoon of leisure at Harrah's.

"You done with the laundry?" I asked when Scott called.

"Yeah. It's all folded and fresh smelling. I used to do my

uncle's laundry all the time. You're going to be pleased. Everything looks really sharp. But, hey, I'm gonna just stop by and use my $5 free play I got over at the Circus Circus," Scott said.

"Do I need to come tackle you? Are you going to piss away more money?" I asked.

Scott laughed and said, "No, I'm fine, man. I'm going to burn through the free play and then that's it. I'm done. I'll be back soon."

Sure enough, Scott burned through the free play and an additional $20 of his own money that he fessed up to, at least. "Man, I gotta stay away from those damn machines. You can't win on those things. But, hey, how's the writing going?" he asked. For the next hour he helped me remember some of the conversations and anecdotes we had heard since we met in Granby. "Dude, I really think you're on to something here. I don't think anybody has any idea what happens on the bus. This could be huge," Scott expressed. I appreciated his help and support. I kept thinking, *Here's a guy that could be my friend for a long time, and I met him on the bus!*

Shortly after noon Scott grew impatient. "Come on! Let's go over to Harrah's. The lounge opens at one." I suspended my writing and, admittedly, became excited at the prospect of being a guest in Scott's world for the next few hours. It was a gorgeous afternoon in Reno: bright sunshine and no humidity. The fresh air and this uncharted adventure were working their magic on me. I felt young and unencumbered for the first time in a long, long time. The bus trip was doing its trick. This was exactly how I had hoped I'd feel when I set out two weeks ago.

At Harrah's we rode the escalator up to the second floor, navigating our way through the maze of noisy slot machines. "Here it is!" Scott exclaimed. "You're my guest. I am so pumped about this. I've had this card for about a year and it entitles you to bring a guest, but I've never had anybody to share this with before. We're gonna have a blast. You can eat and drink anything you want. It's all covered," Scott explained, yet again, before we entered the lounge. As we opened the door, Scott, with great pride, flashed his Diamond card to the hostess guarding entrance to the room. She smiled at him and said, "Welcome." Scott looked back over his shoulder and flashed me a bigwig smile. The room was small, kind of like a hospitality suite in an airport or a hotel. There were maybe a total of six tables and several couches. The room was divided in half with a large, stone fireplace providing the ambience of an old prohibition lounge.

Scott and I grabbed a table. "We came at the right time," Scott said, noticing that there were only a dozen or so people in the room. A bartender named Stanley approached and asked, "Can I get you guys something to drink?" Scott looked at me with an anticipatory grin, so proud that he could host this gathering. "I'll just take a Budweiser for right now," I replied.

"That's all you want? You can have *anything*. Don't you want a martini or some Patron?" It was about 1:15 in the afternoon. I wasn't ready to kick it into full gear yet.

Scott ordered a vodka tonic and then commented, "Just wait. In a little while they're going to bring out some appetizers. It's usually good stuff. Heavy appetizers, like chicken fingers and little sandwiches. You're gonna be in heaven." There was a baseball game on the corner television that had the attention of several barflies. The crowd in the lounge was not what I expected. Scott had built it up in my mind so that I was expecting Donald Trump and some Saudi princes to be in there sipping cognac. Instead, it looked like the same clientele that would attend bingo night at the local Elk's lodge. There were a few men wearing satin jackets. There were several Asian couples sitting on the couch reading the newspaper. For Scott, the lounge was his version of Disneyworld. For the others, it was just a place to hang for a little while to take their mind off how much money they were blowing at the blackjack tables.

I asked Scott if we could go down and place a bet on a baseball game. He said, "Sure. I don't bet on sports, but that would be fun." We headed down to the sports book and I put $10 on the Twins to win. I asked if he would like to sit and watch a few innings and he obliged, but after about twenty minutes, he grew antsy. "Let's go back up to the lounge," he said. As I was a guest in Scott's kingdom, I agreed to follow, figuring I could convince Stanley to turn the game on at the bar. But, before we reached the escalator, Scott said, "I've just got to do this. My luck has to change." He pulled a $20 bill from his pocket and inserted it into the "Deuces Wild" video poker machine. Within ten minutes it was gone. At one point he had built up his winnings to $26. But I got the feeling that Scott had never used the "cash out" button. Scott just shook his head. "I'm an idiot. That happens every time. Why do I do that?" He moaned and groaned, carrying on a conversation with himself all the way up to the lounge.

When we entered the lounge for the second time, the crowd looked much the same, but now there was a lavish spread of chips and salsa, some peel-and-eat shrimp, and nachos. "This is pretty nice, isn't it?" Scott gushed as he ladled a scoop of nachos on his plate. I agreed. We made our way to a small table near the bar. Scott said, "Check her out."

At the bar sat a woman in her late forties, a divorcée named Donna. She had flown in with her boyfriend from New Jersey. She was a well-proportioned woman, wearing a low-cut black cocktail dress. Her blonde chin-length hair belied her age. She was sucking down gin and tonics at a swift clip. "I wouldn't mind hooking up with her," Scott said.

Scott left me at the small table and approached Donna at the bar. I only caught bits and pieces of their conversation, but I could tell that they were trying to impress each other with "Seven Stars" versus "Diamond Club" membership pros and cons. It was like a mating dance for problem gamblers. Donna would cackle and flip her head back, laughing at some of Scott's comments. I saw her gently place her hand on Scott's knee as she spoke, leaning in like she was telling him a secret. Scott pretty much ignored me for the next hour or so, but it was fine. I was enjoying this ritual. Scott was a bus rider, trying to find love wherever he could. Donna made no secret about the fact that she was feeling neglected and abandoned by her "asshole" boyfriend. He was off gambling and left her to get schnocked in the lounge. Scott was an available shoulder to cry on.

Scott came back to the table and said in a low voice, "Check out the Asians over there," pointing to the buffet line. "Can you believe those cheap fuckers?" he asked. "They're over there stuffing shrimp into their purses. They come in here and raid the buffet, steal a bunch of food, and then go back out and gamble. They've got security here, but nobody says anything. Those people do that all the time. The food is supposed to be here for Diamond members to enjoy, and they're abusing it. Pisses me off." Scott was torn between amusement and righteous anger as he witnessed an Asian man putting shrimp into a Ziplock bag that he then stuffed into his backpack. I thought it was hilarious.

A few minutes later Donna came over to our table, making the most out of her ten-foot walk from the bar. She was swaying her hips and smiling at Scott, clearly a woman on the prowl. "Why don't we go over and sit on the sofa?" she asked us. Scott did some cursory introduction, but he was on a mission, and it didn't include me. Scott and Donna sat on the sofa and I sat on an adjacent leather lounge chair. They were sitting very close to each other and Donna's hands were constantly brushing and resting on Scott's legs. He would occasionally look at me and flash a grin, as if to say, "Diamond club membership has its benefits." This went on for the better part of an hour and a half. We were all losing track of time. Stanley kept bringing mixed drinks to Scott and Donna and I was enjoying some red wine. The conversation got more and more suggestive and provocative. Scott solicited Donna, "So, would you like to take this up to your room?"

She smiled at him. "Let's just stay here for a while. I barely know you." Her conviction was forced. I was sure that, after a few more drinks, Scott could be a part-time resident in Donna's Seven Stars suite. They continued the canoodling while I tried to keep an eye on the baseball game on the bar television. When I looked back at the new couple, I saw that Scott had his right hand down the front of Donna's dress, holding her left breast like a piece of fruit. They were kissing and giggling, in their own world.

Scott and Donna were too into each other to notice that the door to the lounge had opened and in walked a well-dressed man who looked to be in his late forties. He had on pleated dress slacks and a pressed dress shirt. About two steps inside the door, he spotted our little caucus in the corner of the lounge and yelled, "ARE YOU HAVING FUN, HONEY?" staring at Donna.

Scott quickly withdrew his hand from Donna's dress and Donna sprung off the sofa to chase after her boyfriend. "Nothing was going on," she pleaded with him as he stormed out. Donna returned to the sofa and said, "He's an asshole. Who cares?" Scott's face was beet red and he decided at that time that it wasn't worth pursuing Donna any further. He didn't want to tempt fate and risk further angering her wealthy boyfriend. He suggested that we go check on my baseball bet. We left the lounge and didn't return, but Donna was the primary topic of conversation for the rest of the evening.

Scott kept asking me if I was enjoying myself, seeking affirmation. He was proud that he had been able to treat me to a day of decadence in the Diamond Lounge. "Was I lying? I mean isn't that awesome? We probably ate and drank over a hundred dollars worth of stuff in there. And it's all free. You can see why I wanted to come out here to Reno." Scott was almost having that conversation with himself so as to rationalize some of the decisions he had made. Scott had professed to me on the bus that he intended to come out to Reno and find a job, and then get an inexpensive apartment. But he gave me a tour of Harrah's and showed me the members' workout facility and accompanying showers. He made the comment, "I can come in here and shower any time I want." It was clear that he was mapping out a plan that would allow him to continue a nomadic lifestyle in perpetuity. "I can eat and drink whenever I want in the lounge. I can shower here in the locker room. What a setup!" he proudly gushed.

Again, I couldn't resist the urge to once again make the comment, "Scott, if you put as much energy into finding a career as you did on this, you would be rich in no time."

"Yeah, I know," he replied with a wistful look, but I could tell he was unconvinced. For Scott, this was the best possible scenario: he could be a permanent guest of Harrah's casino.

After hours of drinking and building up a pretty good beer and tequila buzz, we stumbled back to our room, laughing about our day together. When we got upstairs, Scott asked, "Where did you say that guy yanked you out from under the bus?"

"That was the security guard in Omaha," I replied.

"Well, I'm gonna rock their world," he said in a mischievous manner. He used his cell phone and called the Greyhound station in Omaha. "Hello, my name is Alan Horowitz. I'm an attorney and am calling on behalf of my client. May I please speak with the security guard on duty? . . . I don't care if you're busy. Your security guard accosted my client. Do you think it's okay to lay your hands on Greyhound passengers? There will be a big lawsuit coming your way." Scott had invoked his best New York accent for this phone call. I thought he was a genius, but I was a little uncomfortable with the whole thing. After he hung up, he said, "Man, they can't do that to you. Those assholes think they run the world. Some minimum-wage security guard gets on a power trip and pulls you out from under the bus? No way." I appreciated Scott's solidarity surrounding the injustice in Omaha, but I didn't feel that his indignant-lawyer persona quite matched the severity, or lack thereof, of the Omaha incident.

"Thanks for calling, Scott. Maybe that will make them think twice," I said.

He concluded, "Well, we can call them back tomorrow and press this if you want." I didn't figure legal representation from a non-lawyer was in order. I simply thanked him again as we drifted off to sleep.

We slept hard, whipped after a day of drinking at Harrah's. As the sun broke into our room, Scott started to stir.

"You ever see *The Royal Tenenbaums*? Do you remember when Royal Tenenbaum got kicked out of that hotel where he'd be living for the last twenty years? He says to his wife: 'Ethel, you're making me look like a damn hobo,'" Scott recounted. We both laughed, recalling the absurdity of that movie. But it became clear that, for Scott, this was more than a movie. He seemed to idolize Royal Tenenbaum, a drifter who spent his life trying to beat the system. The character had left behind a string of heartache back at home, but his only mission was to fulfill every carnal desire he had: drinking, smoking, and playing craps. I thought it was kind of sad and kind of funny that Scott was on the same trajectory for his life. Part of me admired his carefree spirit and attitude; part of me feared that he would suffer the same fate as his father and become an alcoholic or a penniless gambler. But, for this two-day interlude in Reno, I couldn't have asked for a better companion.

"Man, I wish you could just stay another day," Scott expressed.

"Yeah, it would be fun, but I've gotta get back on the bus," I explained.

"Where do you think you're headed today?" he asked me. "I don't know. I'm thinking about heading down to San Diego. That would be pretty fun, to go through California and spend a day or two down there," I replied.

"Oh, yeah, that sounds awesome. San Diego is beautiful. I wish I could come with you and we could go to Vegas. I've got the same set up down there. We would have a blast. We could spend a day in San Diego and then head over to Vegas for a few days. The women down there are gorgeous," Scott stated in his best version of a sales pitch.

"Yeah, that would be fun, but I've got to remember why I'm on this trip. I want to meet a lot of people and see who's on the bus," I countered.

"Yeah, I get it. I really think you're on to something. That blog is fantastic. I think people are going to love your book." Scott was supportive of my project. I was excited to have made this friend in the unlikeliest of circumstances. I envisioned Scott and I being lifelong friends whose paths would cross every few years. We could live vicariously through each other's lives.

"Hey, why don't I go downstairs and get us some coffee?" Scott offered. "That sounds great. Here's a few bucks. I appreciate it," I responded, handing Scott some crinkled one-dollar bills from my pants pocket.

"These are called drunk dollars," Scott stated. "You forget that you had them in your pocket from the night before. It's kind of like bonus money."

I laughed and replied, "I'm just going to rinse off in the shower and then maybe we can head back down to Mel's Diner and eat some breakfast before I get back on the bus," I said.

"Sounds good," Scott said.

I let the warm water cascade over my tired, hungover body. My throat was sore and I was dehydrated, but I wouldn't have changed a thing. I felt rough, but was grateful for the last four days of travel and fun with my new friend. After I toweled off, I wanted to hustle down to the sports book and place a $10 bet on a baseball game. I took the elevator down and made it to the counter with five minutes to spare before the game began.

"Ten dollars on the Cubs," I told the man behind the cage. He printed the ticket and held out his hand. I retrieved my wallet from my back pocket and prepared to extract a $10 bill. But, when I opened it, the wallet was empty.

I still had my credit cards, some random business cards, and my family photos, but the slot where my cash had previously been was nothing but a dark hole.

DAYS THIRTEEN–FOURTEEN

Reno, Nevada to Los Angeles, California

Reno, NV-Truckee, CA-Colfax-Roseville-Sacramento-Lodi-Stockton-Modesto-Merced-
Fresno-Bakersfield-San Fernando-North Hollywood-Hollywood-Los Angeles

My heart sank. I had counted my money just before bed and figured I had another few days worth of cash that would get me
down to San Diego. $132 was gone. I knew that Scott had just
ripped me off, but I didn't want to believe it. I felt like someone
punched me in the gut. A security guard was standing next to the
elevator, patroling the slot machines in front of him, talking into
his two-way radio.

"I just got robbed," I told him in a sullen, despondent voice.
"You did? What happened?" he asked.
"It's a long story, but I let this guy stay in my room for the
last two nights. I got in the shower this morning and he said that
he was coming down here to buy us some coffee. When I came
down here to place a bet, I realized that he cleaned out my wallet. That bastard ripped me off," I said, barely able to believe the
words that were coming out of my mouth.

The security guard followed me up to my room and looked around. "Is anything else missing?" he asked.

"Not that I can tell. It looks like he just swiped my cash and bolted." He left my laptop, my digital camera, my bus pass, my credit cards. On the bed were Scott's only possessions. He had abandoned his mesh shopping bag, a bed sheet and pillow he had stolen from the hotel in Colorado, and a Tom Clancy paperback novel. In the bathroom he had left behind a toothbrush, a travel-sized tube of toothpaste, and a stick of deodorant. Scott had vanished.

I went down to the security office and filed a theft report, but I knew that it was a waste of time. Reno seemed to be full of hard-luck, desperate people and Scott would blend right in. In fact, he might have already boarded a bus out of town. I felt like a fool. *How am I going to explain this to my wife? How could this guy do this to me? I thought we were friends.* Those were the thoughts and feelings that consumed me as I packed up my stuff and headed to the Greyhound station. I realized that I was a sucker. I had been had. It could have been worse, but it hurt nonetheless.

I carried all my gear downstairs and went to the cashier's cage to replace my stolen money. "I hate to say it, but it happens all the time," the woman staffing the register explained. Her sympathy was sincere, but she didn't seem too phased by my tale. Intellectually, I could conceptualize that this probably did happen every single day in Reno. But, as they always say, I never thought it would happen to me. I felt violated. I wasn't angry as much as I was disappointed. I was disappointed in myself for being such a fool, and I was disappointed that Scott had chosen to do this. If he had simply asked me for some money, I probably would have given it to him.

I've always considered myself to be a pretty trusting person. I would rather give someone the benefit of the doubt and I hope that others do the same for me. I can't imagine going through life feeling like everyone is out to get me. I typically try to see the good in people. I think most people have something valuable to offer. Until this point in the trip, I had found most of the passengers I'd met to be decent people just struggling to make it in this world. They weren't really different from me in many ways. But Scott made me wonder if I would now have to look at people differently. Would the first thought in my mind now be: *She seems like a nice lady, but is she going to rip me off?*

After paying the $20 service charge to draw out $300 in cash off of my MasterCard, I began the slow, lonely walk back to the Reno Greyhound station. The bright, sunny day slightly dulled the pain. I rolled my duffel bag through the potholes and over the cracks in the sidewalk, paying attention to the inconsistency of the surface. My mind was wandering all over the place, like a boxer in the tenth round. I looked through the alleys and at the corners of the streets wondering if every pedestrian I saw had been a victim of Scott's. I knew it was futile to search for him. He was likely well skilled at what he had just done, elusive as a midnight cockroach.

As I drew closer to the Reno bus station, I saw the unsurprising, customary, huddled masses of beggars and skateboarders gathered outside. "Do you have some money I could have?" one of them asked. I just shook my head and kept walking, amazed at the irony of that request. I would have given them Scott's cell phone number had it not been disconnected. My shoulders slumped and I sauntered into the Greyhound station, convinced that I was a victim of one of the nation's most egregious crimes.

"I need a ticket to get the hell out of Reno," I told Brenda, the plump attendant behind the counter. She was upbeat and asked me where I wanted to go. I calculated the routes and decided to go far away.

"Nogales, Arizona," I told her.

"Wow, that's a long way away. What's going on in Nogales?" she asked in a pleasant, bubbly voice.

"It doesn't matter," I responded in an Eyeore-type voice. "I just had something very bad happen to me. I met this guy on the bus a couple of days ago. We were both coming out here to Reno and he didn't have a place to stay. So I invited him to share my hotel room for a couple of days–"

"And he jacked your shit!" she interrupted.

"Yes! He jacked my shit," I repeated.

"Oh, that's awful. You try and do something nice for someone and they turn around and do that to you. Did you get the cops involved?" she inquired.

"Yeah, I filed a report with the hotel security and I've got a call in to the Reno police department, but I doubt they'll catch the bastard," I lamented.

"Yeah, Reno's full of shady people. Druggies, alcoholics, people pissing away their last two cents in the slot machines," Brenda opined. "Do you have a picture of him or anything?" "Yeah. I forgot about that. Here on my phone. Let me pull it up," I told her, scurrying through my collection of cell phone pictures. "Here he is," I said, holding the phone up so that she could see.

"Oh my God! Linda, come look at this. It's Scott!" she squealed. "Oh yeah. He's a drifter. He's in here all the time. He was hitting on me so bad last time that I told him I was going to call the cops if he kept pestering me. He's a disaster. He's so creepy," Brenda described.

This made me feel even worse. This was not the Scott I had come to know over the past few days. I found him to be interesting, funny, and easy to be around. Brenda described him as a serial scamster. "He's always on the bus," she said. "He's passing through here all the time. He gets a ticket from the cops or somewhere. I don't know how he gets the money to keep riding the bus, but we see him all the time. Linda, wasn't he just in the nut house a couple weeks ago?" she asked.

I had just been had by a vagabond. My mind went back to everything Scott had told me. Was any of it true? Was he really in Macon, Georgia, having wild sex with a nurse last week? Did he really go to college in Ohio? Did his dad really die? How could I have so grossly misread a person? I've always prided myself on being a fairly intuitive person. But my intuition was clearly in need of an overhaul.

"He'll be back through here. You can bet on that. He'll probably wait until he knows that you're out of town. Don't worry, when we see him, we'll call the cops," Brenda said, encouraging me. I found solace in her words. I hoped they had the death penalty in Nevada.

I nursed my sore throat and headache with some Tylenol and lozenges that I purchased at a run-down convenience store a few blocks away. I sat on the metal bench in the terminal for the next hour waiting for my bus. The typical drama of people wandering around, begging for money, arguing with each other, and mooching cigarettes was the backdrop in the terminal. Brenda was kind enough to let me store my bags in the employee area during my wait so that I could at least have peace of mind surrounding my belongings.

The bus ride through Nevada and into Sacramento was uneventful. I didn't want to talk to anyone. I simply wanted to sulk and enjoy the birth of my head cold. I grabbed the very back seat and stretched out, trying to block out everything and take a nap. I awoke to the driver saying that we had arrived in Sacramento. I looked out the window as we passed by building after building on our way to the downtown terminal. Sacramento looked like a ghost town. There was very little traffic downtown and it looked to be a city that had seen better days, void of commerce and activity. The Greyhound station was, per usual, surrounded by the obligatory packs of smokers and people panhandling. The terminal itself was filthy and tired. It was the perfect ending to a perfect day.

I spent most of the layover at a nearby restaurant, a fancy steakhouse, one of the only restaurants I could find that was open.

I figured it was a reward for what I had just gone through. Luckily I had the resources to be able to splurge on a fancy meal. I needed a break. I needed to be away from crooks and the bus, even if for only a couple of hours. When I entered the place, it was full of rich wood tones and white tablecloths. The few patrons were well dressed and enjoying oversized glasses of merlot. Even though I was dressed in jeans and a polo shirt, for a moment I felt like I was in a safe and familiar world. Places like this are not on my family's regular rotation of eateries, but given the two ends of the spectrum, this was closer to what I knew. I could at least let my guard down for a little while.

I wanted a respite, a place where I could find comfort. This steakhouse gave me a chance to lick my wounds while I enjoyed the best meal I'd had in the past few weeks. I know how to soothe myself, with food and drink and comfort. When things get rough, I can typically find a quiet corner of my house to hide out in or settle into my favorite chair and everything feels like it's going to be all right. I wondered about my fellow passengers I'd met on the bus. What did they do when life got rough? It was obvious that some of them took drugs or drank. Others found comfort in transition—I'd met more than a few people who had gotten on the bus to start over, to head somewhere, anywhere, as long as it was new. For them, "home" was being on the move. The stability that I value—a safe home, a loving family, was something that was out of their reach, and might even stifle them. For this month on the bus, I was a member of their community, a community in constant upheaval. I didn't find it to be particularly comfortable.

When I returned to the terminal, I still had an hour to kill before I got on the bus heading to southern California. The scene in the terminal stood in stark opposition to that of the steakhouse where I had just enjoyed a delicious meal. I simultaneously felt fulfilled, after having enjoyed a steak, and guilty, looking around the terminal realizing that not only would none of these passengers likely ever dine at a fancy steakhouse, but they would consider me a wasteful, indulgent fool for having done so.

We traveled through the night, stopping at every dinky town in California on our way to Los Angeles. I was able to sleep for most of the journey, exhausted by the events of the last few days. In Bakersfield the driver kicked me in the legs. It wasn't a loving tap that your mother might give you to wake you up for school. I was kicked like I was a homeless man, sleeping on some forbidden doorstep of a building. "Wake up! We need the seats next to you," the driver said in an abrupt, annoyed tone of voice. I reluctantly slid over to the seat next to the window. An enormous Korean man came and sat next to me. He immediately fell asleep, causing his tree trunk legs to absorb every square inch of open space. He inadvertently started using me as a pillow. I was too tired to do much about it. At one point, I elbowed him because he was snoring louder than I had ever heard anyone snore before. That jostled him, but it was only a temporary fix.

We rolled into Los Angeles in the early morning hours. The sun had come up and the bus station was bustling. It was the biggest station I had seen since I left New York, the fifth busiest bus terminal in North America.[1] There were many gates and an assortment of passengers milling about. The palm trees in the parking lot dressed up the dingy, trash-filled scene, but only slightly. My one-hour layover turned into three, as all buses out of the terminal were delayed because of some accident on one of the freeways. There wasn't really a credible source that informed us of the delays; it was just the product of an unofficial rumor mill that circulated throughout the station.

While waiting for the bus, I was eager to share my story of being robbed with any sympathetic-looking soul. On the uncomfortable, black iron bench in the waiting area, I met an overweight, prematurely bald man named Simon, who was headed to Phoenix.

"I was just out here in Manhattan Beach for a funeral," he explained. "One of my buddies from high school died. It was sad, but it was great to get to see everyone again. We hung out on the beach and drank Coors Light all weekend. It was amazing. I don't know why I stayed away from these guys . . ." Simon's voice trailed off.

Immediately I wanted to share my Scott story with Simon, but I bit my tongue. This trip was about me listening to the stories of others rather than sharing my own. This trip was an exercise in listening rather than talking, and it was probably good for me.

He continued, "I guess I was embarrassed of what I thought these guys would all think of me. I hadn't seen these guys in twenty years. I've done seven years in the pen. I got out last October. I own my shit. I don't blame the drugs, or my shitty childhood, or the state. I was a crackhead. I got high and stole my company's truck. I returned it after a weeklong drug binge, but they came after me anyway. I worked as a surveyor. I'm still looking for work. I don't hide from anything. I tell them, 'Look, I'm the best surveyor you're going to find, especially when I'm not high, and I don't get high anymore.' But nobody's wanted to give me a chance yet. I learned this weekend that good friends are like family. They'll stand by you no matter what. We just loved on each other all weekend. It was a love fest. It was beautiful, man."

Simon was an amazingly open, honest, contrite man who was receptive to sharing his feelings with me, a stranger. For most of us, in social situations we resort to the standard, "Where do you live? Where did you go to school? What do you do for a living?" Those are safe topics and it's the customary dance that we do at dinner parties or when we meet someone at church. But on the bus it's different. I imagine it's a product of realizing that it's safe to unload deep secrets and feelings you have because you know that in another three hours or two hundred miles, you'll never see that person again. It happened over and over again. All I would need to ask was, "Where are you going?" as kind of an ice breaker, and, before I knew it, people were sharing the most personal details about their life with me. I don't necessarily believe that it's because I am a good listener or give off the vibe of being a trustworthy, approachable guy. I just think that all of us really ache for someone, anyone, to listen to us, to care about us.

Simon lived in Phoenix, I learned, and had just been in LA for the weekend. "Arizona is where I did my time. It's home. I have to stay there as part of my parole. But I miss my kids. I haven't seen them or my ex-wife in fifteen years. That's when I got into crack. I was in my early thirties. Can you believe that? It's a disease, man. I threw everything away for that stuff. I miss my kids like crazy. But the good thing is that I'm dating a cougar now. She's awesome. She's five years older than I am. Her name is Maggie and she's smokin' hot, dude. She knows I call her a cougar. She's the best thing that's happened to me," Simon stated.

He then started to wistfully recall some brighter days in his life. "You know, I've seen it all. I grew up in Manhattan Beach and I've done just about everything. I worked as a dockhand, a fisherman, a surveyor. You wouldn't know it now, but I used to be in great shape. I'm still the only one to ever complete the surfboard competition from Catalina Island to the mainland for ten years in a row. You have to lay on the surfboard and just paddle with your arms. It was tiring, but a lot of fun. We would finish up in San Diego and drink a ton of beer."

Simon watched my bags for me while I went to the restroom. Even though I had just gotten burned by a thief in Reno, I trusted Simon. He seemed like a redeemed, honest soul. I didn't realize it at the time, but it was a conscious decision I made to try and trust someone on the bus again. I decided that I wasn't going to change who I was because of what had happened with Scott. I trust people. And if I continued to be so guarded and protective out of a fear of getting burned again, I wouldn't get close to anyone and I would miss out on the whole point of the trip.

On my way to the bathroom, my cell phone rang. I looked and saw that the number was from my wife, Erica.

"Hi baby! How are you doing?" I said.

"I'm good. I miss you," she replied. "Hey, I just got a call from the credit card company about some possible fraudulent charges on our MasterCard. Do you know anything about that?" My stomach flipped and my face got hot.

"Did they leave an 800 number to call or anything?" I asked.

"Yes. Why? Did something happen? Mike? DID SOME-THING HAPPEN?" she persisted.

"Just give me the number and let me handle it. I'll fill you in later," I said.

"Okay. Call me back, though. I want to know what's going on," she replied in an irritated but concerned tone.

For the next twenty minutes I navigated my way through the automated customer service maze and, once I was able to speak with a live person, learned that Scott had written down my credit card number and attempted to extend his pay-by-the-day cell phone plan using my number. The MasterCard guy was gracious and agreed to remove the charges. I felt relieved that Scott hadn't attempted to purchase a car, or a greyhound ticket, or something far more expensive and problematic. I called the Reno sheriff's office to report this latest development but was disappointed in their utter lack of interest in my case.

After procrastinating for another few minutes, I knew I had to face the music. "Hey honey. It's me. I got the charges taken off and I cancelled the card," I reported to Erica in the most upbeat way that I could, hoping that she would just let it drop.

"Who stole your card? What are you hiding? What the hell happened?" she asked in an escalating tone.

"Well, this is going to sound bad, worse than it really is," I began, offering a delay and a chance for her to extend some loving words of support. Realizing that was not going to happen, after a few uncomfortable seconds of silence, I spilled it all.

"You did WHAT? You let a stranger share your hotel room with you?" she asked.

"This is what I meant by 'it sounds worse than it is.' When you put it like that, it makes me seem like an idiot," I reasoned.

"You *are* an idiot. How could you do this? How could you let a complete stranger share a room with you? I am so angry with you. This could have been way worse. Do you know how lucky you are? I trusted you to be safe on this trip. I have been worried about you, but I knew that you would be safe. And you go and do something like this. I trusted you. I can't believe this."

I was pacing around a section of the terminal, occasionally looking back at Simon to make sure that my stuff was still visible. My knees would bend and I would wince with every word of disappointment that Erica was hurling at me through the phone.

"Honey, I'm sorry. I really am. He seemed like a nice guy. I thought we were going to be friends. He just stole all of my cash when I was in the shower. Please don't be mad. It won't happen again," I said, concluding my defense and bracing for the judgment and punishment phase of the phone trial. After a few moments of silence, she launched in.

"You have to *promise* me that you will *never* do anything like that again. You cannot trust people you have just met on the bus. They are on the bus for a reason."

They are on the bus for a reason. They are on the bus for a reason. Those words kept ringing in my head. Erica has never ridden the bus, but she had pretty strong opinions about who she thought was on the bus nevertheless. In her mind, the bus was full of crooks. It was full of poor people, desperate people out to rob me. That really wasn't the case. Yes, most of the people on the bus were poor but they weren't all crooks.

During our conversation I realized that this was *my* trip, *my* adventure. I was doing this alone. No amount of explaining and rationalizing was going to make sense to her. To try and explain it to her felt futile because I knew she couldn't fully understand. It would be like getting the photo album out and showing a friend pictures from your latest vacation. When you look at the pictures from the beach, you can still remember what it felt like, what it smelled like, how the shrimp tasted. But your friend will look at the pictures and maybe ask a few questions to show their interest, but the truth is, they weren't there and they don't have the same perspective. I knew what the bus smelled like. I was the one experiencing the feelings of exhilaration, fear, and adventure. It was unrealistic to think that she could have a full understanding of how I felt. I knew that I would just have to accept my role as the fool in this scenario. No amount of explaining how nice of a guy Scott seemed to be was going to do the trick.

I did understand her anger, however. She had taken on over a month's worth of family responsibilities without her husband. She had sacrificed to allow me to go on this bus trip. I really had no right to expect her to be sympathetic toward me. And Erica's words were sound. They were logical. That's who my wife is. She has great judgment. When we argue, her thoughts are usually well organized. There usually isn't a "winning" of an argument with her. She's the level-headed, thoughtful one in our marriage. She is measured and does things that make sense. Sending me on a month long bus trip already had her teetering on the edge, and I seem to have just pushed her over. I hated to disappoint her.

"You probably weren't ever going to tell me about this. I wouldn't have known unless the credit card company called, right?" There was no good answer to that question.

So, I just said, "You're probably right."

Erica just sighed and chuckled. With one more, "You are such an idiot," and a few more moments of silence and some heavy breathing, she concluded with, "Michael, please be careful. You know I love you."

"I love you too, honey. I'll call you when I get to Arizona."

My shoulders felt a little lighter after having come clean about the Reno heist. I needed to share the whole thing with Simon. Simon was fully attentive to my story, as I had been for his. This was a departure from some of my previous exchanges with bus passengers. I had dabbled briefly in sharing a few stories of my own, but I was reminded that people, by and large, like to talk about themselves. They may listen to what I have to say, but it's more common that they would just nod a little bit and then soon resume to talking about their own stories. Simon was different. He seemed to really care about what happened.

"Wow, dude. That's fucked up. You try and do something nice for somebody and he takes advantage of you like that? But here's the deal. You've got a choice. He's a bad apple, but don't let him spoil the bunch. You can either go through life not trusting anyone or you can run the risk of getting burned by getting close to people. If you can't trust anyone, you'll end up lonely. I've been there man. Lonely is no good."

DAYS FOURTEEN–SEVENTEEN

Blythe, California to Dallas, Texas

Blythe, CA-Phoenix, AZ-Mesa-Tucson-Nogales-Tucson-Benson-Willcox-Lordsburg, NM-
El Paso, TX-Van Horn-Pecos-Odessa-Big Spring-Sweetwater-Abilene-Ft. Worth-Dallas

When the bus stopped for lunch in Blythe, California, near the border of Arizona, Simon and I stepped off the bus and into an oppresive heat. I felt like I had put my face on the vent of a dryer. I asked Simon, "What do you suppose the temperature is?"

"109," he said with a certain precision. "I live in Phoenix. This is nothing, man."

We hustled to Del Taco, across the street from the gas station where our bus had docked. In the cool air conditioning we scarfed down some budget menu tacos and continued telling stories. Simon was excited to get back home and see his "cougar."

We arrived in Phoenix some three hours behind schedule. Maggie was there to greet Simon with a big hug and a kiss. She was attractive and the age difference between them was negligible. Simon introduced me as his friend, then we said goodbye and hugged.

I was sorry to see him go. Simon was the most reflective, thoughtful ex-convict I had met on the trip so far. He was the perfect traveling companion, considering what I had just been through. He was a man on the road to redemption. He had every reason to have just given up and resign himself to a life of self-loathing. Whether the weekend he had spent in Manhattan Beach was an epiphany of sorts, I don't know, but he seemed determined to keep moving forward. He was at peace with the demons of his past and looking toward the future. You've got to admire that about a guy.

The longest stretch of my long trip from Reno to Nogales was behind me, but I still had several hours to go. Because of the delay I had missed the bus heading south from Phoenix. But, in a moment of unexpected accommodation, the Greyhound agent informed me, "we can still get you down there tonight." The agent at the station in Phoenix really cared. He was personable and attentive to my situation. This was rare, but it was surprisingly satisfying to have someone try and help. He made a phone call to a shuttle service and handed me a voucher for a taxi cab. "You'll need to take a cab over to the shuttle service and the bus leaves there in about a half hour. You'll need to hurry, but you can make it." I thanked him and went outside to flag a taxi.

The Greyhound station in Phoenix was located in an industrial area, which was unique. Most stations were located right in the heart of cities' downtown areas. The cab ride over to the shuttle service was about an eight-mile trip through some run-down residential and commercial areas. I had heard about Phoenix being a large, growing city, but I'm guessing that must be happening out in the suburbs. I tried to make some conversation with the cab driver, but he wasn't too interested. He was not happy that I had a voucher. I apologized and told him that was all I had to give him. He said, "Prefiero efectivo." ("I prefer cash.") I said, "I understand."

The shuttle station was tucked in the corner of a deserted strip mall. The entire drive from the Greyhound station to the shuttle station was bizarre. It was around 6 p.m. and there was hardly a soul to be seen. On the west side of Phoenix, there were signs in Spanish all over the place, but buildings looked as if they'd been closed for business for a quite a while. It was eerily quiet. I was wondering if this was a function of Arizona's new immigration laws. Had the police rounded up thousands of people and all that left was this shell of a city?

The shuttle made the three-hour drive to Nogales, a town on the Mexico/US border. There was an absence of the formality and pageantry that accompanies the usual boarding process with the Greyhounds. A guy sitting behind a plastic shield in the station simply told the passengers, in Spanish, that it was time to go. The station room was covered with old, tan wood paneling and had a couple of old gumball machines standing guard. It looked like nothing had changed since 1972. The bathroom had no toilet paper or soap. The terminal was a 20' x 10' gathering space consisting of travelers going to and from the border. Instead of large buses in the parking lot there was just a small handful of different-sized vans.

I boarded the fifteen-passenger van with two other men. On our way out of Phoenix, we stopped in a residential neighborhood to pick up another rider at his house. We pulled right into his driveway as he ran out, hugged his wife, and got on the van. About a half hour later, we picked up another passenger at a gas station. It seemed disorganized to me, but everyone else seemed to know what was going on.

On our way to Nogales, I started talking to the two men seated behind me. I had noticed that they did the sign of the cross on our way out of the parking lot. I trusted that this was a standard religious ritual rather than an indication that they were nervous about us making it there safely. The men looked young. Gregorio said he was eighteen years old. His friend, Francisco, was twenty-six. They were leaving Phoenix for good.

In Spanish they detailed why they were leaving: "We've been here in Phoenix for four years. I work as an auto mechanic. I specialize in repairing vintage cars. Gregorio has been working the whole time at IHOP as a cook. Since this new law passed in Arizona, it has changed. We've seen friends of ours, neighbors of ours, arrested while walking on the street. They've been asked for their documents and then deported." Francisco continued, getting more animated, "I don't understand it. Who wants to work at IHOP? He makes $8 an hour. They say we're taking jobs. Nobody wants to do those jobs. We are supposed to be family. We are brothers. We share this continent. If you go down into Nogales, Mexico, you will be well received. But, yet in your country, you say that you don't want me?"

I didn't know how to respond to them. They seemed angry, defeated, and disillusioned. Francisco told me that he and Gregorio were going back to Cananea, Sonora, Mexico. They had family there.

"Do you hope to come back up here some day?" I asked them.

"Yes, but when it's better. It's not worth getting arrested."

These two guys were very open, although Francisco was clearly the spokesman. It was interesting to hear their point of view on life in Arizona. I felt inadequate and unable to contribute much to the conversation. Mostly I just listened.

We pulled into Nogales late that night. I had a cab driver take me to the Fiesta America hotel, a mile and a half from the border. Hotel options in Nogales were limited. I wanted somewhere relatively close to the border so that I could walk around and gain a little understanding about what life on the border looks like. There was no fiesta happening at the hotel. It was old and tired but seemed safe.

In the morning, I walked to downtown Nogales. I met Marlene, the manager of the Burger King on the Arizona side of the border. She grew up in Kingman, Arizona, born to Mexican immigrants. Her dad got a visa back in the 60s to come work as an engineer at a factory in Kingman, in the northwest quadrant of the state. Marlene and her husband moved to Nogales in 1992 when the opportunity presented itself to purchase a Burger King franchise.

"It's changed a lot," Marlene said. "We used to have tourists all the time, but with the media going on and on about the murders on the border, our business has taken a hit. We hardly see any tourists anymore. The murders aren't even happening here in Nogales. It's like fifteen or twenty miles in where they're seeing the trouble."

I asked Marlene about the impact of the changes in Arizona's laws, where law enforcement officials can request documentation from anyone, without cause.

"They don't really pester people in Nogales. It's over 95 percent Hispanic here and they'd have their hands full if they stopped everyone. They're pretty much just nailing people up in Phoenix," she said.

As I walked around in Nogales, I saw vehicle after vehicle with "Border Patrol" on the sides. They were just driving the streets of Nogales, Arizona, looking for people trying to cross through, over, or under the fences that line that city. The hostile atmosphere made me think about my recurring question that I'd had since that high school mission trip: Why was I so lucky? I had no say in the matter of where I was born and who my parents were. Why was I born on this side of the border? Why was I born in a country where we are free to do pretty much whatever we want? Why wasn't I born in Africa or Mexico instead? It made me grateful, as I strolled the streets of Nogales, that I had a precious piece of paper in my pocket—my driver's license. Hundreds of people cross the border every day in pursuit of a life that I, far too often, take for granted. People die in the desert trying to hide from immigration officers, all because they want to be able to better provide for their families. Most of them are happy to have landed a job like Gregorio's, making $8 an hour washing dishes at IHOP.

In the late afternoon I boarded a Crucero Lines bus (a partner carrier for Greyhound that runs to and from the Mexican border) to head back north. I planned to travel back to Nashville for a few days. I wanted to recharge my batteries and attend a small family gathering in Indianapolis for my grandfather's ninetieth birthday. The Crucero bus took me to Tucson and, from there, I would begin the journey east.

Our bus left Tucson on schedule. We shot straight east on I-10, toward El Paso. Something I learned was that there are multiple border crossing checkpoints on highways in the South. They are not right at the border, though. Usually it's thirty or forty miles in, and the US Border Patrol flags vehicles down and searches them. There are drug sniffing dogs and heavily armed agents looking for contraband and illegal immigrants.

Our bus was stopped about an hour east of El Paso on I-10. The beefy patrol agents got on the bus and announced, "We are with the United States Border Patrol. Please have proper documentation available to verify that you are a U.S. citizen!" Their voices boomed and they were no nonsense. It was about 5:30 in the morning. One agent went to the back of the bus and another stayed at the front. They worked their way toward the middle to mitigate any possibility of confrontation or escape.

One big agent with a crew cut and an automatic weapon strapped across his chest stopped in the row in front of me to question a ninety-five-pound Asian woman. "Can I see your documentation, please?" She just stared at him. In a louder voice, "I NEED TO SEE YOUR DOCUMENTATION!" Silence. "YOU DON'T UNDERSTAND A WORD I'M SAYING, DO YOU? YOUR PAPERS. I NEED TO SEE YOUR PAPERS. HABLAS ESPANOL?" That made me smile because these guys

were obviously trained to deal with Spanish-speaking immigrants. It was an awkward interaction, at best, with this mild
Asian woman.

She nervously fidgeted around and produced something in
the shape of a drivers' license but it was some sort of ID card. The
officer looked at it and just kind of shook his head. I figure that
they have a pretty swift and smooth process for when they catch
illegal immigrants from Latin America, but I wasn't so sure that
he wanted to deal with this case. He just handed her the card back
and said, "Thank you." She smiled and tucked the card away.
A large African American woman in the seat behind the Asian
woman was amused by the whole encounter and said to me, "I
think she knows more English than she's pretending. He almost
snatched her ass straight off the bus!"

I guess it makes politicians and concerned citizens feel better that we have these checkpoints with officers, mirrors, and
dogs, securing our border one Greyhound bus at a time. But from
the hundreds of miles that I traversed along the border during my
trip, I can say I don't see Greyhound as being a major player in
the human smuggling game. It was mostly just the same as in the
rest of the country–a bunch of weary travelers, heading to new
towns, looking for a new start on life.

On this leg of the journey I met a young man named James.
He was thirty-two years old and on his way to Dallas. James was
the first person I met who made a conscious choice to ride the bus
instead of flying. He had the financial resources to fly; he was just
being cheap. "I saved $120 by taking the bus, but this is a disaster,"
he remarked after the long delay at the immigration checkpoint. He
was starting to realize that it's difficult to put a price tag on time. The
$120 seemed to be a heavy price for spending the better part of two
days on the bus instead of taking a two-hour flight.

James was headed to Dallas for a continuing education
event. "I'm an auctioneer. I've been doing this for most of my

life. My grandpa was an auctioneer and he taught me the trade," James replied.

"Do you have to have formal training for that?" I asked.

"Oh yeah. I went to auctioneer school in Mason City, Iowa. There's some really good money in this, but you kind of have to pay your dues. My goal is to become a national champion," he said.

Now that's a niche career, I thought to myself.

James was a good-looking guy with an easy smile. He wore a short-sleeved denim shirt that hinted at a rural upbringing. He said that he had just broken up for good with his girlfriend of nine years. They had been on-again, off-again for much of that time and were actually engaged for four of those years. He said he moved to Phoenix to get as far away from her as possible. He seemed like a pretty happy guy, unencumbered and excited about his future as an auctioneer. "If I keep going at this, I can make a nice living. This continuing education is part of the deal. I have to keep my accreditation and keep working my way up. What I'd love to do is get involved in specialty auctions. I love muscle cars and they've got only like a dozen of these really high-end auctions each year around the country. I know a guy who only does those things and he makes well over six figures," James explained.

"How does it work? Do you work on commission or do you get a flat rate to be an auctioneer?" I asked. "It depends how it's set up. Usually you'll get a fee to be there, but then you get commission on top of that. The key is knowing where to set the price for an item. It doesn't matter if you're auctioning off a piece of crap table or a million-dollar home. You've more or less got twelve bids. That's what the studies show. The psychology of it is that an auction will generally last about twelve bids. So if you lowball the initial bid, you're shooting yourself in the foot. If you set it too high, you start to hear crickets. There's an art to it."

I was fascinated. "Do you really talk a million miles an hour or is that just on television?" I asked.

"Oh yeah. I practice every day. I've practiced every day of my life. I love it. You have to learn how to do it. It's not easy. I have to use a lot of filler words. A good auctioneer can size up the room and get the most money possible out of people. The higher the final price, the more I get paid. That's why I want to work my way up and pretty much stick to high-end auctions. You don't have to work that often and you can make a killing," he said.

James was an interesting guy. He was quick-witted and had a pretty good sense of direction for his life. The heartache of his breakup was now just a memory. He said that being around all the beautiful girls in Phoenix has made the transition pretty easy. James was fascinated by my story of riding the bus. He peppered me with questions about the people I'd met and what it was like to ride the bus. I entertained him for a while with tales from the road. Once he learned of my story, he started to get into the spirit of analyzing human behavior and said, "What do you think the deal is with the Asian woman? You think she's really here legally?" I smiled, feeling that I had met a kindred soul. If I lived in Phoenix, I would love to hang out with James. I've never had a friend who was an auctioneer. I thought that would be entertaining, at least out at a bar with my buddies.

When we finally pulled into Dallas, we were extremely late due to the Border Patrol interaction and a few stops that were longer than planned. People slowly started filing off the bus, rooting around and grabbing their belongings. James and I stayed in our seats, letting the traffic subside. It was his destination, and he wasn't in too big of a hurry. As we looked out the window, we noticed the small Asian woman lugging two gigantic suitcases into the parking lot. There to greet her was an overweight, middle-aged, balding Caucasian man. The two embraced and kissed. Then, they began the twenty-foot walk to his emerald-green BMW. He opened the trunk and helped her load the suitcases. It was an odd scene.

"What do you suppose is going on there?" I asked James.

He chuckled and said, "Mail-order bride, for sure."

The large African American woman who was sitting behind the nearly-deported woman overheard James's comment and chimed in, "If I came from China and my new husband stuck my ass on the bus, I'd just head right back across the ocean and go home. Hell with that noise."

DAYS SEVENTEEN–TWENTY-ONE

Dallas, Texas to Des Moines, Iowa

Dallas, TX-Texarkana, AR-Malvern-Hot Springs-Benton-Little Rock-Forrest City-
Memphis, TN-Jackson-Nashville-Clarksville-Madisonville, KY-Evansville, IN-
Mt. Vernon, IL-St. Louis, MO-Columbia-Boonville-Kansas City-Des Moines, IA

From Dallas I rode the bus home to Nashville. It was a fairly uneventful trip. I chose to mostly sleep and not interact with anyone. Luckily the bus was relatively empty and all of the stops were scheduled—one of the few times on my trip that this was actually the case. I got home in the middle of the night and found my car waiting for me in the parking lot of the Greyhound station. As I began the drive south on I-65, I felt odd. After having spent a couple of weeks on the road as a passenger, I was now in control of my speed and direction, not dependent on anyone to get anywhere.

As I pulled into my driveway, a feeling of peace came over me. I was back in my world. I felt safe and steady. Gratitude rushed over me as I looked at the lights shining from our front porch. When I had shown Scott a picture of my family on the way out to Reno, with a touch of envy, he said, "You've got the American dream." His words hit me anew as I realized that I had left behind dozens of wandering bus travelers back at the station. My life was stable compared to almost everyone I had met over the last couple of weeks. I have a wife and kids who love me. I have a nice home in a safe neighborhood. A comfortable bed and hot breakfast awaited me. It took about 6,000 miles of bus travel to make me remember how lucky I was, but I remembered at that moment. I've got all I need, and then some. I am indeed living the American dream.

Out of courtesy and a distorted sense of martyrdom, I slept on the couch for a few hours until everyone in the house started to stir. Erica came downstairs and gave me a big hug and kiss. The coffee pot started grinding the beans on cue and, while I had only been off the bus for a mere six hours, it seemed like I had never left home. Erica poured me a hot cup of coffee in the Greyhound Museum mug I had mailed home from Minnesota. My boys awoke and gave me hugs. My stories of life on the bus took a backseat to learning about what was going on with them and their new year at school. Erica had let the Reno incident drop, thankfully, and we focused on doing normal family things throughout the weekend. I enjoyed a few home-cooked meals and ran a few errands. It was good to be home, but it was a reminder that, despite how many problems and worries I thought I had, the stability and love that surrounded me at home have proven to be more valuable to me than anything. The bus helped me see that.

Taking my family to Indianapolis for my grandfather's birthday party was a major change of gears after having spent three weeks on the bus. He would only turn 90 once, and, out of a sense of duty and love of family, we spent a nice day with aunts and uncles, my sister, parents, and grandparents. It was a little awkward, as all of them were aware that I was in the middle of a bus trip across America. Aside from my aunt, sister, and one cousin, nobody quite knew what to say about my trip. It was hard to explain my journey to a generation of people who were farmers and rarely took vacations, much less would have ever considered taking a thirty-day bus trip for the hell of it. It seemed foolish and wasteful to them, I'm sure. But everyone was polite about it. The questions directed my way were brief and cursory and I responded with similarly superficial answers. The day, after all, was about my grandfather.

After sleeping in my own bed for a couple of nights, I was encouraged and buoyed by those close to me to get back out and finish my trip. My neighbors lectured me about the Reno robbery, but they also said that I shouldn't let that stop me. A few days at home helped put things into perspective. I realized that Scott was indeed probably the one bad apple. I had certainly felt out of my comfort zone for most of the bus trip, but I hadn't ever really felt like I was in danger. Erica told me to take off my wedding ring and not reveal any personal details about me or my family. There was still a seed of doubt in her mind about this loose cannon scamster that was still floating around out there.

"Don't tell anyone you're writing a book. Don't tell them where you live. Don't tell them that you're married or that you have kids. Just make up some story about how you're just traveling around out to see the country," she advised. I humored her and left my wedding ring on our dresser and promised that I would be more discreet about my identity, for her sake. She couldn't understand. My neighbors couldn't understand. This was *my* trip. I was the one who was living this, not them. To them, I'm sure I sounded foolish and naïve. I listened to their counsel, but knew that I would probably keep on putting myself out there. *Still, I will try to be more careful,* I told myself.

My neighbor, Bart Bass, cut out of work for a couple of hours and drove me to the Greyhound station on Monday morning. I decided that I would travel back out west. I had no desire to come within arm's reach of Reno, but I did want to go see the Pacific Northwest. I had never been to Seattle before. So, feeling refreshed, I decided to embark on the longest run of my journey. I would

leave Nashville at 10:30 on Monday morning and was scheduled to
arrive in Seattle on Wednesday evening at 6:00. Bart dropped me
off and offered the same refrain I'd heard many a time now: "Man,
you're crazy."

As I entered the terminal in Nashville, I was proud of myself.
I had made the same walk from the parking lot just a few weeks
ago, feeling like a doe in the woods. Now I was a salty veteran
of Greyhound travel. I knew where to go for my ticket. I felt as
comfortable getting in line as I did lining up at the cafeteria in the
fourth grade. The fellow travelers who awaited me were like long
lost friends I hadn't seen all summer vacation.

It was a hot day. Thankfully the bus was nowhere near capacity as we traveled up through Evansville on our way to St. Louis.
Seated across from me was a young woman who looked to be
about twenty years old. She was wearing sweatpants and a white
T-shirt. She wore glasses and had her blonde hair pulled back in
a ponytail.

Jessica was headed out to Idaho. "I started my trip in South
Carolina, so I've already been going for over a day. My mom lives
out there. I'm going to move back in with her," she said.

"What were you doing in South Carolina?" I asked.

"I was in college. But I'm dropping out and moving back
home. I just feel bad wasting my mom's money when I don't really
know what I want to do yet," she offered. I had long thought the
point of college was to waste your parents' money while you figured out what you wanted to do with your life, but I didn't share
that with Jessica. "I was studying biology, but I hated it. I'm going
to try and go get a job where my mom works. She does medical
records for a hospital there in our hometown. It pays pretty well.
She says she thinks I can get a job."

I figured there might be more to Jessica's story than she was
letting on. Why would you want to leave college where you're
surrounded by friends, beer, and pizza to go sort through medical

records? But she wasn't offering up anything else, seemingly content to sit and play with her cell phone.

"So, why are you on the bus instead of flying back to Idaho?" I pressed.

"It's too expensive. I don't really have the money, and I didn't want to ask my mom for it," Jessica explained. With that, she made it clear that the conversation was over. "I need to check some e-mail," she said, which was a polite way of saying, "I'm done talking to you."

While Jessica wasn't interested in becoming best friends, we were traveling companions of sorts for the next few days, and by the time we made it to St. Louis, she had warmed up a bit. "Will you watch my cell phone while I go to the bathroom?" she asked.

"Sure, if you'll return the favor when you get back," I replied. That was a gesture of trust that I appreciated. I was comforted to know that at least for the next two days, I could urinate without fear of people stealing my stuff. I'm sure she felt the same way. Jessica had remarked earlier that this was her maiden voyage on a Greyhound.

As we waited for our bus to Kansas City, I learned that she actually had lived in South Carolina with her sister but they didn't get along. "She's older than I am and just bossed me around all the time," Jessica shared. She figured it would be a nice break to be back at home with her mom, eating her homecooking and not having to worry about bills and classes.

We got back on our bus, where a boisterous, foul-mouthed African American man named Brandon was standing in the aisle, blocking the back third of the bus, not concerned with the seating needs of any of the other passengers. He had cornrows and reeked of cigarette smoke. I simply said, "Excuse me," and without taking a breath in his conversation with a fellow passenger, he nonchalantly moved to the side to grant me passage to the row behind him. I overheard him say, "The fucking cops in Virginia suck, man.

They'll pull you over for anything and throw your ass in jail. The courts suck, too, man . . ."

Brandon went on for twenty minutes, through the driver's "welcome, no drinking, no smoking" speech, informing anyone who would listen about the various trials and tribulations he had experienced with courts in Virginia, Texas, and California. And then, in a clarifying remark, he said, "You know, when I was nine years old, my dad gave me a drink of whiskey and an ounce of cocaine for my birthday. Can you believe that shit?" Brandon's childhood sucked, he pointed out, and to his slightly increasing crowd of bus disciples, he announced that he wasn't a quitter and that he had overcome all of the hardships in his life.

Brandon didn't stop talking for three hundred miles. I didn't really need to personally engage him in conversation to get his story. He was sharing it in a loud, profane way with anyone who would listen. "I'm on my way to Kansas. Practice starts soon. I told the coach I had to tie up some shit with the courts in Dallas."

"Where do you play?" asked a semi-interested traveler.

"Ottawa. It's a Division II school in Kansas. I'm the starting point guard. I grew up in Camden, New Jersey, but I wanted to get the fuck out of there. They offered me a scholarship out here," Brandon explained. When no one offered comment on Brandon's accounting of his basketball ability, he just continued without provocation. "I don't know if I'm going to make it to the NBA. I mean, I'm good. I'm real good. But, I'm only 5'11. You gotta be taller than that to play in the NBA. But I've had some European scouts checkin' me out. I've heard that they pay real good over there, like 15K a game, man. If somebody comes and offers me that kind of coin, I'm droppin' out of college tomorrow. Plus, I hate the practices. Coach wants me to run suicides"—basketball conditioning drills—"I've already told him, 'Fuck that. I ain't runnin' no suicides.'"

At every possible opportunity, Brandon got off the bus and lit up during the smoke breaks. I had to wonder if that were part of the reason that he didn't like to run suicides. That would be hard on a smoker. Brandon had tattoos all over his arms and neck. I'm sure if he wore less revealing clothing than baggy jeans and an oversized white T-shirt, we could have seen more body art on display. He had a chip on his shoulder, but he flashed a smile that I'm sure has gotten him out of a few jams in his lifetime. He did occasionally listen to the tales and travails of other passengers, offering profanity-laden support.

It was late at night when we pulled into Kansas City. Brandon bid farewell to everyone as he headed to the smoker's pit. Jessica and I stood by the cell phone charging station guarding each other's gear as we took turns going to the bathroom. On my way to the men's room, I noticed a promotional poster on the wall. It read, "Come Join the Greyhound Team." Beneath that enticing headline were several bullet points. "Great benefits," "Competitive salary packages in the low $30's." I know that we are in the midst of a recession, and jobs are hard to come by, but there is no way on God's green Earth that I would be willing to drive a steel tube around this country for $30,000. It would be a lonely profession at best, dangerous and unfulfilling at worst. It's a thankless job. Drivers are the face of the company for thousands of passengers who are constantly being inconvenienced and arriving late to their destinations. They have to put on brave faces and wear their vests and neckties. Aside from Donna, every driver I had met viewed their job as strictly a way to pay the bills.

In the terminal a young man approached me and introduced himself as Jamie. He stood about six feet tall and had blond hair that was spiked up. I had seen him on the bus from St. Louis, but I was busy listening to Brandon's exploits and Jamie was seated several rows forward. He said he was headed back to Des Moines. As we boarded the bus headed north to Des Moines, Jamie asked in an elementary-school kind of way, "Wanna sit together?"

"Did you listen to any of that stuff that Brandon was saying?"

I asked Jamie as we took our seats toward the back of the bus on the right hand side. "Supposedly he's some star basketball player. He was talking about how he's going to play in Europe and get rich," I elaborated.

"Yeah, he's full of shit, dude. You can't believe anything people say on the bus. I don't know why people have to lie, but they do it all the time. That guy maybe played basketball at one point, but he's full of shit," Jamie professed.

"I'll tell you what. I've got an Internet connection on my phone. Let's look up the school he said he's going to and see if we can find the basketball roster," I suggested, proud of my idea. After a couple minutes of searching and finding the Ottawa basketball team, Brandon's name was nowhere to be found. "Huh," I sighed, playfully expressing my disbelief.

"See what I mean? Full . . . of . . . shit" repeated Jamie, shaking his head.

Brandon wasn't alone in his bravado. There is something about being on the bus, full of people that you've never met and will likely never see again, that can tempt a person into taking on a different persona. It's a lot harder to do in your hometown, around your friends. You can try and shed that nickname that you were given in high school, but if they called you "Booger" back then, they'll probably always still think of you as "Booger." It's hard work to make even a slight change in who you are. It's usually a major production. Friends who have known you for your whole life will resist calling you by a new name or even changing their opinion of you. The bus is different. You've got a captive audience, and you can just try out a new identity, crafting crazy stories about yourself, and no one is the wiser.

"Have you ridden the bus before?" I asked, wondering if Jamie's analysis of truth telling was a byproduct of frequent bus travel.

"Yeah, one other time. I was riding from Des Moines to Atlanta.

It was crazy. This cute little black girl sat down next to me and she started giving me a blow job," Jamie recalled.

"Are you full of shit, like Brandon?" I asked him playfully.

"No, this was legit. She just started talking to me and we started making out, and next thing I know . . ." he explained. "She put a blanket over her head and it was kind of dark on the bus. But here's the thing. I didn't even get to finish. We stopped for a smoke break and to pick up some people and I got off and smoked. When I came back on the bus, she had moved a couple rows back and started sucking off some other guy. Can you believe that? At least I was first," he stated.

Jamie had been in Atlanta, where his folks lived. "Actually, my parents split up, and my mom moved to Florida and my dad stayed in Georgia. They split up when I was a kid and each one of them married someone who already had kids our age. So it was kind of cool. I got to grow up with half brothers and sisters who were pretty close to my age," Jamie explained. "We get along great. It wasn't always easy, though. I got into some trouble as a teenager. But we're pretty close now."

"What kind of trouble did you get in?" I pushed.

"Well, several things. Nothing real bad. I just always seem to be the one that gets caught. When I was a teenager, I got busted stealing from a Coke machine. My cousin is the one who had the key and worked at a store that had the machine, but we both went in and stole the change. I was the one who got busted. Then, another time, I helped my friend Alan steal a car. He had this awesome TransAm that he traded in at a lot for a Datsun 280z. It wound up being a piece of crap. So we went to steal the TransAm and we brought it back Alan's farm. We stole the engine out of that thing to put it in his Datsun. Then Alan set the car on fire on his farm to make it look like somebody else stole it and was making a statement. Wasn't that brilliant? But I didn't get tied to that, thank God. Alan ended up getting busted and had to trade a tractor back to the car lot to make it right. The guy didn't press charges, though.

"That was just piddly crap, though," he continued. "I got busted later on for stealing stuff. I had this buddy who worked at Target. He convinced me that he could steal a bunch of stuff out of there and they would never know. So we made out of Target with several bags full of stuff. And, of course, they had video cameras and we got busted. Since it was more than $500, it wound up being a felony. My dad hooked me up with a good lawyer; a friend of the family, so I didn't have to go to jail. I had to do a bunch of community service, though," Jamie recounted.

"Man, it sounds like you've kind of been in the wrong place at the wrong time," I sympathized.

"Yeah, there's some of that. But a lot of it was just stupid decisions when you're young, you know? I mean all this went down when I was a teenager. But I have run into some trouble as an adult too. I've gotten busted with pot. The first time wasn't a big deal—I had half an ounce. They tagged me with a misdemeanor, which wasn't that bad. But the second time, I got caught with four ounces, so I got nailed with possession and intent. Intent is huge. They wound up putting my ass in jail. My dad suggested that instead of spending money on bail, we should use it on a good attorney. So I sat in jail for four months. I wasn't too happy about that. Then, on the day of my trial, the lawyer that we had hired didn't even show up. He had something else going on. But he sent a partner of his and, luckily, this guy really knew his shit. He got the whole thing cleared up. I wound up pleading guilty to a lesser charge, and with time served, I just had to serve some probation. But, that's all in the past now," he concluded.

"Well, that's good," I affirmed. "What do you do in Des Moines?"

"Right now I'm waiting tables. It's not a career, but it's something. I love living in Des Moines. I came up here after a few semesters in college because I had a buddy that lived up here. I've bounced around in a few different restaurants and bars. The great thing about Des Moines is that it's a big enough town that there's always something going on, but it's small enough that you're likely to run into someone you know. I don't know what I'm gonna do, though. I'm thinking about becoming an LPN. I've talked to Kaplan about their program. But I've heard from multiple friends that they're going to phase out the LPN program altogether. There would be no point in that. I don't want a degree in something that I can't use," Jamie explained.

"I've also thought about becoming a paramedic. I heard that they don't get paid for shit. Can you believe that? I would think that those guys would be raking it in, but they don't. So I'm thinking about becoming a physical therapist or getting into radiology or something. I need a niche job where I can get paid well, you know?" Jamie had put a lot of thought into all of this, but he didn't seem to be in too big of a hurry. "I'm 32. I know a lot of people have it figured out by now, but I was kind of a late bloomer."

Jamie related to me that he had been in several lengthy relationships, but the girls that he had typically dated had reaffirmed his patterns of self-destructive behavior. "But I finally found a girl that I can see myself with for a long, long time. In fact, that's why I'm on the bus. She's getting her D.O. from a school in Des Moines, and she has to do a bunch of rotations. There are too many students in Des Moines, so she has to go to different cities. I just flew to Detroit. She had wrapped up a rotation in Flint and had to head to St. Louis to do another one. I told her I would drive her car down to St. Louis. She doesn't like to drive that much. So I got her set up in an apartment there and then had to take the bus back to Des Moines. She's only going to be there for two weeks and then she'll come back to Des Moines," Jamie explained.

"That was pretty nice of you. You must really be into her if you're willing to get on a Greyhound for her," I weighed in.

"You ain't lying. But, no, seriously, she's super cool. She's got her shit together. She's good for me. She's an Asian girl from California. I worry that I don't fit in too well with her family. They're really into academics and math and stuff. Her dad died a couple of years ago from an aneurysm on an airplane. It's really sad. That shook her up pretty bad. Their family is super tight. She wants to move out to California after she finishes all of her rotations. I don't know about California. The weather's awesome and the beach would be cool, but people out there have really strange opinions on things. I was thinking maybe we could move to Seattle or Las Vegas, somewhere really progressive. That would be a good compromise," he expressed.

"Would you miss your family? I know Des Moines isn't that close to Georgia or Florida, but it's closer than Seattle," I countered.

"Yeah, I've thought about that. I'm fairly close with my dad, but he's supportive. He's met her and really likes her. Plus we talk on the phone pretty often. It's weird. My dad has always been one to encourage me to make my own decisions. Growing up, he wasn't heavy-handed. He would lead me to think about what I was doing and the consequences of my actions. He would say stuff like, 'What led you to that conclusion? How does that make you feel?' He's really good at helping me think things through," Jamie reflected. "It's kind of strange, though, because we've reversed roles lately. My dad is actually asking my opinion on things now, kind of like we're friends. Get this: he was a truck driver for years. He had his CDL and everything. He was gone a lot when I was growing up, but he loved driving his truck. Then he got in a few accidents. Some were his fault and some weren't, but he got scared. He was worried that he would hurt someone, so he walked away from it. Then he starts his own business—it's a printing and embossing business. He's done pretty well with it, but he really misses driving trucks. So, I asked him, 'What makes you happy?' He was quiet for a few seconds and then opened up to me about how he misses the road and how he had just gotten scared. I told him to follow his heart. So he's going back to get re-certified and to get his license again. It was kind of nice giving my dad advice," Jamie shared.

As we were stopping for a smoke break, Jamie and I noticed one of the passengers seated a few rows ahead of us. He had long red hair and a matching goatee. When he got up to exit the bus, we realized that he stood over 6'5. "What do you suppose his story is?" Jamie asked me.

"I don't know. He looks like he might be foreign," I suggested.

"Yeah, I overheard him talking. He's got some kind of accent. I'm gonna find out," he said. I stayed in my seat, spacing out, watching the passengers get on and off the bus. After a ten-minute break, Jamie sat back down next to me and declared, "I was right. I mean, I was close. I was guessing Irish. He's Scottish. He's got a huge accent. He was out there burning a joint. He says he stays stoned all the time. He's like a giant, stoned leprechaun," Jamie chuckled.

The conversation quelled for the remaining few hours. Jamie and I drifted off periodically as we made the trek to Des Moines. He was a good companion and a great storyteller. He made me feel welcome back in the world of the Bus People as I began the second half of my journey across America.

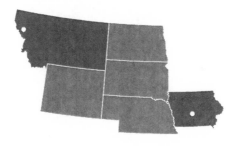

DAYS TWENTY-ONE–TWENTY-THREE

Des Moines, Iowa to St. Regis, Montana

Des Moines, IA-Omaha, NE-Vermillion, SD-Sioux Falls-Mitchell-Oacoma-
Vivian-Kadoka-Wall-Rapid City-Spearfish-Gillete, WY-Buffalo-Sheridan-
Billings, MT-Livingston-Bozeman-Butte-Missoula-St. Regis

After a brief layover, I chased a Benadryl with a swig of Mountain Dew and got comfortable for the relatively empty bus headed to Sioux Falls, South Dakota. We traveled through the night. I was pretty much out of it while we stopped at a few dinky towns in Iowa and South Dakota before arriving in Sioux Falls around 8 a.m.

The Greyhound station in Sioux Falls was a converted motel lobby, part of a stand-alone building that fronted a few hundred abandoned motel rooms. There was a carpeted waiting area with a television and a makeshift gift shop, where I purchased a deck of Mt. Rushmore playing cards as a thank-you gift for my neighbors who drove me to the Greyhound station in Nashville. An odd and lingering chlorine/cigarette smell hung on the carpet and drapes, an aftertaste of years gone by. While this station had a little more of a homey feel to it, the bad news was that we would be stuck here for a four-hour layover.

I dodged traffic across a four-lane, divided road to have breakfast at the Sheraton and to do some writing. I saw Jessica and a couple of young female passengers enter the restaurant about twenty minutes after I did. They proceeded to order countless Bloody Marys for the next hour and a half. Jessica's two companions were rough. They were large women who wore hooded sweatshirts and had tattoos galore. The more they drank, the louder and more profane they got. There was a family on vacation a few booths away that was treated to a chorus of f-bombs until the waitress and manager came over and asked them to hold it down. Jessica seemed embarrassed, but the other two were nonplussed. They left shortly after their admonishment. Jessica went to the atrium and hooked up her laptop, checking her Facebook page and e-mails. After a few cups of coffee and an omelet, I wheeled my bags into the spacious men's room in the lobby and took a birdbath, trying to wash off as much bus filth as possible.

When I walked back over to the station, I saw the two large drunken women slumped in a chair, resting their heads on each other's shoulders. Jessica was listening to her iPod. In the waiting area I saw about a half dozen teenagers being instructed by two women holding folders of material. I eavesdropped on their conversation and learned that these young people had just completed a stay in a drug and alcohol rehabilitation center and were being put on a bus to different destinations. The two case workers were going over details with them about where they would be staying and where to report for work once they got there. None of the teenagers made much eye contact nor seemed enthused about getting on the bus. The case workers spoke with motherly enthusiasm, but it didn't seem like anyone was buying it.

Shortly after noon our bus began the westward trek across South Dakota. West of the Mississippi, as the states get larger, the towns and buildings get fewer and farther between. The drive across South Dakota was interminable, only to be matched by the drive across Montana. There was very little to look at out the window, other than the pretty farmland and more rolling hills the farther west we traveled.

We stopped in the town of Mitchell, South Dakota, and I was flooded with memories of a family trip we took when I was a boy. My father had business in Montana at Glacier National Park, so my parents, my sister, and I packed up our 1978 Buick LeSabre for the two-week trip together. As we were driving across South Dakota, I remember my sister and I imploring my father to stop at the Corn Palace. There are signs all across the state beckoning the weary traveler off the road with the promise of a magical place: "Only 325 more miles to the Corn Palace." "Only 180 more miles to the Corn Palace." By the time we got to Mitchell, we couldn't contain our excitement and anticipation any longer, and my dad caved. What we found was a building much smaller than we had imagined, walls covered with corncobs, secured with lacquer. There were rows and rows of trinkets and cheap crap for purchase. I remember talking my parents into buying me a Wooly Willy game where I could add facial hair to a drawing of a man by dragging magnetic shavings around with a little red pencil. It entertained me for hours.

But on this Greyhound trip there would be no Wooly Willy, no stop at the Corn Palace. Instead we stopped at the Loaf-N-Jug, connected to a gas station. On the side of the Loaf-N-Jug, toward the back, was a red neon sign on the exterior of the building that read "Casino" in cursive. I stuck my head in the room and saw about twenty slot machines in a dark room that reeked of smoke. There were a couple of elderly people—one with an oxygen tank—playing video poker. Whenever I've pictured a casino, in my mind, I've always thought of the movie *Rain Man*, of Raymond dressed in his fancy suit, riding down an escalator to play cards at a swanky hotel. This "casino" was tired. It looked like the owner of the gas station had just popped up some drywall and built an extra room in order to profit off the desperation of closet gamblers.

On the sidewalk I saw a young woman eating out of a Tupperware container. She was dining on what looked to be a mixture of beans and rice in a soupy, foul-smelling concoction. I introduced myself. Her name was Rachel, and she was headed to Rapid City, South Dakota. She shook my hand with a firm grip and calloused hands. Rachel was an attractive woman, in her early twenties, but she was dirty and un-kept. Her hair was stringy and greasy and her outfit consisted of scrub pants, a T-shirt, and a denim button-down shirt acting as a jacket. She had piercingly beautiful blue eyes and looked very fit. As we boarded the bus, I sat next to Rachel, hoping to hear her story.

"What's going on in Rapid City?" I inquired.

"I'm meeting some friends there. We are biking across the country," she replied.

"Like motorcycles?" I asked.

"No, bicycles," Rachel said, smiling, revealing a beautifully white set of teeth. "We started in California and we are trying to hit the forty-nine states. Hawaii would be too difficult," she laughed. "There are four of us. We started in Northern California. We all went to school together and we're trying to raise awareness for a sustainable future. We've already hit California, Oregon, Washington, Alaska, Idaho, Montana, and North Dakota," she said in matter-of-fact fashion.

"So, why are you on the bus?" I asked.

"Well, I'm coming back from Kansas City. That's where I'm from. I just attended a wedding for a childhood friend. I biked ahead of my group for about a week and got far enough ahead that I took the bus down to Kansas City, went to the wedding, and got right back on the bus to meet up with them. I have to take the bus to Rapid City and then hitchhike up to Sturgis. That's where they're meeting me tonight. I left my bike at this woman's house.

She was working as a nurse at the hospital in Sturgis. I stopped in there last week and asked if she knew of anywhere that I could store my bike. She was so nice. She let me come to her house and shower, keep my bike there, and she even gave me a ride to Rapid City to the bus station," Rachel recalled.

"But why are you on the *bus*?" I pressed. "Why not fly up here or rent a car or something?"

"I'm not a fan of single occupancy vehicles. They're terrible for the environment. That's one of the reasons we're biking around the country. We're speaking at elementary schools and other places to show people that there are alternatives to travel that don't pollute the earth. We are also an overweight, apathetic country. Getting on our bikes for a year and a half seemed like a good way to lead by example. It's great exercise and we get to see the whole country. Plus, I chose the bus because you get to meet all sorts of characters," Rachel espoused, revealing a similar desire to mine. I shared with her that I, too, was on a mission, albeit a less altruistic one.

I learned, as I was digging my greasy fingers deep into the bag of beef jerky I had just bought, that Rachel is a vegetarian. In many ways, she is the prototypical "granola"—a somewhat affectionate term I learned in college to describe educated people who choose to make statements about many things in society by not bathing and not eating meat. "What's the longest you've gone on this trip without a shower?" I asked.

"I'd say thirty days or so. But I don't mind being dirty," Rachel answered. Rachel was out to save the world, but in a pleasant way. I couldn't help but wonder, however, if her act would change or if she would tone it down once she got married.

"My folks pretty much think this trip is crazy. I'm from Johnson County, Kansas, which is really nice. I went to school out in California at Humboldt State. I just graduated last year and am still trying to figure out what I want to do. This seemed like the only time I might ever have to do a trip like this. So, after I talked with them a while about it, they were pretty supportive," she explained. I suspected that Rachel has always been a bit of a thorn in her parents' side. She is obviously well educated, attractive, and motivated, but she was probably the kind of teenager that gave her parents grief when they threw a soda can in the trash. They are undoubtedly successful, professional people who have given their all so that their daughter can follow in their footsteps. Instead, she has chosen to ride her bike with three buddies for eighteen months, hitchhiking, staying with strangers, and doing God-knows how many other things that would make her parents cringe. I imagined them at dinner parties, rolling their eyes and explaining in exasperated tones to their friends how their daughter was on a yearlong bicycle adventure around the country. But deep down I bet they are secretly proud of her.

Rachel was exactly the type of person that I envied back in my post-college years when I was a newlywed. While I opted to start out on life's path with a wife and career aspirations, I wish that I could have had an experience like Rachel was having. Not showering and bicycling across the country wouldn't have been at the top of my list, but floating around for a year, seeing the country, and not having many responsibilities would have been a once-in-a-lifetime opportunity. Rachel seemed to understand that. She, at twenty-three years old, had a "save the world" attitude, but I think deep down she knew that this probably wouldn't last forever. She had a chance to do something, and she took it.

Rachel was obviously not the typical bus passenger. She *chose* to take the bus, not as some penny-pinching decision, but for the sheer sport of it. While Rachel came from a life of affluence, she made a decision to be a part of the bus community. She, even at a young age, realized that there is much to be learned about stepping outside her world and getting to know people from other backgrounds. Rachel would probably be the first to admit, too, that she had some things in common with the people on the bus. While largely unspoken, there was a tinge of discomfort when she referred to her relationship with her parents. That is something that was probably universally true of bus people, and, honestly, is probably universally true for all of us.

I have always wanted to please my parents. I have listened when they've given me advice. The worst thing they could say to me was, "I'm disappointed in you." I've always kept an eye toward my folks, wanting to make sure they're proud of me. My parents both grew up on farms in Indiana. They both graduated from college, which, in the late 1950s, was a major achievement. They prided themselves on carving professional careers for themselves and raising my sister and me. Hard work, education, and prudent decisions were part of the ethos of our family when I was growing up. Getting a wild hair and going on a bus trip like I was on was not something that they would have ever imagined for me and, honestly, did not enthusiastically embrace. But, like Rachel, I had wanted to follow my own path and seize an opportunity.

Sometimes I wonder if I've learned anything from my relationship with my own parents. Will I encourage my children to follow their dreams, or will I give them subtle little messages about what *I* think they should be doing with their lives? It's a parental balancing act. We want to protect our children from stupid decisions and heartache, but some things our kids will just have to experience. I hope I just give them the tools to deal with what life throws their way. I want them to be happy. I think Rachel's parents, and my parents, ultimately want the same.

I said goodbye to Rachel in Rapid City. We were supposed to have a forty-five-minute layover in Rapid City, but we were behind schedule, for no real apparent reason, and the announced layover was reduced to ten minutes. I felt an intestinal storm brewing, undoubtedly a result of a two-day diet of beef jerky, Doritos, and soda. I navigated through the bombed-out construction zone that was the Rapid City bus depot to find that the one stall in the men's room was inhabited by a homeless man who had passed out. I crouched down slightly to see a pair of black boots in front of the commode. There was some urgency to my need for a toilet, so I rushed up to the ticket counter and explained my dilemma. "That happens all the time. Drunks go in there and pass out. Here, I'll let you in the employee bathroom. But don't tell anyone about it," said the woman at the counter. "It'll be our secret," I said as I hurriedly rushed into the pristine bathroom. It was the most luxurious four minutes I had spent in the last two days. I knew that I didn't want to be stranded in Rapid City, but I trusted that the woman working there wouldn't let the bus leave without me.

As we left Rapid City, our bus had suddenly swelled to near capacity. There were families, couples, and wayward souls all heading out west. The trip to Billings, Montana, was quiet, except for the noise of rubber scraping across the windshield as the driver used his wipers to keep a visible patch of space in front of him. The dark, drizzly night gave the bus a sad, reflective mood. Nobody was really talking to each other, despite the big crowd.

From Billings we began the interminable voyage across the southern belly of Montana in the dead of night. I was exhausted. While the goal of this project was to ride around the country, learn about who's on the bus, listen to their stories, and communicate them with the world, sometimes I just needed to sleep. This was one of those occasions. I opted to just keep my head on the pillow, enjoying the two seats that I had eminent domained two states ago. I tried to pretend I was sleeping while a train of four or five new passengers got on the bus at our stop in Bozeman. I was really hoping no one would choose the seat next to me. But he did.

The guy said, "I sit here?"

I huffed and puffed and moved my bag to the floor and crammed myself into the small space next to the window, and then, in a moment of genius, I started coughing. I started coughing like I couldn't stop. I said to my new seatmate: "You can sit here if you want, but I'm sick. Really sick. I think I have the pig flu." He just smiled and sat down next to me. I later learned that he didn't speak much English. Unfortunately, the father of six in the row in front of me did speak English. "If my kids end up getting sick, so help me. . . ."

I dropped the act and just accepted that I would be awake until I said goodbye to my new seatmate Jesus, who would get off in Missoula. Jesus was on his way north from Ogden, Utah, to Missoula, where someone had told him that there was work to be had. He had previously worked for several years as a mechanic in Phoenix before his brief stint doing construction in Utah. He asked me if there were a lot of Mormons in Missoula. I told him that I did not know.

I later fessed up to Cameron, the large, African American father of six sitting in front of me, that I didn't have pig flu or any kind of flu. I just wanted to sleep. "You gotta do what you gotta do, man," he said to me with a smile as we enjoyed a cup of coffee in St. Regis, Montana. I explained to him that I was traveling the country writing my book about my experience. "You are straight up crazy, man," he giggled. "I just spent the last two weeks on this damn bus. My kids and I went to Detroit for my grandparents' birthday. They're ninety-eight and we don't know how much time we got left with them. So I busted myself out buying these bus tickets. I'm never taking the bus again." Cameron is about the fiftieth person I heard make that proclamation during my trip.

Cameron's kids were really well behaved. You could tell he was doing a great job with them, considering the required vigilance that it took to make sure that no creepy strangers talked to his kids, to make sure they were fed, to take them to the bathroom, and to try and keep them from misbehaving on the bus. Earlier in the night, Cameron went off on his daughter who raised the armrest and couldn't get it back down. "Why would you do that? I just put that fuckin' thing down and now you raised it up again. What's wrong with you?" Cameron was at his wits' end. I got the feeling that he usually didn't use such colorful language with his kids, but two weeks on the bus will do that to a person.

At the coffee stop I said, "Cameron, your kids are amazing. They are doing so well. I don't think I could have handled a trip like this when I was nine years old."

"Thanks, man. It's just that they start acting squirrely and I worry they're going to bug everyone on the bus," he explained.

I understood. I have worried my whole parental life about that same thing. There's nothing worse than thinking that other people are thinking you are a crappy parent or have no control over your kids. I can remember leaving Chili's one night before we finished dinner because my fourteen-month-old son was flipping out and making a lot of noise. My wife got upset with me and said, "He's a kid. They do these things. Just walk around with him."

"But we're ruining everyone's night," I said. "Nobody wants to listen to a screaming kid. Everyone's looking at us." So we angrily got in our mini-van and left. In retrospect, I was the idiot. It wasn't that big of a deal. It's just that in my own delusional world, I thought that my child's behavior in Chili's was a reflection of me as a parent and, thus, me as a human being.

"Well, you're probably the only one who's stressed at all. It's because they're your kids. Just relax. You're almost home. They're not bothering anybody. They're doing great," I assured him. Cameron appreciated that and seemed glad to have a new friend for the last three hours of his trip. We talked about parenting, sports, and life. Cameron shared that, in four days, he would finally be marrying his girlfriend of nineteen years, the mother of his six children. He was excited, and had a beaming smile as he explained that they were going to get married by some lake in Eastern Washington with a large canopy of pine trees all around. We finished our coffee and walked across the parking lot of the gas station. Cameron encouraged his kids to stay close. He and I continued talking with each other until we arrived in Spokane, his destination, where I got to meet his fiancé and snapped a picture of the whole family, reunited and ready for a new beginning. Cameron had made it–he had endured a two-week road trip to visit family. It was a major accomplishment.

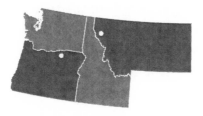

DAYS TWENTY-THREE–TWENTY-FOUR

St. Regis, Montana to Stanfield, Oregon

St. Regis, MT-Kellogg, ID-Coeur D Alene-Spokane, WA-Moses Lake-
Ellensburg-Seattle-Ellensburg-Yakima-Sunnyside-Pasco-Stanfield, OR

We changed drivers in St. Regis, Montana, the self-proclaimed "Fly Fishing Capital of the World." Joan was the new driver who would take us all the way to Seattle. She was an average-looking woman, probably in her early fifties, with a nice smile and a pleasant speaking voice. About a half mile out of St. Regis, heading west on I-90, Joan asked over the PA system, "Would you all like it if I shared a little bit of the history about some of these towns while I drove?"

There was very little reaction from the fifty-five passengers on board. Finally, after an uncomfortably long silence, one person yelled out, "Yeah." That was all Joan needed. For the next eight hours she peppered us with history, biology, geology, geography, and recreational nuggets of information. It was all included in our bus fare. It was the first time I had seen a driver do this. It was like having a museum docent taking us across the entire state of Washington.

Joan started in about the tamarack trees. "The large pine trees you see are the tamaracks. They only grow west of the continental divide, which is somewhere around Butte. Their needles actually turn yellow and orange in the fall and they lose them. They grow new needles each spring. If you look off to the left, you'll see some trees that were snapped in half by a wind blast . . . WAIT, DO I SMELL CIGARETTE SMOKE? THERE IS NO SMOKING ON THE BUS!"

"It was me," said a heavily tattooed guy about halfway back on the bus. He had just spent twenty minutes in the bathroom. "I pooped, and so I lit a match. Sorry."

I think he was smoking, but the match story was a good cover. Joan let him have it: "What do you think they would do to you if you did that on a plane? Would you do that on a plane? They would be waiting to arrest you. What made you think you could do that?" The offending party said "sorry" a couple more times and then just stared out the window as Joan continued berating him from behind the wheel.

After five minutes or so, Joan had cooled off and then gently resumed. "The fire of 1910 claimed many lives here in Kellogg, Idaho. Some people survived by hiding in tunnels under the mountain. A man named Pulaski is credited with saving scores of people. In fact the firemen have a safety procedure now named, 'the Pulaski'. Over to the right, you'll see the mine that was the site of the tragic collapse in 1975 . . ."

At this point my mind wandered and I started doing some calculations. While Joan was speaking, of the fifty-five passengers, I would say fifteen were drunk or high, twenty were sleeping, twelve more were either arguing with the person next to them or talking loudly on their cell phones, and there were maybe eight of us remaining who were dialed in to Joan's symposium on all things Idaho, Montana, and Washington.

"Over there on the side of the road you'll see some large

orange signposts. You'll notice that they are twelve feet high," Joan observed, pointing out large thin sticks by the side of the road. "They put those there so that the plows know where the side of the road is during snow season. This area can get between 400 and 450 inches of snow each winter. I actually like it when the drifts are really high because that blocks the lights from oncoming vehicles," Joan explained to an increasingly disinterested audience. "I've driven this route for years. Sometimes they have to shut down I-90 completely. I've been re-routed to Portland and I've had to turn around in Ellensburg it's been so bad," Joan continued.

At a smoke break in Moses Lake, Washington, I suddenly felt sympathy for Joan. She was bright, very knowledgeable, and had been driving this bus for the last thirty years of her life. She's had to deal with snowstorms, moose in the road, and match-lighters on the bus. She did all of this for an audience of uninterested, strung-out bus passengers. I wanted her to know I appreciated her efforts to inform and entertain us. I felt an intrinsic obligation to affirm Joan, to once again play the part of the eager student. My dad got his PhD in zoology, and any ride in the backseat of the Buick LeSabre was incomplete without comments from my dad like, "Hey kids, do you see the ruby crested nuthatch?" "Where?" "Over there. Don't you see it?" "No." "It's a male. He's sitting on the power line." I rarely saw the birds, but, my dad kept trying to get me and my sister interested in birds and trees and thirteen lined ground squirrels. I wanted my dad to love me, so I did my best to seem interested.

I guess I wanted Joan's approval too. I moved from my seat next to a guy who I was sure was suffering from tuberculosis, to the front row of the bus. I wanted Joan to know that someone appreciated her efforts. I asked her many questions, and occasionally regressed into being a smart ass, a bad habit I sometimes have.

"Cle Elum is the next town we'll be passing. It means 'swift water' in Indian," Joan offered.

"Joan, how would the Indians even know about Swiss people?"

"No, no, no. *Swift* water."

Joan loves driving the bus. She's had the Washington and Oregon runs for the entirety of her thirty-year career. She started the same week that Mount St. Helen's blew up, in May of 1980. She grew up in Massachusetts, but went out west with a friend the summer after she graduated from high school and never came back. In a private conversation after she had put the PA mike down, she shared, "It was during the John Denver craze. There was this romance of the mountains. I fell in love with it. I love it out here. Washington has everything. Within three hours of Seattle, you can be in the mountains, on the beach, in the desert, or picking apples. What other state can say that?"

I liked Joan. I really did appreciate her. She shared about her genealogy studies, how she once "nicked an elk" with her bus (I doubt the elk felt 'nicked'), how her brother got cellulitis from accidentally eating some turkey poop on their farm in Massachusetts, how her same brother had once gotten Lyme Disease from a tick, and how Washington exports tons of Timothy Hay to Japan.

"I notice there are a lot of Japanese people on the bus around here," I said.

"Yeah, this seems to be where they all come. They come over here for college. I'm always carrying Japanese students on my bus. They study at Central Washington and the University of Washington. There's a huge Asian influence here," Joan explained.

"What got you interested in giving the history talks while you drive?" I asked. "I have really enjoyed it and I feel like I've learned a lot," I said, fishing for a sign that Joan was feeling sufficiently appreciated.

"I like sharing some of this stuff with the passengers. Most people are having a bad day on the bus. Maybe I can make it a little brighter," Joan expressed. She was the West Coast's version of Donna. She made the long drive across the state of Washington fly by. Joan is a credit to Greyhound. I wonder if the corporate offices know about the diamonds in the rough that they have out on the road, like Joan and Donna. I hope somewhere, somehow, these drivers understand that their attitude and pleasant dispositions matter.

"I'm hoping to get to the Mariners game tonight," I shared with Joan as we closed in on downtown Seattle. We were running a little behind schedule and Joan got off the interstate in Seattle to avoid some of the highway traffic, opting instead for back roads. The traffic was still terrible. "Where are you staying?" Joan asked me.

"The Westin. Is that close to the ballpark?" I asked.

"Not really. But we should get there about 6 and the game doesn't start until 7, so you should have time to take a cab." Joan was interested in my journey and, by the time we pulled into the Greyhound station in Seattle, she had given me instructions on what to see and where to eat during my twenty-four-hour stay.

"It was great meeting you," I said after giving Joan a sideways hug.

"You too. Good luck," she returned with a smile.

I hustled the five-block walk to my hotel, quickly checked in, and showered. I did take a moment to look out the window of my thirtieth-floor room to enjoy a quick view of the city. It was beautiful: a bustling city, water, and Mount Ranier in the distance. I can see why people love Seattle. It was breathtaking.

I flagged down a cab and took the hilly ride to Safeco Field. I bought a ticket from a scalper for $20 and sat on the first base line, not too high up. The late summer air was crisp and cool—a gorgeous night. I arrived before the first pitch and started walking around the concession area. I ordered a cold Budweiser and a Dungeness crab sandwich. That was the first time I had ever seen that kind of combination at a baseball game, but it worked. It was amazing. The game moved by at a snail's pace, and the Mariners lost to the Angels, but it was an absolutely beautiful place to see a baseball game.

After the game I grabbed a taxi and was soon in my bed, exhausted from three solid days on the road. I pulled the shades and slept hard–drool-on-the-pillow hard. In the morning I wrote for a bit and then toted my bags back to the Greyhound station, hoping to make the 12:30 bus headed to San Diego. When I got to the station, an hour ahead of time, I learned that the bus was already sold out. The terminal was filthy, crowded, and chaotic. I asked the man at the counter about the next bus out of town and he said that there was one around midnight that could get me going toward San Diego.

"What about Las Vegas?" I asked him.

"You could take the 7:50 bus tonight to Salt Lake," he replied. I called an audible and decided that Vegas might be a nice destination. Now I had seven hours to kill in Seattle.

Since it was another chamber-of-commerce kind of day, I walked toward the water. On a Thursday afternoon, the Pike Place Market was bustling. It was just like I had seen on television, with guys wrapping fish and street vendors bustling about. There was a quartet of African American men in front of the Starbucks doing a heartfelt a cappella version of "Under the Boardwalk" before a growing audience. I sat and had a nice lunch by the water and thoroughly enjoyed the hubbub of the area. There were plenty of people with signs and strange clothing who look like they came straight out of Berkley in 1970. It was a sunny day that just breathed life.

I arrived back at the Seattle terminal at 7 p.m., and the line behind door #2 was already spilling out the door onto the sidewalk. The Seattle Greyhound terminal was typical, although it appeared to be severely undersized for the amount of traffic that moves through the place. The floor was brick-colored tile and sticky. There were spills and stains that appeared to have been there for months. About 40 percent of the vending machines and phones had "out of order" signs taped to them. It was crowded and didn't smell very good. I went to the men's room and passed by an African American man standing in front of the sinks. He had on dirty clothes and a red mesh ball cap,and was cradling a big oil can of Busch beer. He was talking to himself, and then looked at me and mumbled something. I just proceeded to the urinal.

As I walked out of the bathroom, I observed an obese woman with a cast on her foot. She was using her good foot to push a scooter around the waiting area. She had on pink, dirty sweatpants and a baggy T-shirt, her salt-and-pepper hair wild and unharnessed. She was doing laps around the black metal benches in the seating area. Nobody paid her any attention. It was a circus.

People in line were already agitated. It was getting close to our departure time for Salt Lake City, and the bus was nowhere to be seen. At about 8:30, I walked up to the ticket counter. "Do you know what the deal is with the 7:50 bus?" I asked the guy.

"No. It's late. The bus isn't here yet," he nonchalantly replied. He didn't care. Nobody really seemed to care—except the people waiting for the bus. In fact, I believe that there are some employees who take secret pleasure in watching the misfortune and inconvenience of others. Their curt answers and insincere smiles seem to give them away.

On the sidewalk there were several clusters of people just hanging out, drinking and smoking. Greyhound stations are popular gathering spots for this kind of activity. The passengers waiting in line wove through small groups of transient people who were getting high. I witnessed a domestic dispute between an extremely intoxicated African American man and his girlfriend. He was staggering on the sidewalks, yelling profanities, trying to provoke people into a fight until his anger turned toward his girlfriend. "You better watch your mouth, bitch! I've got a gun," he exclaimed. The Greyhound passengers watched this exchange develop with some yelling at the man to "shut the fuck up." Everyone in line was complaining about the delay. When I reported to the interested parties that "the bus is late and they don't know when it will be here," people just shook their heads and lit cigarettes.

I looked forward in the line and saw my friend from the bathroom holding a bus ticket. I couldn't believe he was going to be on the bus. He kept working his way back to everyone in line: "You got a cigarette?" He would wobble as he stood and would stare at people for an uncomfortably long time, his eyes struggling to focus. Everyone blew him off and he just kept trying. I figured the security guard would stop him before he could get on the bus. That turned out not to be the case. Our bus finally arrived, just before 9:00, and we started boarding. The security guard was having a discussion with the man in the red cap, but he let him on. We all filed on the packed bus. Before we even left Seattle, I could hear activity from the back of the bus, about five rows behind me. The lady who had been riding the scooter and the African American guy were going at it, arguing about space issues. Things calmed down, but not for long.

About forty-five minutes outside of Seattle, as we were climbing up toward Snoqualmie Pass, I started to smell cigarette smoke. This is against the law, as the driver explains at the start of every trip. "Stop smoking! You're going to get kicked off the bus!" I heard coming from the back. It wasn't another passenger chastising the smoker; it was the smoker herself. The lady with the cast and scooter was yelling at herself. She flicked her lit cigarette under the seat in front of her. A college-aged guy picked up the cigarette and ran to the bathroom to throw it down the toilet. When he came back from the bathroom, he announced to those of us who were staring toward the back: "She's yelling at herself. It must be one of her personalities or something. She's nuts."

With all of the hubbub, our driver, Curtis, pulled over on the side of the interstate and turned on all the lights. He made his way to the back of the bus. After surveying the situation and getting a report from the young man who had discarded the cigarette, he told the woman: "You need to stop smoking or I'll have to kick you off the bus."

"Shut up," she told him. "Shut up and drive the fucking bus!" Curtis looked at her and then looked around at the other passengers. It was silent except for the verbal assault from the smoker. I could see the wheels turning in Curtis's head. Several drivers told me that they hate calling the police to come intervene for bus behavior—that involves a lot of paperwork and really slows things down. Curtis chose the path of least resistance and turned around and went back behind the wheel. The woman briefly calmed down, but the buzz and chatter in the back of the bus between the surrounding passengers slowly escalated.

The resolution didn't last long. About five minutes later the woman started kicking her feet against the wall of the bathroom, screaming: "I don't want to go to Pasco! Just drive the fucking bus. Shut up! Shut up!" She was talking to herself and getting louder by the minute. I've never seen anything like it.

It got worse. "You shut up! Get your black ass off the bus! Get your n***** ass off the bus!" She was screaming now. Everyone started standing up and turning around to see what was going on. She had singled out the Busch drinker and was berating him for no apparent reason. She was yelling at him, dropping racial slurs that made everyone come unglued. People started yelling at her: "Shut up lady! Settle down." Suddenly and without warning, she got up out of her seat and sucker-punched the African American man in the mouth.

Curtis pulled the bus over and turned the lights on. As he came to the back, the woman started charging at him like an angry rhinoceros. Curtis, who was a smallish man, tried his best to diffuse the situation, but this woman was far gone. She barreled over Curtis and ran toward the front of the bus.

"Let me off the fucking bus! Let me off. LET ME OFF!" she screamed. As she made her way to the front gate, an elderly man began swinging his cane at her head. He connected a few times but that didn't slow her down. It was like giving a two-thousand-pound bull a half tablet of Valium. They decided to open the gate and let her off. There was panic and people were screaming, "Don't let her off! She's going to run on the interstate! She's gonna get hit by a truck!" But nobody really tried to stop her. She took off running up the shoulder of the road, headed for nowhere in particular. Curtis nervously fumbled with his cell phone and called 9-1-1 as he chased after the woman.

Peering out the front window, I saw the man she had punched chase her down the road and lunge at her ankles. Curtis was in tow behind the two of them. The lunge was successful and all three of them crashed onto the gravel shoulder like linebackers. Curtis and Mr. Busch were sitting on top of the woman, keeping her from running off. She was large and violent. They stayed on top of her for about five minutes until the police showed up. The Washington State Troopers immediately cuffed her. The large officers were able to pick her up and carry her to the cruiser. At this point, I was out on the side of the road watching this go down, unable to contain my curiosity.

She was bucking and kicking as they shoved her head into the back of the police car. It took three officers to wedge her into the backseat. Once they had shut the door, they looked at each other and sighed deeply. They looked a bit disheveled from the scrum. Then they gathered information from bus passengers for the next twenty minutes. Everyone was eager to get off the bus to add in his or her two cents, but most were excited about the bonus smoke break the episode provided.

Everyone was given an incident report to fill out. Most people wadded it up and threw it under the seat in front of them. Some people did artwork on theirs. A couple of dutiful people handed in the form. I did not. I was tired. My trip out to Seattle had been scenic and tranquil with Joan serving as our guide. My trip out of

Seattle was scary as hell. The rest of the trip went smoothly, but there was a buzz on the bus, and not just the typical chemically induced buzz. This was a night we would all remember forever.

With the original delay and the unplanned riot, we wound up being over two hours late into Stanfield, Oregon. People missed connections left and right. One guy was going to have to stay in Stanfield until two the next afternoon to catch the next bus going in his direction.But nobody seemed to get too upset about the delays. "Shit happens," as they like to say.

DAYS TWENTY-FOUR–TWENTY-SIX

Stanfield, Oregon to Las Vegas, Nevada

Stanfield, OR-Pendleton-La Grande-Baker City-Ontario-Nampa, ID-Boise-Twin Falls-Burley-Tremonton, UT-Ogden-Salt Lake City-Provo-Cove Fort-St. George-Las Vegas, NV

We didn't see daylight until we got into Idaho.

The new bus out of Oregon still had a handful of people who originated in Seattle, but mostly it was a new crop, unaware of the bizarre events of the night before. We would stay on the same bus all the way into Salt Lake, making stops in Boise and Twin Falls. Usually it was a handy and convenient thing not to have to switch buses very often. But this was the foulest smelling bus I had been on yet. The odor emanating from the toilet was unbearable. It was a stench of urine and shit that was making everyone on the bus comment about it. This bus was in a league of its own. One woman remarked, "Damn, that's nasty. Somebody done banged that bathroom up!" I had never heard that expression, but it fit. During a smoke break, I complained to the driver who said, "Oh, really? Okay, I'll have them clean it up in Boise," which was still several hours away. I returned to my seat, which was way too close to the bathroom for my taste, and breathed through my mouth, trying not to wretch.

Idaho was gorgeous. The rugged mountains and bright sunshine were a welcome reprieve from a night spent in a dark, scary bus. Luckily, during our forty-five-minute stop in Boise, the driver did arrange for someone to clean out the toilet. But it wound up being not much better than a few sprays of Glade, masking the fumes rising from about five pounds of human feces. Still, it was an improvement. We loaded back up and made our way into Twin Falls for a lunch break.

"If you look to your right, you'll see the site where Evel Knievel made his famous jump over the Snake River Canyon. He didn't make it and had to parachute out," the driver informed us. Everyone was scrambling to look out the window of the bus and glimpse this nugget of history. Joan's tales of forest fires and walking trails had hardly woken people from their slumber, but mention Evel Knievel and apparently you've got a captive audience.

"I thought it was the Grand Canyon that he jumped over," someone shouted up at the driver.

"Nope," he countered over the PA. "This was the place."

We arrived in Salt Lake City around dinnertime. After a brief respite, I boarded the Las Vegas bus and grabbed the very back seat, hoping to stretch out and catch a little sleep after two solid days of travel and chaos. There were a couple of passengers I recognized from Seattle on my bus. I felt a bond with them. We were the survivors of the Crazy-Lady-Snoqualmie-Pass incident.

As I took my seat, I noticed a young man approaching in what looked to be a full-on prison uniform. He chose to sit right next to me and introduced himself as Daniel, but said most folks called him D.

I was amazed on my journey by how many people I met who had done prison time. I've always heard on the news about overcrowding in prisons, but until this bus trip I hadn't met too many people who had been incarcerated for any length of time. That certainly changed during my thirty days on the bus.

While Daniel had boarded the bus in Salt Lake City, his journey had begun six hours earlier. He was on his way home to Las Vegas after a two-year stay in the Nevada State Penitentiary. The bus doesn't run directly from Northern Nevada down to Vegas—the majority of Nevada is government-owned scrub-land. Instead, one must travel hours east to Salt Lake. Daniel just dealt with it. After two years, what was an extra eight hours?

I discovered that often prisoners were released and given a bus ticket to their hometowns. According to the Federal Bureau of Prisons, between 2005 and 2007 the agency purchased 84,600 bus tickets for inmates.[1] This does not include the thousands upon thousands of tickets that state prisons buy for their recently released inmates. It would be nice if family were there to pick them up on the day of their release, but for the men I met, they were on their own. Once again, Greyhound was a cheap, convenient way to get people where they needed to go.

Daniel was dressed in blue pants, kind of like scrubs, blue Vans-style shoes, and a blue button-up shirt.

"Why did you wear your prison clothes on your way home?" I asked him.

"I left my other clothes there at the prison for the guys that really need them," Daniel explained.

Daniel was a twenty-two-year-old African American man. He was soft spoken, affable, and was eager to talk with me. Earlier in the day, Daniel had been released from prison in Winnemucca, Nevada. He did most of his two years there and said it was by far the best prison he's been in. "It's like bunny camp there, man," he expressed. "There's no problems there. People just mind their own business. The food's pretty good. The guards don't bust your balls too much. It's bunny camp." I didn't know what to make of that. Daniel had been in five different prisons in Nevada during his two-year sentence, so, he had a frame of reference on prisons, I guess. "Nevada ain't a bad place to do your time. You don't want to do time in California. Prison sucks there. I've got friends who've been in over there. And, you definitely don't want to do time in Texas. They'll fry your ass down there."

Daniel said he did a few days in the prison in Lovelock, where they keep O.J. Simpson. While O.J. was acquitted by a jury of his peers in the murder of his estranged wife and her boyfriend, he couldn't stay out of trouble. A few years ago, he and some buddies went after a guy in a Las Vegas hotel room for stealing some of his memorabilia. He was convicted of kidnapping and sent up the river for a number of years. "He's in PC, man—protective custody. Nobody messes with him. He's in there with child molesters and stuff. He's on lockdown for twenty-three hours a day. Only one hour a day he gets to lift weights and run around. I heard he's buyin' new shoes for everyone in the prison with him."

Realizing that the opportunity to chat with D was far more important than sleep at this point, I started digging a little bit. "So, if you don't mind me asking, what were you in for?"

"Burglary and larceny," he said. I'm not sure what the difference between the two is, but I'm sure a lawyer could explain the nuances. All I know is that D was involved in some pretty serious stuff. He had been knocking off jewelry stores in Las Vegas for quite a while by the time he got caught. "I was working with this other dude. We would go into the stores and ask to see stuff out of the case and then, after we'd get the clerk all confused, we grab a handful of jewelry and we'd bolt. Sometimes we'd take girls in with us if they were asking for IDs. The girls would go in ahead of us and would ask for the jewelry out of the case and then we'd punch the girls or knock 'em down, take the shit, and run out of the store. Then the girls would act like they didn't know us when the cops came. That worked pretty well. But the other guy and I split up. He started doin' his thing and I started doin' my thing. On the night I got caught, I learned that the night before, the owner of the jewelry store he was hittin' shot him and killed him. I didn't know that. So I went to do my thing and I noticed a black dude and a white dude outside the store. They were in an unmarked Dodge Ram. They came in and I just put my hands up. They tried to pin that murder thing on me, but I didn't know anything, for real. They kept after me in interrogation. 'What did you know about this? Did you have anything to do with his death?' I kept tellin' 'em I didn't know nothin' about it. They finally let up, and because I didn't have a gun, I only got two years. It wasn't too bad."

D explained that probation is no good. "I'd rather just do my time and get paroled. Probation seems to last forever. You gotta check in with your probation officer all the damn time. Be here. Be there. I hate it. The cool thing about parole is that when you're done, you're done. I've only got a few months to check in with my parole officer and then I can do my thing."

"What did your folks have to say when you went away to prison? Were they upset with you?" I asked.

"My mom died a long time ago. I'm close with my dad. He wasn't happy with me but he was like 'just do your time.' That's really all he had to say about it," D said. "He came to visit me a couple of times when I was in prison. I'm hoping to do what he does. He taught me how to work on cars growing up. I love it. I'm gonna call him when I get home and see if he can teach me some more stuff and then maybe I could start my own repair business. But he lives in California, so I don't know how soon I'll be able to get over there to see him," D explained.

"Ladies and gentlemen, we're pulling into Provo now. Sorry about the delay, but with all the road construction, those things happen. Please just take ten minutes to go out and grab something to drink or smoke a cigarette," the driver announced, interrupting my conversation with D. We slowly waddled off the bus, spilling into the parking lot of a gas station at dusk. D leaned up against the bus and lit a Marlboro Light. "These things would go for like $3 a pop in prison," he stated, exhaling a long plume of smoke.

"You gotta smoke I could bum?" asked a scraggly traveler. Without responding, D just reached in his pack and withdrew a cigarette and offered his lighter. Of the bus smokers, some carry their own cigarettes and others mooch off the first visible smoker they see at every stop. D was just glad to be free, so he was in a generous mood.

"Hey, where are you guys going?" mumbled an extremely thin woman. She approached D and me, wobbly on her legs, swaying forward and back. She was struggling to keep her eyes open.

"Vegas," replied D. He looked at me and raised his eyebrows, letting out a little grin as we watched this woman stagger ever closer to us.

"Me too. Maybe we could sit together. My name's Tammy" she slurred, reaching for D's hand. He gave her a light handshake and then she turned to me to shake my hand, but never took her eyes off D. "Did you just get out today?" she asked.

"Yeah," he responded.

"Where were you in?" she continued.

"Nevada," he said. D was keeping his answers brief, but Tammy was pressing on.

"That's cool," she said. "I have a friend that just got out. He was in there for nine months and nobody came to visit him. Can you believe that?"

Tammy was fidgeting with her backpack and speaking in slurry fashion, going on and on about nothing in particular as the driver beckoned us back on the bus. D and I hustled back to our seats, anticipating the theater that would be Tammy's arrival on the bus. Tammy climbed the stairs and immediately proceeded to the rear of the bus, where D and I were sitting. She bounced off the seats like a drunken human pinball, using them as a padded boundary to navigate her way toward the back. We had spread out to occupy all three of the seats in the back row.

"Can I sit in between you guys?" she asked. Luckily, D spoke up.

"I think there's an open seat right here," tapping the right hand seat in front of us. Tammy didn't balk and sat down.

"I want you guys to be my bus buddies. Every time I ride the bus, I have to find my bus buddies. Will you be my bus buddies?" Tammy asked as she started reaching in her backpack, not really caring to get an answer. She pulled out a bottle of prescription medication. "I'm taking Percocet," she told us as she popped a couple of pills in her mouth and washed them down with a gulp of Mountain Dew.

"Do you have some medical problems?" I asked her.

"I just had a tooth pulled today, so I'm taking these to deal with the pain. I'm in a lot of pain," she replied. "I'm going to have to have all my teeth pulled. I've been taking pain meds for the last twelve years and I haven't always taken them the right way," Tammy explained.

"What do you mean, 'the right way'?" I countered.

"I've had twenty-nine blockages in my stomach and over a dozen surgeries, so I've gotten hooked on painkillers and sometimes I snorted them. I would smash them with a hammer and snort them and the dentist told me that my teeth are rotted out because of it," she said, matter-of-factly. "Do you want one?" she asked me.

"No, I'm good. Thanks, though," I replied. Tammy flipped open her cell phone and mumbled something. She continued to alternate between rummaging around for Chapstick, drinking Mountain Dew, playing with her phone, taking pain pills, and rubbing her face for the next six hours. Tammy was a nervous, strung-out mess.

Tammy had high cheekbones and pretty blue eyes that were only visible when her eyelids would strain to open far enough so that I could see them. She was thin and had long brown hair that was tucked under a green military-style hat. She was probably really good looking before she had fallen into the pit of addiction. I later learned that narcotic pain medication often causes constipation and blockages. So it was kind of a chicken-and-egg thing—I didn't know if Tammy had to take the pills because of her stomach blockages or if she had the blockages because she was downing Percocet like it was out of a pixie stick.

"I should be there after midnight. I don't know. The bus is running late. But, hey, I met these two really nice guys who agreed to be my bus buddies," Tammy rambled into the phone. "I just told them that you're going to be my bus buddies," she whispered loudly to D and me as if she were keeping some sort of a secret. "Well, I've got enough for a while, but find a different pharmacy if they're giving you shit about it." Tammy continued into the phone, orchestrating some plan to procure more pain meds in Nevada. "Okay. I'll talk to you later," Tammy concluded, flipping her phone shut. She ran her hand through her hair and rubbed her nose with her fingers. "God. I hurt so bad," she shouted out in an exasperated manner for anyone who would listen. The man seated next to Tammy had put in his headphones and was trying his best to ignore her.

Tammy reached back and put her hand on D's knee. "You got a girl back in Vegas?" she asked him. D looked over at me and grinned, shaking his head.

"Yeah. I got a girl," he answered.

"You excited to see her? You gonna give it to her good tonight?" Tammy asked and let out a deep, throaty laugh, amused by her ability to envision some good just-got-out-of-prison sex.

D shook his head and said, "We'll see". I imagine D had been thinking about that night for the last two years of his life.

As Tammy got up to use the bathroom (her first of many trips to the bathroom throughout the night), D looked at me and said, "That girl's trippin', man."

"She sure is," I agreed. "So how long have you been with your girlfriend?" I asked.

"About four years," Daniel replied.

"That's cool that she's stuck with you. Are you nervous about how things are gonna go when you see her?" I asked.

"Nah, man. We're solid. She came to visit me some and we talked on the phone. She's my girl. I told her I'm leaving my old ways behind. I don't want to fuck this thing up," he explained.

"Did she know what you were up to when you were robbing the jewelry stores?" I asked.

"I think she probably knew something. I'd give her a $20,000 necklace and she'd be like, 'Where'd you get that, D?' I'd tell her 'I got it for you 'cause I love you.' She didn't ask no more questions. But she probably knew somethin' was up. She was pissed when I got caught and had to go away. But we're cool now."

After about ten minutes Tammy emerged from the bathroom. A young Hispanic boy was waiting patiently in the aisle while Tammy was in there doing God-knows-what. She plopped back down in her seat and immediately went for her Chapstick and another dose of Percocet.

"God, I'm in so much pain," she announced again, perhaps justifying her constant consumption of drugs. "When are we going to stop? I need to smoke so fucking bad," Tammy continued. She was a stream of lamentations lobbed into a vacuum of bus air.

"So do you have family in Las Vegas?" I asked Tammy. "Yeah, my brother is down there. He and his wife are super cool. I love to go see them. But, I'm actually going down there to get some more pain pills. They've got some connections," Tammy explained.

"Have you lived in Provo for a long time?" I asked.

"Yeah. I'm divorced. Hey, let me show you a picture of my kids," she said as she reached again for her phone. Pulling up a picture, she showed me the phone and identified each of her five children. They ranged in age from seventeen to seven years old.

From the look of the picture, the kids were well taken care of. They wore matching denim shirts and the picture was taken in front of a beautiful rock backdrop. "They got married about five years ago. My husband was an abusive asshole. And now he's remarried and I hate her. She's like Molly Mormon and she totally looks down on me because I'm strong and independent," Tammy explained. "My kids live with their dad and his bitch of a wife. He made up all this bullshit about me being an unfit mother. But, I still get to see the kids a lot. I'm really close to them. They are my world," Tammy stated.

It was a sad conversation. Tammy said that the chips have been stacked against her. She had recently lost two jobs and is having trouble getting hired on anywhere else, although she admitted to not really looking all that hard. "I loved working at my last two jobs. I worked at a gas station in the morning and then at a pizza place at night. The gas station owner's wife was all jealous of me, worried that I'd run off with her husband and she made him fire me. The pizza place was great. I loved it there. I wasn't making that much money, but I could pay my rent. Then they had to downsize, and since I was the last one hired, I was the first one fired," Tammy explained.

Tammy had clearly made a ton of bad choices, but it was painfully apparent that she was now just a prisoner to her addiction. It consumed her every waking moment. I was glad to learn that she still had contact with her children, but, at the same time, I was troubled to hear her rationalization and denials that would inevitably become her undoing. Tammy seemed glad to have D and me nearby to listen to her story.

We made several stops through the night. Each stop was the same. D would smoke a cigarette and complain about Tammy's neurotic behavior. Tammy would bop around smoking and complaining about how long the trip was taking and how bad her body hurt. After we left St. George, most of the bus fell asleep. D was exhausted and leaned his head against the window. Tammy took that opportunity to come sit right in between the two of us. At this point she started rubbing my leg.

"Where are you staying when you get to Vegas?" she asked me.

"I've got a room on the strip," I replied, vaguely.

"Which hotel?" she pressed.

"I think it's Treasure Island," I replied, having a bad feeling about where this was headed.

"What would you think about me crashing with you? It's going to be late when we get there. I don't really want to wake my friends up," she lobbied.

"You know, that would be fun, but I've already been robbed once letting a stranger share my room with me. That would be tough to explain having it happen twice," I countered.

"But I'm not a stranger. I'm your bus buddy. We could really have some fun," Tammy said as she started moving her hand higher up my leg. She looked at me and smiled.

"I'm gonna have to pass. As fun as that sounds, I've made a promise to myself not to do that again," I said, restating my position.

"Well, that's too bad. But, hey, we could have fun on the bus. You ever heard of the mile-high club?" she asked.

"Yeah, I've heard of it. But, isn't that reserved for airplanes?" I shot back.

"Yeah, but we could do it on the bus. What's the worst that could happen? They could kick us off the bus? I'll go back to the bathroom and you come in a couple minutes later, okay?" Tammy plotted. D was overhearing all of this and couldn't control his snickering. Tammy was oblivious.

"Thanks for the offer, but I'm gonna pass," I explained.

"That's too bad. I'm *really* good," Tammy said in her closing attempt at bus seduction. She got up and went to the bathroom to change from jeans and a black shirt into a velour lime-green jogging suit.

"Why don't you hit that?" D asked. "She wants you bad."

"D, she wanted *you* bad until you fell asleep." That made D cut up.

"This is the craziest damn bus ride I've ever been on. She's a trip, man."

As Tammy surfaced from the bathroom in her new outfit, awaiting her was a woman pushing her baby in a stroller toward the bathroom. This was a woman I had seen in the bus station in Seattle, part of the original crew who had survived the Snoqualmie Pass Incident. The woman didn't need to use the bathroom. She simply had a question for Tammy.

"You got one of those Percs?" she asked.

"Yeah," Tammy said, reaching for her pill bottle.

The woman was rocking the stroller gently back and forth to keep her baby quiet. "How much?" she asked Tammy.

"Twenty", she answered. With a quick transaction, she took the pill from Tammy and washed the pill down with her own bottle of Mountain Dew. Tammy's makeshift pharmacy had served its purpose.

D looked at me, shook his head for the five hundredth time and just said, "Crazy, man."

Tammy sat back down, thankfully having given up on her advances toward me. She pulled a bottle of nail polish from her bag and started painting her nails. It was dark on the bus and she was doing a terrible job, smearing polish on her fingers. It was a sad display. She asked me to hold her little flashlight for her while she painted her nails. D continued to pretend that he was asleep against the window while I served as a technician for Tammy's manicure. "I'll wait for this hand to dry and then I'll do the other one," she said to me. After three or four minutes of blowing on her nails and waving her hands around, Tammy gave in to the night and fell asleep. Her other nails were never painted.

The driver woke us up as we neared the Las Vegas skyline. In the desert, from the window of our bus, I could see the neon welcoming me to a place of rest. As we approached the station, Tammy tried one more time to convince me to allow her to stay in my hotel room. D luckily jumped in and started talking about how excited he was to be home.

"I'm going straight in a cab and getting the hell out of here. The police station is right across from Greyhound. I don't want no part of that, man."

Tammy chimed in, pretending to be a knowledgeable ally, "Yeah, Vegas cops are assholes."

We said goodbye in the terminal. I hugged Tammy and wished her well. She scribbled her phone number on a scrap of paper. It read, "Tammy, the one you know you want in Provo" above her phone number. Daniel came up to me and said, "Be cool, man". He gave me a hug with a fist bump on my back, and we said goodbye. I traipsed off into the night, eager to recover from one of the wildest rides of my life.

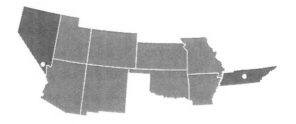

DAYS TWENTY-SIX—THIRTY

Las Vegas, Nevada to Nashville, Tennessee

Las Vegas, NV-Henderson-Bullhead City, AZ-Kingman-Flagstaff-Phoenix-Mesa-Tucson-
Benson-Willcox-Lordsburg, NM-Deming-Las Cruces-El Paso, TX-Van Horn-Big Spring-
Abilene-Ft. Worth-Arlington-Dallas-Mesquite-Garland-Greenville-Mt. Pleasant-Texarkana,
AR-Hope-Malvern-Hot Springs-Little Rock-Forrest City-Memphis, TN-Nashville

After relaxing for a day at Treasure Island, I moved over to the
Palazzo, a newer casino that featured hundreds of hotel suites. I felt
like the guys from *The Hangover* as I surveyed my living area with a
beautiful view of the Las Vegas strip. The atmosphere stood in stark
opposition to the thirty-three-hour wild bus ride from Seattle. The
woman who checked me in at the front desk was quite interested
in my story of bus travel and expressed to me that I would have to
come back to the Palazzo someday and do a book signing.

On this Labor Day weekend, the Palazzo was populated by
hundreds of people wearing red shirts. They were Wisconsin fans,
in town for the Wisconsin/UNLV football game. As I sat down
on one of the big comfortable couches at Emeril's Sports Book, I
started talking to a Wisconsin fan who was seated to my right. He

was there with his girlfriend. They had traveled from Madison, Wisconsin, for the weekend.

"Why aren't you at the game?" I asked.

"It's too damn hot out there. It was 109 at kickoff. We went over there to tailgate but said, 'Screw it. Let's go watch it at the casino.' We've got some money riding on this game. I hope the power doesn't go out this time," he said. "When we played here several years ago, we were favored by like ten points. We were killing UNLV and then sometime in the third quarter, some dude drove his truck into the power station and the game was called off. It was just before it was an official game, according to the casinos. I guess they were going to take a huge loss and then this guy crashes his truck and the lights go out. It was all over the news. I can't believe you never heard about it," he ranted.

The next day was Labor Day. I woke up feeling rested and, after lounging by the pool for most of the afternoon, I took a cab over to the Greyhound station for the 7 p.m. bus heading east. I was planning to travel through Flagstaff and continue on I-40 all the way back to Nashville. The Las Vegas Greyhound station was bustling. It was a holiday, but it was busier than I had expected. There were some down-and-out-looking characters, a few families, and some people with large boxes of belongings, all hustling to get a good spot in line. I splurged and paid the extra $5 for priority seating. I was ready to get home and wanted to make sure I had a spot on the bus. The driver started taking tickets about forty-five minutes after our scheduled departure time. He was an elderly African American gentleman who was in no hurry whatsoever. He slowly removed people's tickets from their sleeves, examined them, and deliberately handed them back to the passengers.

We started rolling south on I-15, well behind schedule. Our layover in Flagstaff was going to be fairly tight as it was, and the fact that I had a man who was about two steps removed from a coma behind the wheel didn't give me a feeling of confidence that I would make the connection. But, as is always the case with bus travel, there was nothing I could do about it. I boarded the bus and hoped for the best. The bus was crowded but quiet. Nobody really spoke to each other. We all just wadded up sweatshirts against the window and tried to catch some sleep.

Several hours later I woke to our driver's voice saying, "Ladies and gentlemen, welcome to Flagstaff. If you were planning on heading east out of Flagstaff, that bus has already departed, so you'll need to continue on with me down to Phoenix and we'll get you on another bus." His tone was unapologetic and matter-of-fact. I looked at my watch and realized that we were over two hours behind schedule.

"Why are we so late?" I asked to the passenger on my right.

"He must've driven forty miles an hour," the man replied.

As I got off the bus, I asked the driver, "What happened? Why did I miss my bus? I'm supposed to be in Nashville on Wednesday afternoon."

"We were late getting out of Las Vegas," was his reply. He answered without emotion, not even making eye contact with me as he took a long drag off his cigarette.

"This is messing up my trip. I'm going to be late," I explained to him, well aware that he had zero interest in my inconvenience or the inconvenience of any other traveler. He just stared at me and puffed away on his cigarette.

I shook my head and walked into the terminal to buy a soda. I tried to find a sympathetic traveler. "Can you believe this?" I asked to a heavy-set woman fishing through her purse for change.

"It's the same old shit," she replied. "Hey, do you have some change I could borrow?" she asked, already having dismissed the fact that we were going to have to ride an extra three hours out of our way.

"Sure," I responded, and handed three quarters over to her.

Without a word of thanks, she deposited the change and retrieved the Mountain Dew from the bottom of the machine.

I got back on the bus and resigned myself to the fact that this leg of the trip would be a fitting conclusion to my total bus experience. There was no way I was going to have made it from Las Vegas to Nashville without incident, much less on schedule. We arrived in Phoenix around dawn. Our driver instructed those of us who had been "re-routed" to go up to the ticket counter and make alternate travel plans. This was his way of saying, "My shift is over and I have no interest in dealing with any of you." Rather than arguing further with the driver, I joined about a dozen other passengers in a line at the ticket counter that already snaked around out into the main waiting area. After a twenty-minute wait I was greeted by an uninterested customer service agent who informed me that the next bus heading east would be departing in a mere three hours. Rather than taking a straight shot east on I-40 all the way to Nashville, I was now going to retrace my steps I had taken a few weeks ago and pass through Tucson and El Paso on I-10 before the endless trip across Texas. I had been scheduled to arrive in Nashville at noon on Wednesday. With the change in plans, I was now on pace to make it home at about 2:00 in the morning on Thursday. I knew that even that ETA was very much in question, as a lot can happen between Arizona and Tennessee.

The daylong journey across southern Arizona and New Mexico was uneventful. We arrived in El Paso around dinnertime, staying on our newly revised schedule. The hour layover in El Paso gave me time to charge my phone and call Erica to let her know that I would be arriving in Nashville in the middle of the night. She was understanding and helpful and said that she and a neighbor would have my car waiting for me. I told her that I was tempted to bag the last forty-eight hours of the trip and hop on a plane. She encouraged me not to quit, that I would regret it if I were to bail, having come this far. As I was on the phone, I looked over and, near the ticket counter, a scruffy man was stumbling around, asking people for change and cigarettes. I overheard someone saying that he had been in the station earlier in the day, but had suffered a seizure and was taken away by paramedics. As our bus was boarding, I noticed him getting on. I assumed he had gotten medical clearance to keep traveling.

About an hour out of El Paso, we were stopped at the same immigration checkpoint my bus was stopped at fourteen days ago. The routine was the same. Heavily armed, burly patrol agents boarded the bus; one in the back and one in the front. They worked their way toward the middle of the bus asking to see documentation from every passenger. A young black man was sitting toward the front and the agent's progress stopped as he seemed dissatisfied with the papers the man had shown him. "Sir, I need to see a passport or social security card, a driver's license, birth certificate, something like that." Everyone was staring at the interaction. The other agent, having satisfactorily verified the nationalities and status of the back half of the bus, joined the conversation. The bus was silent except for the two agents and the young man. The young man was rooting around in his backpack, looking for paperwork. After about ten minutes, the agents escorted him off the bus and took him to the hut by the side of the road. As our bus was pulled over by the side of the road, I observed agents checking the undersides of trucks with mirrors attached to long sticks and German Shepherds sniffing around. It was a thorough checkpoint and, unfortunately, it appeared that our bus was going to be a casualty of stricter immigration patrol.

Our driver stood outside the bus, smoking and chatting with government workers. Finally, after a forty-five-minute delay, the driver got back on the bus and we started easing back on the highway. I noticed that the young man never rejoined the bus. He was being detained, evidently until he got his paperwork cleared up.

Someone from the front of the bus passed word back that he was from Belize and didn't have any documentation on him, so we left him. Nobody seemed very sympathetic. Instead, people were concerned that they would be missing connections in Dallas because of the delay. That wound up being the case.

We rode all night through Texas, arriving in Dallas in the afternoon on Wednesday. We realized that about half of us had missed our connecting buses because of the border patrol standstill and leisurely smoke breaks that extended our trip. So now I had to wait for the next bus heading east out of Dallas, which would be in five more hours.

The Dallas station had a cafeteria, not unlike that of an elementary school. There were hot dishes and an assortment of desserts. A woman dressed in a white coat and a hairnet scooped me up a plate of chicken, rice, and beans. A stocky man in a gray T-shirt and baseball cap approached the serving line and looked at my plate. "That looks pretty good, man." I agreed. As I spoke with him, I noticed an angry-looking scar on the front of his neck. The incision was red and puffy. Having just recovered from my own cervical fusion a year earlier, I knew that's exactly what he had gone through.

"How long ago was your fusion?" I asked.

"About two weeks ago," he replied as we carried our trays over to a table. "How did you know?" he asked.

"I had mine done about a year ago," I informed him.

He introduced himself as Tucker.

"Why are you not wearing your brace?" I asked.

"I don't want my neck muscles to get weak. They wanted me wearing that brace. I wore it for a couple days and then said, 'Screw it,'" he explained. Tucker was about six feet tall and barrel-chested. He was unshaven and looked rather rough.

"Were you in a car accident?" I asked.

He shot me a stare and there was an uncomfortable moment

of silence. "No, man. I got blowed up over in Iraq," he said with a tinge of anger.

"Oh man. Sorry to hear that. How did it happen?" I asked.

"We ran over a bomb in our tank. I was messed up pretty bad," he said, showing me a few scars on his head. "It was about a year and a half ago. I was in the hospital in Germany for a few months. I just had this neck surgery here in Texas a couple of weeks ago. Hey, how long were you on pain pills?" he asked me.

"Probably for a month. Maybe six weeks," I replied.

"Really?" he asked incredulously. "I'm in a ton of pain. They told me it would be a lot longer than that," he said.

Tucker withdrew two pill bottles from his pocket. "This is OxyContin. I take two of these a day. This other one is Percocet. I take one or two of these every few hours. I been taking it since the explosion," he shared. "The army takes good care of me. I get all my pills at the base. It doesn't cost me anything."

"So where are you headed?" I asked.

"I'm going home to Mississippi for three weeks. I'm gonna see my folks and my daughter. She's fourteen now. She lives with her mom, but we've got a real good relationship. I'm excited to see her," he explained.

"Well, if you're gone from the base, how do you keep your medications filled? Do they give you refills or do you have a doctor back in Mississippi who's going to be checking on you after the surgery?" I asked.

"No, I can't go to another doctor. The guy just checked me out back on the base. If you get busted trying to get pills from somebody else, they'll kick your ass out of the army," Tucker explained.

"Well, thanks for serving our country. I'm sorry you got hurt. I bet you saw a lot over there in Iraq," I said.

"You don't need to thank me, man. I was just doing my job. But, it's hell over there. We're over there trying to help these people out and there's folks trying to blow us up and kill us. It's nuts, man," Tucker stated.

"Do you think it's working? Are we making progress?" I inquired.

"Hell, no. We don't have any business being over there. As soon as we leave, that place is gonna go to hell. None of us understand why we're over there." Tucker was brutally honest. He had been on three different tours. He was in his mid-thirties and had seen the progress and conflict firsthand. He was almost killed serving his country, and he wondered about the cost: "I'm not going back. I'm going to get an honorable discharge before too long. I've given my blood, sweat, and tears to that war, but I don't know that it's made a big difference," he lamented.

"Well, I really appreciate it. I don't know a lot about what's happening over there, but I admire guys like you," I said.

Tucker said thanks. I could tell he was hurting. His bravado and mannerisms were masking a lot of pain. He had dropped out of college fifteen years ago and made a decision to serve in the military. It was obvious from our discussion that he was wrestling with a laundry list of what-could-have-beens. He was excited to reconnect with his daughter and try to find work as a contractor.

"When I'm done with the army, I'm gonna move back home to Mississippi and see if I can't go into business with my dad. I know a lot of people around there and I love building houses. There's real good money in it. My dad will help me get started with it." Tucker said with sincere optimism.

We continued chatting for an hour or so, sipping black coffee and talking about how crazy the bus was. Out of the blue, Tucker offered up, "Hey, about these pain pills . . . I order them online from Canada. I've got a place that this guy showed me on the Internet. They show up on my front door in a black bag. I can't live without 'em."

I just nodded. It seemed pretty obvious that the price Tucker was paying for his wartime injuries might turn into a battle with addiction. He was gobbling up pain pills at a frightening pace as we sat together in the terminal. Not only was he severely injured in a foreign country, he was probably haunted by memories of the death and destruction he saw there too. He seemed as if he were a man carrying deep pain, a product of war that rarely makes the news or the papers.

As we discarded our trash and made our way back to the waiting area, we noticed the same scruffy man I had seen in El Paso. He was lying on the floor by the ticket counter. Paramedics were just entering the door. The man's khaki pants were soiled and he was flopping around, in the middle of another seizure. Nearby passengers just stared at him, no one daring to get too close. I was hoping that, this time, they would take him to the hospital and keep him there until they got his condition under control.

Tucker and I put our bags down on the ground and sat on the floor, leaning against a wall. All of the uncomfortable black iron bench seats were already occupied. The station was packed with travelers, all coping with delays of one type or another. Everyone was grouchy and trying to make the best of their wait. Although spacious, the Dallas station struggled on this day to hold the volume of passengers that had accumulated in the terminal. As Tucker and I sat on the hard floor, a female Greyhound employee wearing tan pants, a white button-down shirt, and a neon green vest walked up to us. "Gentlemen, I need you to move your bags and feet out of the walkway. It's a violation of our fire code." So Tucker and I moved our bags closer and curled our legs up so as to not clutter the walkway. The woman's warning to us was stated out of irritation. I had seen this before, but I was on the homeward leg of the trip and just looked at Tucker and shook my head.

Finally Tucker and I joined several dozen other passengers on a bus bound for Memphis, where his mom would pick him up.

Tucker and I talked most of the way through Arkansas. He drifted off to sleep a few times and then would wake and take some more pain medication. He looked generally uncomfortable. We talked about sports and girls. He was a good companion for the long ride. When we crossed the Mississippi River around midnight, I knew that I was only four hours from home. I was praying that there would not be another unforeseen delay that would mess up my connection home to Nashville. I was already about twenty hours behind schedule.

When we arrived in Memphis, I helped Tucker pull his suit-case off the cart and reminded him that he really wasn't supposed to be lifting more than twenty-five pounds. I encouraged him to try and follow the doctor's orders. We hugged and wished each other well. Thankfully, I only had about forty-five minutes before my bus would be leaving for Nashville. As I entered the jam-packed termi-nal, I saw two long lines already snaking through the building. Both were for buses headed to Nashville. I was grateful that I would be a re-boarder and would not have to mess with the long lines. I walked over to the gift shop and bought a deck of Elvis playing cards to give as a token of thanks for my neighbor who had helped out some with my kids while I was on this bus trip. As I started walk-ing back toward my gate, I witnessed an African American woman who worked for Greyhound throwing a major fit.

"Huh-uh. No way. No way are you going to do that in my station. You get sick on my floor and you gots to go!" She was lay-ing into a young woman, about twenty years old, who was sitting on a bench with a pool of vomit splattered around her feet. The woman was hunched over, holding her head in her hands. She had a friend next to her who began to lobby with the Greyhound worker that her friend "just wasn't feeling well." But the worker wasn't having it. "No way, honey. She's drunk. She needs to get her ass out of my station before I call the cops." With that, her friend helped her up and they stumbled out the front doors of the station into the Memphis night. A young man in a Greyhound vest appeared with a mop.

After a three-day journey from Las Vegas, I too felt like puking all over the floor of the station, but I knew that the end was near. I boarded a bus filled to capacity, finally heading home. A family of five was seated in the row across from me and behind me—a mother and father with three children looked to be at their wits' end. For the four-hour ride to Nashville, they were trying to placate their two older children, who looked to be about three and five years old, as well as their infant daughter, who screamed bloody murder for the better part of the ride. It was about 3:00 in the morning and we were scheduled to arrive around 7 a.m. The bus was full of people trying to sleep. An elderly African American woman seated in front of me was losing her cool.

"You all need to shut that child up!" she declared.

The parents were tired looking. The mother was yelling at the father to keep the baby quiet. The father yelled back at her, "What do you want me to do?" I felt bad for them.

I remember those days. There's not a whole lot that you can do to calm down a grouchy infant. When the pacifier, something to eat, a bottle, singing and rocking all failed, usually my wife and I just started yelling at each other. We knew we couldn't take out our anger or frustration on our son, so we would just bark at each other and blame the other for the situation. This poor couple was clearly in that spot. Their kid would not stop fussing and everyone on the bus was trying to sleep. You could just feel their tension and stress as they tried to console their baby, but my sympathy and patience level were at rock bottom. All I could think about was getting back home to my own family.

Driving in on I-40, Nashville's lights had never looked so bright and inviting. I breathed a sigh of relief as I stepped off the bus. My first breath of the summer night's air, which usually felt soupy and heavy, was just what I needed. I breathed deeply, taking in a lung full of air that promised reunion and comfort and exhaled the last molecules of bus residue. My car was waiting for me, a beacon of freedom and independence shining in the dim parking lot.

This trip was over. I was home.

EPILOGUE

For the last month my body had been jostled, cramped, and contorted on the large, constantly vibrating bus. Slipping into my waiting Pontiac, I felt my body relax into the driver's seat of my car. It fit like a glove. As I pulled out of the Greyhound parking lot in Nashville, I kept an eye on the row of buses in my rearview mirror. They got smaller as I headed west on Charlotte Avenue.

In the days following my return home, it was difficult to immediately go back to business as usual. It was unfair to expect my wife or friends to share in my nostalgia or to sit captive while I told bus story after bus story, but I was constantly reflecting on my interactions with these various characters over the past month. I couldn't help but work to put all the pieces together in my mind of what I'd seen and experienced and the people I'd met. So, who are the people on the bus?

Becky was leaving a boyfriend in Minnesota and heading back to Texas, hoping life would be better. Tyler was traversing the country hoping to start a lucrative pot farming business in California. Jessica had bailed on college and was looking for a fresh start back with her mother in Idaho. Daniel was finishing a two-year prison sentence, hoping to reconnect with his dad and learn how to fix up cars. Ordell was seeking reunion with his girlfriend in Omaha, sure that things would be different this time around. Burt, the unemployed folk singer, was on his way back to Reno in search of the steady employment that had eluded him for the last decade. Joe and Art were just using the bus to get from point A to point B.

But the one thing they all had was hope. Whether the hope was founded or an illusion, the bus was a visible representation of their dreams for a better life. They were leaving somewhere and headed somewhere new. They were confident that tomorrow would be better, that the grass would be greener elsewhere, and that allowed them to persevere and deal with the discomfort and inconvenience of days-long bus travel. I've come to believe that the bus is more than a vehicle–for many, it's a symbol of something bigger. For many, it's hope.

We are all eager to be a part of something greater than ourselves. We want someone to listen to us. This experience gave me a chance to sit in a seat of privilege and hear people's stories. Many people were visibly longing to connect. They wanted solidarity, to feel that somehow they were not alone. They sought community with one another on the bus, however random that community might be.

Twenty years ago I rode the bus to try and chase down the love of my life. Today, I realize that I don't have to chase anymore– I have her. It is a blessing that I never deserved. After a month of traveling and hearing stories upon stories of people who are searching for community and happiness, I was reminded that I have that at home. I have a wife and children who love me unconditionally. I have a life of relative stability. I have problems. Sure, we all have problems, but I know that I have the resources to deal with most of my problems. For many of my fellow bus passengers, that kind of support may always be out of arm's reach. I realized that I had, too often and for too long, taken all of that for granted. Maybe it took a month on the road, traveling with people who are good folks, but dealing with addiction, poverty, and estrangement, to remember that I am a lucky guy.

I will remember the passengers I met, just as I did from my trip two decades ago. Every time I'm on the interstate and see a Greyhound bus barreling down the road, I will wonder about who's inside. What are their stories? Where are they going? Are they lonely? Are they hopeful? Their stories will stay with me forever.

Maybe The Allman Brothers and others have inaccurately portrayed the backseat of a Greyhound bus as a place of romance and adventure, but they may not be too far off either. It is quite a place to get to know the country.

NOTES

DAY ONE: *Nashville, Tennessee*
1. Greyhound.com, "Historical Timeline," http://www.greyhound.com/en /about/historicaltimeline.aspx.
2. Greyhound.com, "Greyhound Facts and Figures," http://www.greyhound .com/en/about/factsandfigures.aspx.
3. U.S. Department of Transportation, Research and Innovative Technology Administration (RITA), "TransStats," http://www.transtats.bts.gov.

DAY TWO: *Nashville, Tennessee to Righmond, Virginia*
1. Centers for Disease Control and Prevention, "Adult Cigarette Smoking in the United States: Current Estimate,"http://www.cdc.gov/tobacco/data _statistics/fact_sheets/adult_data/cig_smoking/index.htm.

DAY THREE: *Richmond, Virginia to Wilmington, Delaware*
1. Greyhound.com, "Greyhound Facts and Figures," http://www.greyhound .com/en/about/factsandfigures.aspx.
2. Ibid.

DAY THREE: *Wilmington, Delaware to Pittsburgh, Pennsylvania*
1. Greyhound Coupon Code, www.greyhoundcouponcode.net.

DAYS THIRTEEN–FOURTEEN: *Reno, Nevada to Los Angeles, California*
1. Greyhound.com, "Greyhound Facts and Figures," http://www.greyhound .com/en/about/factsandfigures.aspx.

DAYS TWENTY-FOUR–TWENTY-SIX: *Stanfield, Oregon to Las Vegas, Nevada*
1. Budget Travel, "Federal prisoners are transported via public bus lines," http://current.newsweek.com/budgettravel/2009/06/the_feds_send _inmates_between.html.

ACKNOWLEDGMENTS

Special thanks to my family: Erica, Russ and Mitch. You let me leave home for a month on a crazy journey. I missed you all while I was gone, but you made me appreciate what I have at home. The bus can be a lonely place, full of people searching for community and unconditional love. You reminded me that I have that at home. I love you.

Thanks to Lori Jones, my editor. You were patient with me for months and gave me invaluable feedback and direction. I am proud of this book and you made it so much stronger.

Thanks to my designer Mary Hooper at Milkglass Creative. Your creativity, imagination and willingness to snoop around the bus station with me proved that you believed in this project.

To my proofreaders: Doug Haddix, Phil Hazelton, Jim Tate and David Hood. Thanks guys for your attentive eyes, helpful commentary and absolute support throughout the whole trip. It meant more to me than you'll know.

Finally, thank you to all of the drivers and passengers that made this trip what it was. I can't name all of you. In fact, I changed most of your names. But, if you happen to read this book and remember our conversations, thank you. Thank you for opening up to me, for sharing your stories and for inviting me to be in community with you. I will never forget these thirty days.

ABOUT THE AUTHOR

Mike Pentecost is a graduate of the University of Kentucky, where he majored in business management. He is an ordained Presbyterian minister (PCUSA) who lives in Nashville, Tennessee, with his wife, Erica, and two sons, Russ and Mitch. He has written essays on his time in the ministry. *Bus People* is his first book.